Troublesome Behaviour in the Classroom

Discipline problems are never far from teachers' minds, and are widely believed to be increasing in prevalence and intensity. Mick McManus describes the range of causes, remedies, research, and theory on troublesome behaviour in schools, testing each for its practical value to teachers in ordinary classrooms and schools. He looks at troublesome behaviour from nursery to late teens, and from the irritating to the violent, developing a systematic approach to solving problems in classrooms that is practical and easy to implement. He shows how troublesome behaviour can be understood in terms of pupils' motives, their domestic, peer-group, and classroom contexts, and demonstrates that it can be coped with through teachers' skills, techniques, and attitudes.

Troublesome Behaviour in the Classroom

A Teachers' Survival Guide

Mick McManus

First published 1989 by Routledge
11 New Fetter Lane, London EC4P 4EE

Published in the USA by
Nichols Publishing Company
PO Box 96, New York, NY 10024

Reprinted 1990, 1993

© 1989 M. McManus

Phototypeset in Linotron Times by
Intype, London

Printed and bound in Great Britain by Mackays of Chatham PLC, Chatham,
Kent

British Library Cataloguing in Publication Data

McManus, Mick, *1943–*
  Troublesome behaviour in the classroom:
  a teachers' survival guide
  1. Schools. Classroom. Discipline
  I. Title
  371.1'024

Library of Congress Cataloging in Publication Data

McManus, Mick, 1943–
  Troublesome behaviour in the classroom: a teachers' survival
guide/Mick McManus
     p. cm.
  Bibliography: p.
  Includes index.
  1. Classroom management. 2. School children–Discipline.
3. Problem children–Education. 4. School discipline. I. Title.
LB3013.M387   1989
371.1'024–dc19
                                                              88–34313
                                                              CIP

ISBN 0–415–03910–X (hbk)
ISBN 0–415–03911–8 (pbk)

To my wife June,
who has never been a bit of trouble,
and to our children Sally, Jimmy, Maggie and Bob,
who have.

Contents

List of tables and figures

Tables

Figures

Preface

This book began as an inquiry into why some schools suspend many more pupils than others. The results were unexpected. There was no support for the view that big schools had more discipline problems than small schools; that urban schools had higher suspension rates than suburban schools; nor was there evidence that poverty and domestic disadvantage in a school's catchment necessarily led to more pupils being excluded for behaviour problems. Visits to schools gradually provided evidence that high suspension rates were not a simple reflection of indiscipline, but were often the unintended consequence of taken-for-granted disciplinary procedures.

As data accumulated I came to believe that some teachers had ways of perceiving and coping with problems that made their schools better able to accommodate and influence difficult pupils. Over a period of three years working at Leeds Polytechnic I developed a course which aimed to help teachers adopt the perspectives and strategies which seemed to be effective. Although the research was conducted in secondary schools, there was widespread interest from primary and middle schools in methods of coping with troublesome behaviour, and most courses had members from all sectors.

Despite my misgivings about finding common ground for teachers from nursery, infant, primary, middle and high schools, this diversity turned out to be a benefit: indeed, some of the most rewarding meetings were with teachers from a local authority that has long had a policy of grouping teachers from all sectors into neighbourhood pyramids. Others in the field have noticed this too (Hanko, 1985: 145). This is not to say that there are no differences in techniques and approaches between sectors, and where applicable these are specified in the text. It is my firm belief, however, that the skills of good teachers from nursery to university are more similar than disparate. In a major American study, Evertson and Emmer (1982) found that with primary and middle school age-groups effective procedures were broadly similar. The differences noticed were adjustments to age, subject and type of grouping rather than differences in 'qualitative principles'.

This book outlines the research, describes the in-service course, explains the sources of its ideas, and shows how schools can teach themselves. Some parts of Chapter 2 have appeared in *Research in Education* and *School Organisation*. Exercises are included, together with advice on their management for the course leader or staff-tutor. One way of conducting a series of training meetings would be for the staff-tutor to introduce each session with an outline and explanation of each chapter. The exercises are best begun in small groups so that everyone has a chance to talk through their ideas. Plenary sessions draw the meetings together. The suggested duration of each phase should be regarded as a minimum, but having a time limit helps to focus and discipline discussion. Some pages of this book, those containing summaries and exercises, may be copied in small numbers for use by one trainer within one institution: they are most useful to participants if distributed some days before meetings to allow time for reading and reflection.

The course owes a lot to my twenty years' experience with troublesome teenagers in schools and units; but most of all I have profited from the help and friendship of teachers in schools, and colleagues in the polytechnic. Listing them all here would fill more than a page, risk leaving some out or, worse still, including those who want nothing to do with it. I would like to mention Phil Simpson, Ted Bowskill and Gerry Vernon for the confidence they had in that aggressive young teacher I used to be. As for the rest – friends, even if you read only this far, you can be sure you are on the list.

Chapter one

Concerns, causes and remedies

The literature offers a bewildering collection of definitions, estimates of prevalence, claims about trends, historical evidence, and speculations upon causes and cures. The popular view that disorder in schools, like disorder in society, is a recent phenomenon has often been contradicted by reference to historical sources. Curtis (1963) records some of the frequent disturbances at the ancient universities, whose students were in many respects the equivalent of present day secondary pupils. For example, at Cambridge in 1261 there was a fight between scholars from the north and south; unlike twentieth century two-nations disputes, this one led to plunder and burning. At Oxford, on St Scholastica's Day in 1354, a pub-fight ended with many dead and wounded; a similar riot broke out in Cambridge in 1381. School rules are a clue to what behaviour might be expected from thirteenth century pupils: at Westminster, boys were forbidden to play tricks on townsmen and not allowed to carry bows, sticks or stones. The fifteenth century Cambridge graduation ritual for a Master of Grammar, who sought a licence to teach, placed discipline on an equal footing with learning. After the candidate had 'argyude as shall please the Proctor' he was provided with a 'Rodde' and a 'shrewde', that is, mischievous, boy whom he then 'bete openlye in the Scolys'. In this way, says Curtis, 'the newly fledged master approved his ability to teach in a grammar-school' (1963: 65). Most sixteenth and seventeenth century pictures of schoolmasters, says Curtis, depict the master with a birch or rod.

A number of serious disturbances followed the abolition of certain 'papist' holidays after 1565. In 1587, pupils used armed force to occupy Edinburgh High School as had happened earlier in Aberdeen. In 1595 magistrates were called to regain control of the same school and a town councillor was shot dead in the process. Raikes was partly impelled to found his Sunday schools by the 'wild and mischievous behaviour' of children on their day of rest. Evidently some of it continued for Raikes had discipline problems: in one incident, a badger was let loose in the schoolroom. The horrors of eighteenth and nineteenth century public schools have been described by Gathorne-Hardy (1977): for example, in an 1818 riot at Eton, pupils smashed the desk of their headmaster Dr Keates.

It may be said in mitigation that these examples come from more brutal times in which such incidents did not carry the horrifying implications that they would in the twentieth century. In the eighteenth century Coram was moved to found his hospital to rid the streets of abandoned and dying babies and even as late as the 1890s they were said to be a common sight (Schostak, 1986). However, there is evidence that past violence was not viewed lightly at the time. Concern about increasing disorder among the young led, in 1847, to the establishment of a House of Lords Select Committee to look into the operation of the criminal law in respect of children. Evidence included statistics showing a rising conviction rate among those under 21, and some witnesses blamed the ragged schools for it (Curtis, 1963: 302). In 872 at Malmesbury school, in an early example of violence towards teachers, the pupils of the unfortunate Scotus Erigena stabbed him to death with their pens. As commonly happens with twentieth century incidents, this too was disputed and Curtis comments that the report has been the subject of controversy as to its trustworthiness.

What is troublesome behaviour?

Disagreement and uncertainty about the amount of troublesome behaviour is common and this is allied to the difficulty in arriving at a definition which all can agree is interpreted and applied consistently. Doyle says the key to understanding misbehaviour is to see it 'in the context of classroom structures'. He defines it as 'any behaviour by one or more students that is perceived by the teacher to initiate a vector of action that competes with or threatens the primary vector of action at a particular moment in a classroom activity' (Wittrock, 1986: 419). In the effort to recognize the subjectivity and relativity of teacher perceptions, this definition makes anything potentially misbehaviour.

In a class which has been left to its own devices, so that the teacher can catch up with marking, a pupil who asks for some work to do would be misbehaving. Conversely, if the teacher does not notice the bored pupil cutting his or her books up, that is not misbehaviour. For as Doyle's definition says, anything that interferes with the teacher's state of mind is misbehaviour. The definition of disruptive behaviour offered by Galloway et al. (1982) is similarly flawed: '. . . any behaviour which appears problematic, inappropriate and disturbing to teachers'.

Another attempt, which appears to remove the subjective element by defining disruption in terms of its effect upon (ordinary) teaching and the (normal) school is that by Lawrence et al., (1977, 1984): 'Behaviour which seriously interferes with the teaching process and/or seriously upsets the normal running of the school.' As many teachers say when asked for examples of such behaviour – it depends what you mean by seriously. Distinctions between maladjustment and disruption are similarly problematic. There is a popular view that maladjustment is a pathological medical condition and disruption is rooted in moral deficiencies. Individual pathology plays a greater or lesser part in each pupil's behaviour, but there is no line between those who are typed as maladjusted and those typed as disruptive. Similar errors were made in identifying pupils with learning difficulties prior to the abolition of categories of handicap following the Education Act 1981. For example, many came to believe that pupils could be sorted into remedial, ESN(M) and ESN(S) types, but these categories evolved from historical and administrative arrangements. They encouraged the view that problems were solved because they had been identified, and where a pupil proved unamenable in a particular placement, there was a tendency to seek a fresh place rather than a fresh policy.

Hewett and Blake (1973) wrote that the 'most pressing need is for a reliable system of definition and classification of emotional and behavioural disorders'. We still do not have one, and they were wrong. To rely on definitions and categories to suggest remedies is to divert attention from observation of the individual and his or her circumstances. There are no easy solutions, so we have to think.

In a survey described in Chapter 2, I asked fifty teachers to indicate on a list of thirty-eight items the pupil behaviours they thought were 'serious threats to good order'. There was total agreement on only one item: 'Hits teacher'. Five teachers ticked every item; five queried the meaning of serious or declined to tick any. The difficulty of definition is captured in an autobiographical anecdote by Blishen (1980):

> There was a boy in class two who was, I had to conclude, an advanced delinquent – yet his offence was barely definable. The nearest I could come to it was to say that he turned sitting down into a comedy.

Becker (1963) was only slightly exaggerating when he wrote, more directly than Doyle, that:

> . . . deviance is not a quality of the act a person commits . . . the deviant is one to whom that label has successfully been applied; deviant behaviour is behaviour that people so label.

Labels and classifications spring from theories, often held implicitly, and it is true that they may tell us as much about the labeller as about the labelled. This does not mean that labels, categories and definitions are purely arbitrary: the distinctions, especially if they stick, must have something to do with that which is being observed. As Pring (1976) says, words like 'cats' and 'dogs' tell something about the classifier, but they also tell us something about the nature of cats and dogs. Defining and measuring the seriousness of misbehaviour is not a matter of applying such a simple distinction: it is more like trying to decide which dogs are light grey and which are not. No objective definition which would reduce the measurement of disruption to a simple counting process is possible. This definitional obscurity, unsatisfactory as it may be, is an important clue to one of the ways in which the problem of troublesome behaviour might be tackled. There are at least two parties to any disruptive incident. Both contribute to its being defined as serious or not, or indeed to whether it becomes defined as a disruptive incident at all.

In the light of these definitional problems, it is not surprising that there are no reliable statistics on troublesome behaviour. The Pack Report (HMSO, 1977) on truancy and disruption in Scotland concluded as much. When figures are gathered, they are disputed: if too low for the critic's liking they are said to indicate teachers' unwillingness to risk censure in an atmosphere of hostility towards a beleaguered profession; or they may be dismissed as from a tainted source – headteachers covering up their school's shortcomings. If too high, then they are said to be the exaggeration of interested parties seeking additional compensation and resources. Hargreaves *et al*. (1975) recorded only one act of violence to staff during their research, as did Lawrence *et al*. (1977) during their work in a secondary school. In their four year study discussed in Galloway *et al*. (1982) twelve of 266 suspensions were for violence to a teacher. A survey by the DES in 1975 (DES, 1980) found the level of violent acts to be 7.68 per 10,000 pupils, and the level of acts of rowdyism to be 3.81 per 10,000 pupils. With a school population of around eight million it is easy to see how a low rate of disruption could generate a daily supply of horrifying anecdotes. Reviewing research, Johnstone and Munn (1987) conclude that possibly one quarter of teachers are worried by disruption but very few are seriously worried. Surveys by teachers' unions invariably produce more dramatic results, but it is difficult to know how to allow for sampling distortions: perhaps replies come only from those who are worried. The NAHT claim (reported in *The Times*, 17.6.88) that there are ninety-five assaults on teachers every day, if taken at face value, would indicate that the number had tripled since the DES survey in 1975.

The term, assault, is emotive, a legalistic category carrying the implication of serious harm: it distorts reality when applied to such things as pushing past a teacher to escape punishment, or being kicked on the shin by an infant in a tantrum. Lawrence *et al*. (1984) sought information from Europe on disruptive behaviour and uncovered a patchy but broadly similar mix of concerns and uncertainties as exists in Britain. The problems giving most general concern were bullying, vandalism, refusal to obey teacher, bad language and difficult classes (but not difficult schools). The type of offences that most often appear in the press – alcoholism and violence to teachers – were bottom of the list. Only in France was violence to teachers high on the list of concerns. Writing of the situation in America, where school violence is popularly believed to be widespread, Doyle refers to national surveys which show that serious incidents 'are generally rare in most schools' and most often occur out of classrooms (see Wittrock, 1986: 418). There seems to be no reason for Davies to modify his conclusion (quoted in Jones-Davies and Cave, 1976) that although much disruption is awkward and undesirable it is still a minority sport.

Common sense remedies

A glance at history puts present problems into a less stressful perspective. It also prompts us to consider the value of the simple solutions that are popularly offered for indiscipline in schools. Brutal punishments do not seem to have been effective: while some pupils were being flogged at school, some of their non-attending peers might be awaiting capital punishment or transportation for non-violent crimes. Even if rigid and complete discipline were achievable in a school by force, it would not necessarily transfer with the pupil to fresh situations. Goffman (1968) has documented the varied strategies available even to asylum inmates to enable them to protect themselves from unwanted influences: for example, withdrawal, rebellion, 'playing it cool'. We can be sure that pupils are at least as inventive. Wills (1967) hoped pupils would devise a moral system of their own which was 'not unacceptable to society' and which they would stick to and value: 'It is possible for a person under discipline never to display a single symptom and go out into the world untouched.' Davies and Maliphant (1974) conducted an extraordinary experiment to measure the effectiveness of 'distinctly unpleasant' electric shocks in teaching 'refractory' pupils and ordinary pupils a simple skill. The refractory individuals received significantly more shocks than their more amenable fellows but the effects were short lived. The authors suggest that this is typical of the ineffectiveness of punishment upon them in ordinary life.

Discussing troublesome pupils, Laslett (1977) points out that the cause and source of punishment are easily confused. Punishment does not discourage misbehaviour but reinforces the pupil's view of adults as treacherous. In a research review, Topping (1983) concluded that punishment was ineffective and could aggravate problems. For a few distressed individuals, seeking punishment may be a part of their problem not a solution to it; others are denied the opportunity to make amends. Laslett therefore suggests that management is a more useful concept than punishment. A pupil is put in the care and under the close supervision of one person, perhaps a personal tutor or senior member of staff, where difficulties can be sorted out without the interference of an attendant audience: close proximity encourages a helpful exchange of information. Wills (1945) also thought punishment took away the valuable opportunity for the offender to make restitution. He also suggested that punishment led to the exclusion of moral thinking in favour of book-keeping calculations related to the possibility of being caught, and the likely price to be paid. This encouraged the attitude that misbehaviour could be paid for, the slate being wiped clean for fresh villainy. A similar claim is sometimes made about the function of the sacrament of confession and it is equally unconvincing; in any case, the argument applies as well to restitution as it does to punishment. At the other extreme from punishment, permissiveness is equally unhelpful. In a pioneer study, Jackson (1968) noted that to survive in classrooms pupils needed to learn turn-taking and patience: teacher as gatekeeper created the experiences of denial, interruption and distraction for pupils. Delamont (1976) produces the often quoted figure of one minute of teacher's time per pupil per forty-minute lesson and comments that research is needed into how pupils spend their minute. Many pupils need help in learning how to use the other thirty-nine. Something of this sort is implied in Laslett's (1977) suggestion that troublesome pupils should be occasionally exposed to less tolerant adults than their teachers.

Common sense causes

The advice in this book is intended to be useful in the teaching of all pupils, from the naughty to the seriously disturbed. No-one should assume that classroom management skills, or the social and institutional pressures of classrooms and schools, are irrelevant to the treatment of pupils believed to be severely disruptive or maladjusted. Many teachers take it for granted that the treatment of pupils who have behaved very badly over a long period is a medical matter. Certainly, any other form of approach may seem hopelessly time-consuming and uncertain in its effects: to listen, think and help can be an open-ended, unrewarding and exhausting enterprise. It seems self-evident that some pupils have something bio-chemically wrong with them, and common-sense to leave medical experts to find the most soothing cocktail of tranquillizers. Teachers have grown accustomed to deferring to experts of various kinds, and take it as axiomatic that medical advice is safe, scientific and objective. Doctors have only recently lost the right to decide whether a child needed special schooling or not. Teachers are rarely cast in the confident role of experts and do not find it at all remarkable to be told to consult specialists.

Much of the drift of a book on disruptive behaviour, written by two doctors, is in this vein (Holman and Coghill, 1987). Members of powerful professional groups are accustomed to having weight attached to their views on matters outside their specialism: for example, a scientist's opinion of religion, a doctor's views on parenting, a university teacher's policy for primary school maths. We defer too easily. Part of my argument is that teachers need to increase their confidence in their own expertise, and therefore to give only what limited credence is due to members of other professions when they pronounce upon school matters: much of what they have to say is pure tautology. For example, we are told: 'The prime purpose of schools as places of learning can be furthered by reducing impediments to learning, especially in children unable to learn' (Holman and Coghill, 1987: 220). In another inconsequential passage we learn: 'A teacher of 35, 15 years in the profession, when told by the head to get her hair cut saw this as a threat to her identity'; and well she might. However, a more serious threat to teacher identity is posed by politely accepting any kind of flim-flam from outsiders. A healthy scepticism is needed: the observations of those who have distinguished themselves in other spheres can be every bit as insubstantial as comments from any other person stopped on the street. To say that teachers should have confidence in their own expertise and not accept other specialists' opinions uncritically is not to say that teachers should regard their own medical and psychological knowledge as complete and sufficient. Laslett (1977) warns against teachers as amateur psychologists but notes that teachers' contact with pupils is greater in duration and variety than that of any other professional. That being the case, teachers are best placed to understand pupils' problems and should take a central role in assessing the advice of others, whose contact with the problem can rarely be other than peripheral.

The notion that problem behaviour can be solely attributed to chemistry, whether internal in the genes or external in food additives or petrol-lead, has a powerful hold over the imagination, comfortably placing the responsibility elsewhere and offering an easy solution. It is important to be clear about the relationship between biology and behaviour if only to rid ourselves of impossible dreams in respect of miracle cures. Biology cannot cause behaviour. We use the word cause in many ways and easily deceive ourselves about the reasons why of things. To make the argument clear, consider the relationship of biology to behaviour in a larger context. For example, a news report may say that famine, resulting from a crop failure, is causing starvation and food riots. In the wealthy countries we see such reports as fitting a well-known pattern: some countries have too many people, climates that grow too little food, and inefficient governments – it is a natural disaster. It is nothing to do with us but, having been moved by television coverage, we will contribute what we can. But is the crop failure the cause? We know that the world is over-supplied with food and transport as well as the necessary botanical knowledge. A famine is not a result of natural events but of social ones: food could be redistributed and resources reallocated but we do not choose this uncongenial solution.

Behaviour problems are sometimes thought about in similar ways: a pupil has got into a wild state and gone beserk again; she has too much aggression, too little self-control, and ineffective parenting – one of life's losers. It is nothing to do with us, but we will try to make sure she takes her tablets. It is tempting to let nature take the blame, but biological conditions cannot be any more than a background feature: their behavioural outcomes are the result of being channelled by experience. There is a view that we all have an aggressive drive that is essential to our independence (Storr, 1968): repression is therefore disapproved of and the solution is said to lie in encouraging positive aspects of aggression. But this view assumes what it seeks to explain. Aggressiveness does not have to be an innate drive necessary for survival: many people survive and even command others without being aggressive; it is tautological to postulate an aggressive drive and then prove its existence by describing any sort of personal effectiveness as aggression. Aggression in schools is better understood as a strategy that a pupil has learned to use as an effective method of expression or a way of achieving his or her goals. The focus needs to be on individual perspectives, relationships, and situational constraints, not the supposed defects in individual pathology. This is not to substitute what Dyke (1987) describes as psychoanalytical determinism for the biological kind. Bastide (1972) notes how a psychoanalytical focus on individuals leads to a sociological interest in relationships: early life influences are social; for traumas of infancy to affect the present they must be reawakened and maintained in the present.

No-one is born with a predisposition to hitting teachers: in a life of parental neglect and societal indifference, one pupil may find that violence is effective, another that teachers are a safe target for the hate they feel for their family and themselves. There is no genetic configuration that causes a particular misbehaviour: misbehaviour is social and exists not as a natural entity but only in a relationship, or potential relationship. Bastide (1972) argues this point even for insanity. In chronic and serious cases the use of drugs may be the only feasible strategy. Tablets are less labour-intensive than straitjackets, and the alternatives are unthinkable: full, preventive, social and financial support for families at risk, and ready assistance for those whose get into difficulty. Often enough, it is more comforting for the parent too: the belief that one's child has a medical problem is less threatening than accepting that our parenting is at fault. Of course all treatments have a cost. Passed from one expert to the next, defined as a psychiatric or mental health problem, prescribed first this and then that, it is not surprising that some pupils grow dependent and anxious: and every recurrence of their problem behaviour confirms their growing and reasonable belief that they are not as others are, and must face a life of troubles, isolation, possibly madness. Their problem is as much a result of our omissions as their flawed inheritance. It matters very much that we avoid the error of assuming that pupils receiving medical attention are beyond the reach of teachers' understanding and skills.

Our beliefs about the nature of a condition have real consequences. Bastide (1972) describes how a religious sect, the Hutterites, interpret bouts of depression as a visitation by the devil. They stay with the afflicted person and give social support until, as they see it, the demon gives up and leaves. Of course, unbelievers will point out that the companionship of others has lifted the spirits, not driven off a spectre. But that is not a point worth worrying about: whatever their reasons, the Hutterites have settled on an altogether better treatment for depression than anything available on prescription. Most important of all, their strategy re-integrates the sufferer into the community: much medical or quasi-medical treatment abandons the victim to treatment in isolation. Schostak (1986) likens some drugs to riots: one acts inwardly to destroy the self, the other outwardly to destroy reality. In the matter of troublesome behaviour, medical interventions are like charity concerts for starving countries: a temporary relief and a welcome distraction from fundamental moral deficiencies in the way we exercise our social responsibilities. As we shall see in the next chapter, some schools, like the Hutterites, view troublesome behaviour, and their responsibilities towards it, in ways that keep their pupils in their community.

Courses aimed at helping teachers manage disruption in the classroom generally fall into two groups: those that assume teacher skills are at fault and need remedying (for example, Chisholm *et al.*, 1984); and those that assume that disruptive behaviour can be unlearned through a programme of behaviour modification (for example, Cheeseman and Watts, 1985). Teachers can adopt the skills and strategies in these programmes without necessarily changing attitudes that may themselves be contributing to their problems and the stress they feel. Useful as these approaches may be they are incomplete without consideration of the meaning of pupil behaviour and the hidden motives and anxieties that it may reflect. At a simple level there is the testing of teachers' rules and resolution; the displaying and defending of personal identity; the establishment and maintaining of a place in a friendship or peer-group; and the straightforward relief of tedium and tension. Some teachers read these activities as personal attacks or as proof of a supposed rising tide of disorder. They may be disabused and reassured by the evidence in such texts as Beynon (1985), Denscombe (1985), Hammersley and Woods (1984), Schostak (1983), and Woods (1980).

At a deeper level there are the influences of domestic and personal experiences which can dispose some pupils to unskilled and inappropriate strategies: struggles for attention, power or revenge; using the teacher as a safe target for feelings that belong to another person, place or time; seeking refuge from reminders of traumatic experiences in wild behaviour;

camouflaged or inept attempts at friendship and destructive testing of any relationships that may be formed. Many teachers find themselves driven to pessimistic fatalism with severely disturbing pupils. Confrontations seem unavoidable and security may be sought in unbending and autocratic domination: pupils may be required to march in step or not to march at all; the result may be a synchronized but stressed and brittle atmosphere. Understanding may be gained through such texts as Balson (1982), Cronk (1987), Dreikurs (1957), Hanko (1985), and Stott (1982). Such knowledge permits a more dispassionate and analytical stance and can be used to produce an agenda for staff discussions focused on pupils or groups whose behaviour is causing problems. A possible list of tasks for such meetings might include: to retrieve and identify pupils' motives and strategies; to discover the sources of their need for attention or feelings of hostility; to uncover any teacher behaviours, classroom factors or school influences which may be unintentionally maintaining unwanted behaviour; to devise and agree a consistent, whole-school approach to particular problems.

This book is intended to provide a basis for teachers to begin their own casework discussions in their own schools. It is from a teacher addressed to teachers: the people who know and can help troublesome pupils. It is not intended to be a contribution from a 'tip and run' expert (Hanko, 1985). It is my hope that those who read it and begin to work in the ways described will integrate it into their practical experience: they should become unable to separate what they know from experience and what they read in the book. Sharing ideas, experiences and worries helps teachers become inured to and insulated from disruption; they may be less easily provoked and less likely to fall back on coercion and punishment. In a perfect example of the disarming approach, Kohl (1970) remarks: 'I like defiant, independent and humorous people and my preferences naturally come out in my teaching'. To be encouraged and enabled to use more detached and disarming strategies is to be able, should we so wish, to remain composed, dispassionate, impassive. And where such strategies predominate in a school the climate, ethos or atmosphere may be described as harmonious: many parts are played and varied tunes are possible. Pupils of every demeanour and disposition may feel valued in the care of serene and shatterproof professionals.

The deficiencies of explanations which rely on single causes are recognized in the more accessible guides that are now available (see Denscombe (1985), Docking (1980), Fontana (1985), Furlong (1985), Laslett and Smith (1984)). Explanations for troublesome behaviour can be approached from two directions. On the one hand, we can begin with the pupil and his or her individual characteristics, personal perspectives and family circumstances; on the other we can look at the social and cultural milieu in which schools and classrooms are maintained and teachers go about their work.

Whichever end we begin at, the quest for understanding leads us to glance towards, if not to travel to, the other. There is a similar range in the remedies offered for disruption in schools, but the fit is imperfect. Those focused on the pupil employ behavioural psychology, with its emphasis on straightforward rewards and punishments, or cognitive approaches which take account of the pupils' perspectives and motives. Those beginning at the societal end of the spectrum might emphasize the unequal distribution of chances in life, the selective functions of schools, the shortages and competitiveness in the classrooms, and the resulting dilemmas and frustrations for teachers – many of whom see themselves as demoralized losers in a critical and unrewarding environment. Teachers stand on the boundary where pupils' problems and society's contradictions meet: to them falls the task of motivating those who have the skills that will be rewarded and mollifying those who do not. Some of the bad teachers blamed for indiscipline in schools are those who find this task beyond them. For some observers, confident that our social policies are fundamentally right, the weakness of such teachers renders them unfit for the profession.

In arguing for a broad and inclusive approach to problems in schools we are up against some terminology from which dangle simplistic theories and explanations. For example, the term, disruptive, implies that the problem is caused by only one person. Sometimes the term is used in such a way as to suggest that it identifies a particular type of disorder – as distinct from maladjusted, delinquent or naughty. There is little to be gained in pondering these refinements. In general, I have used the phrase troublesome behaviour and I do so, not to identify a specific syndrome, but in the hope that its neutrality carries no implications about aetiology or treatment. Worse still is the emphasis in some texts, and in the titles of two of them, on classroom control. Fontana (1985) suggests using the phrase in the sense of controlling an aircraft rather than a string of donkeys or a cage of lions. Another way of looking at it is to see virtue in increasing a teacher's power in the classroom: power is here understood as energy, a force from which pupils as well as teachers benefit. Davies (1984) claims that pupil deviance results when they are in danger of losing struggles in the classroom; giving the teacher more control may involve giving the pupil more power: absolute power and absolute powerlessness corrupt absolutely. Control of oneself and a feeling of empowerment are important in social relationships: defensiveness distorts perception, isolates individuals and destroys relationships.

Troublesome girls?

Just as this book applies to minor as well as serious forms of troublesome behaviour, it is also about both boys and girls. Girls are heavily underrepresented in exclusion statistics and are commonly considered to create fewer problems in schools than boys do. If true, it may be a consequence, not of innate temperamental docility, but of strategic adaptation to the world as they see it. Aggression does not pay off for girls in the way some boys find it does for them. Other people's social and cultural expectations make other strategies more effective for achieving their goals. Although it is usual to deny that boys and girls are treated differently, schools do seem to use gender as a basis for classification. King's (1978) infant teachers, asked why boys and girls should line up separately, were baffled by the question; Delamont and Galton (1986) recorded secondary pupils being classified by sex up to twenty times per day. During observations in a nursery, I witnessed one of those points at which the teacher's unconscious teaching finally got through to the pupils:

> Teacher (checking register): 'We'll call the girls first this morning.'
> (As each name is called the child stands.) 'Now let's choose a boy
> to count the girls. Sutpahl, you this morning.' (As he counts, each
> girl sits down again.) 'Now we'll call the boys' names. That's unusual,
> the boys are all together in a row this morning.'

In this way the biological category of sex is transformed into the social category of gender. This achieved, it is quite likely that goals and strategies will come to differ. Perhaps girls see education as a road to freedom or as an irrelevance in which failure is unimportant (Fuller, McRobbie, quoted in Furlong, 1985). Put simply, maybe our society teaches boys and girls that different strategies pay off, and then rewards them differentially. This would account for the common claim that when a girl is troublesome or aggressive, she is more vicious and tenacious than a boy would be. As boys learn that aggression in males is rewarded, they may also learn ways of avoiding it and limiting its damage. For most girls, violence is taboo, and in not learning to use it at all they do not learn to use it with discretion: perhaps those few who strike out for independence, strike out more and strike out for longer. Other explanations centre on the different group sizes in which boys and girls find friends (Davies, Meyenn in Woods, 1980a). The games boys are encouraged to play require large numbers, girls are expected to engage in less energetic activities, and are often found in groups of two or three. A boy who falls out with a friend will lose only a small percentage of his social circle, a girl may lose it all. In these circumstances intense feelings are to be expected, and it is not surprising that some girls' friendship crises seem endless – to the despair and bewilderment of teachers and parents.

Davies (1984) argues powerfully for another view. She challenges the belief that girls are less deviant in schools and suggests that their deviance is as great but takes different forms. Both sexes seek to exercise power but they do so in different ways. Perhaps boys, like convicted persons, are not the only offenders but only those who are caught: the 'failed offenders' (Phillipson, 1976). Davies found girls to be conformist 'only in certain areas – the institutional rules of the school in terms of attendance, misbehaviour and damage, and the technical goals of achievement in terms of conscientiousness and presentation of work' (Davies, 1984: 14). That is a formidable list of areas to be conformist in. Girls were said to be as bad as boys in respect of smoking and lack of uniform. In my survey of fifty teachers, reported in Chapter 2, covert smoking and inappropriate clothing were bottom of the list of teachers' concerns, which possibly accounts for girls not being regarded as serious problems. Davies says that girls were more deviant in respect of asserting 'more independence in the creation of personal time and space around the school'. Where bored boys might flick paper, girls would avoid work by pretending to write. Davies' evidence seems to confirm not her own argument but the popular view: girls cause less trouble in schools. Her list and examples clearly show this.

Deviating in ways that cause minimal annoyance and disruption to the routine is what is meant by conformist action. This does not imply intellectual conformism, but this is not seriously suggested, nor is it possible to imagine what possible evidence could be proof. If girls do choose to deviate in non-provocative ways, this may be a result of their different perceptions of others' actions and intentions. Girls may be the equivalent of deviance-insulative teachers, and boys closer to deviance-provocative (see Chapter 2). Davies' interesting Script theory seems to explain it all. Many scripts, or generally expected routines of behaviour, are for only male or female characters. Boys and girls can adapt or ad lib and they can act each other's scripts; but when they do, like drag artists and principal boys, they can get it horribly wrong. Further, if girls' scripts include the drama 'Being more understanding than boys', then it may be that teachers offer them more honest explanations than they think worth the trouble with boys. Cronk (1987) argues convincingly that a lack of such explanations results in misunderstanding and misbehaviour. When pupils are persuaded that teachers are doing their best, they co-operate. Taken together, these two writers seem to have sorted out the mystery of the missing girls.

Outline of the book

The next chapter describes some of the research and other work with troublesome pupils that helped develop the methods argued for in this book. Where reference is made to real schools, teachers or pupils, their names, situations and peripheral details are altered. The material for this chapter was gathered over a period of several years: some of the schools have closed, some teachers retired, and most of the pupils are now adults.

Chapter 3 is a detailed account of teaching skills and qualities that are said to be associated with freedom from troublesome behaviour in classrooms. The chapter describes ways in which this knowledge can be used to help teachers in difficulty, and to improve the understanding of experienced teachers who are content with their classroom effectiveness. A major problem confronting those who see the solution to indiscipline in improving teacher skills is the disagreement about what counts as a good teacher. Wragg (1987) quotes a review by Barr:

> Some teachers were preferred by administrators, some were liked by pupils, some taught in classes where there were substantial pupil gains, and generally speaking these were not the same teachers.

In a profession where more than two thirds now have more than twenty years' experience, it takes a reckless bravery to insist on colleagues following one's own prescriptions. Good teaching is difficult to quantify because values intrude in a way they do not in more technical professions. And yet there is, as we shall see in Chapter 3, an abundance of research on good teaching. Much of it presupposes that it can be identified first and its characteristics listed later: we know it when we see it. Disagreements about teaching skills are similar to moral disagreements in that arguments about low level rules in specific contexts are confused with disputes about general principles upon which we all agree. For example, there can never be consensus on whether it is always right or wrong to tell lies or not. Faced with an armed desperado asking after the whereabouts of one's friend, most of us would apply a precept of higher generality and tell a lie. One of the exercises following Chapter 3 is an opportunity to think about general skill categories in teaching: discovering them is a task uniquely suited to the teaching profession. Success in this as yet unaccomplished work would form the foundation of a code of professional expertise. Empowering teachers in this way, far from weakening others, would enhance the knowledge, understanding and personal effectiveness of us all.

Chapter 4 considers the classroom scene from the pupils' point of view. The argument here is that pupils' attitudes, motives and strategies are invariably (some would say always) rational and reasonable in respect of their experiences and circumstances. Even apparently senseless activities, such as openly being drunk in school, have been represented as rational responses to an educational experience perceived as economically worthless (Willis, 1977). In a contrasting book, Robertson (1981) emphasizes the role of teachers' authority in combat with pupil motives, which he says are to seek excitement, attention, work-avoidance, and peer-group status through brinkmanship. Different pupils will of course have different motives and this chapter considers all the possibilities. A dispassionate and developmental view is encouraged. Understanding the sources and motives of pupil hostility insulates the teacher from personal hurt and helps in the achievement of order and co-operation.

I depend heavily here on the writings of Balson (1982) and Dreikurs (1957). Their emphasis is on addressing, not the surface behaviour of troublesome pupils, but their underlying motives. This kind of reflectiveness is often scorned in favour of the behavioural approach (the manipulation of rewards and punishments) or even the common-sense tactic of 'Shut up and do as you're told'. There is a feeling that reflection is misplaced on a battle ground: teachers would rather get their hands on something simple, effective and quick. I am convinced, and I hope readers will be too, that a reflective and analytical disposition does not preclude action nor necessitate relinquishing control. It puts depth and precision where there is often shallowness.

Interestingly, an American study of teaching styles and student behaviour concluded that there was some empirical support for approaches to discipline modelled on the work of Dreikurs. Discipline techniques were categorized as authoritarian, behaviour modification, common sense, instructional, permissive, intimidation, group process and socio-emotional climate. The latter pair were found to be 'positively related to on-task behaviour' (Wittrock, 1986: 422). Such studies cannot fully allow for differences in classes' original orderliness, however. The strategies recommended in Chapter 4 help teachers come to terms with the inevitable difficulties faced in classrooms. In this respect they are effective irrespective of their effects upon pupils, and although empirical support is welcome, it is not essential. I regard this chapter as the core of the book.

Whereas the book as a whole concentrates on prevention, Chapter 5 focuses on responses in threatening situations of stress and confrontation. The advice derives from earlier chapters, so to some extent coping with confrontations and stress offers a relatively clear empirical test of the book's philosophy.

Chapter 6 describes two contexts, knowledge of which helps in the understanding of pupil behaviour. These are the classroom itself which has its own particular dynamics and constraints; and the school, its climate, ethos and organizational arrangements. It concludes with a case study which raises issues discussed throughout the book. The effect of schools' methods of allocating pupils to groups was first shown by Hargreaves (1967). The stigmatizing label indicating a low ability stream is more powerful than anything actually spoken by a teacher, and many studies have confirmed this. Less rigid streaming seems to lead to less polarization of attitudes. However, Willis' (1977) work suggests that some pupils, whose opposition is more deeply and historically rooted, are able to see through organizational camouflage and educational myth. Others suggest that pupils can be kept in ignorance of their academic status until the time of fifth-year examinations.

Chapter 7 discusses how teachers responded to the in-service work upon which this book is based, and explains how teachers and schools can teach themselves.

For explanations to be complete, and remedial strategies to have any hope of success, they must not depend on a single cause and a single remedy. To do so is often the first step towards abandoning responsibility. If a pupil is believed to be brain-damaged, hyperactive, or from a hopelessly ineffectual or irredeemably criminal family, then the school may see little point in trying to help, or may offer minimal help in a destructive atmosphere of pessimism. Pupils and classes vary in their behaviour: from 'a pack of hungry half-starved wolves with the math and English teachers' to 'docile lambs with their science teacher' (Wittrock, 1986: 409). It follows that any explanation that rests entirely on them cannot be complete (Hargreaves, 1975). Similarly, it is futile to settle on explanations that blame capitalism, unemployment, television, the school or bad teachers. Pupils are not inanimate objects, malleable and ductible, responding in predictable ways to external stimuli: if they were, simple and effective treatments would have been found long ago. Pupils and teachers interpret the world of experience, both internal and external – a world of experience, not a narrow, solitary patch – and it is upon these understandings that they act.

Troublesome pupils cannot be understood without considering them in several spheres: individual, family, classroom, school, community and whole society. All these spheres have the individual pupil at the centre. In one sense we are all sociologists: thinking about ourselves and our position in the world is to be forced to consider relationships. What C. Wright Mills called the sociological imagination, exploring the relationships between public issues and private troubles, is essential in the understanding and management of troublesome pupils. To view problems from only one perspective is not so much incomplete as distorting (Andy Hargreaves in Woods, 1980b).

Enlightenment is a valuable aid to seeing problems, not as opaque and oppressive, but as interesting puzzles to be solved – even if we conclude that on some levels no direct action is possible. Shedding light on the network of causes and social relationships makes them visible, accessible and less frightening than when they remain unseen forces in the darkness. Accepting and understanding our constraints is a form of gaining control of ourselves, a form of autonomy. In one sense we are never powerless and no social or educational problem is hopeless. All teachers are part of the education system and therefore no teacher should ever feel that decline is out of control and nothing is being done. Pessimism is out of place. A teacher who is concerned about education is that part of the system that is thinking and is saving itself through them.

Chapter two

Exclusion from school

Many studies over a long period have found correlations between disruptive or delinquent behaviour and domestic deprivation, family disorder, erratic parental discipline, poor attainment or ability, as well as being male, teenage and working class. Furlong (1985) and Galloway et al. (1982) contain summaries of this work. Looking specifically at exclusion, York et al. (1972) found excluded pupils to be 'severely disturbed psychologically and have serious educational handicaps'. They also noted family disruption and parental delinquency and located the cause of exclusion firmly in the pupils, their domestic circumstances and their failure 'to meet the demands of school life'. Teachers and headteachers were explicitly excluded from the equation. York's pupils did not include any short-term excludees and almost all had already been referred to a hospital psychiatric department, making them untypical of troublesome pupils in general. Galloway et al. (1985) whilst agreeing that there is a 'high rate of psychiatric disorder in excluded pupils and their families' notes the 'strong evidence for the importance of school variables in determining exclusion rates'. In his Sheffield secondary schools, five out of the thirty-nine accounted for more than 50 per cent of excluded pupils over a three year period. In a similar survey I found that five of forty-nine schools accounted for 30 per cent of excluded pupils in one year. Although Galloway's research did not identify any specific school factors responsible for differing exclusion rates, he concluded that policies on exclusion were idiosyncratic to each school. He suggested that the practice of pastoral care, as distinct from its formal organization, was a possible factor: this proved to be the case in my survey. Longworth-Dames (1977) found no significant differences between the personalities of excluded pupils and their peers, as measured by Cattell's High School Personality Questionnaire. However Stott's Bristol Social Adjustment Guide showed a higher level of hostility and failure to inhibit impulses (inconsequence) in excluded pupils. Pupils who had changed schools did not always exhibit the same extreme behaviour in their new setting which the author puts down to the pupil's modification of their behaviour in a new school. This may be so, but it could also be a difference in the perceptions of a new and more resilient teacher filling in the questionnaire.

That the domestic cultural environment may help or hinder school attainment patterns is generally regarded as self-evident. It is a simple explanation readily illustrated to the satisfaction of many teachers (Chessum, 1980). The theory of social learning proposed by Bernstein (1971) has made its way into teachers' thinking in various forms. More recently Brice-Heath (1986) described the educational consequences of a mismatch between domestic adult–child interaction and that between teachers and pupils in the classroom. An interesting feature of this case study was the clear evidence that, for first grade pupils, the home environment was richer and intellectually more complex than the classroom. In the domestic environment adult questions referred to whole objects, events, causes, effects, comparisons. At school, the teachers asked only the names and features of things: this is similar to the distinction Barnes (1969) makes between closed and open questions. There are likely to be behavioural consequences where there is misunderstanding: pupils, baffled, may withdraw or, feeling resentment, assert themselves in unwanted ways.

My enquiry began with data on the suspension rates of nearly fifty high schools in a large city. A school's rate of suspension is an imperfect guide to the degree of disorder or harmony within it. In all my visits to schools I saw no sign at all of the disorder and decline that outside commentators sometimes claim characterizes the system. Whatever the relationship between suspension and disorder, a school's ability to retain its pupils is a significant achievement in itself and differences in effectiveness in this respect are themselves worth investigating. Raw suspension rates alone are insufficient for comparing schools because it is usually supposed that some school catchments contain more pupils presenting problems than others. However, schools which were comparable in many factors turned out to have widely differing rates of suspension.

Table 2.1 Correlation coefficients

	Susp.%	Free meals%	Number on roll
On free meals%	0.47		
Number on roll	−0.35	−0.45	
Poor Attendance	0.45	0.80	−0.29

Table 2.1 shows the correlations among all the data. The outstanding correlation is between poor attendance and the proportion of pupils qualifying for free meals. In this table poor attendance was a measure of the percentage of pupils attending for less than 80 per cent of the required time – that is, missing an average of one day a week. A correlation of 0.8 means that approximately 65 per cent of poor attendance can be explained

by this free-meals statistic. In a similar study Galloway *et al*. (1985) found a slightly higher correlation between poor attendance and free meals. He found a correlation of 0.89 with the percentage of pupils missing more than 50 per cent of their schooling: that is to say, poor attendance on this scale seems to be 80 per cent attributable to poverty in the school's catchment, as measured by free meals. There was, however, no strong relationship between school processes and attendance. This suggests at first sight that a school's attendance rate is a given over which school policy can have little effect. The lack of relationship may be a statistical artefact, however, produced by the fact that school attendance policies differ less than catchments do: almost all the schools visited had rigorous attendance policies and regular checks on absentees. Attendance rates are normally taken as outcomes of school policies in measures of school effectiveness. It is worth noting that if attendance is in fact more properly a measure of catchment, then differences in attendance would partially explain differences in other outcomes.

The correlation, between free meals and suspension, of 0.47 indicates that only about 20 per cent of a school's suspension rate can be attributed to catchment poverty. This leaves a large margin that must be explained by something else: more importantly, these other factors, unlike local poverty, are more likely to be under the school's influence if not its total control. Behaviour in school is known to be related to the general atmosphere, ethos or climate of the school irrespective of catchment (Reynolds and Sullivan in Gillham, 1981; Rutter, 1979). Reviewing research, Graham (1988) notes that in Gray's (1983) research 'intake explains behaviour in school the least, and academic attainment the most'. One suggestion that I sought to investigate was the role of the school's referral system for discipline problems. The procedures used by a school may unintentionally escalate minor problems into major confrontations in which the authority of the school may be perceived to be at stake. This is documented in Lawrence *et al*. (1977) who described 'a fast route which, started at the level of exclusion from class . . . could lead to . . . suspension'. Further examples are in Galloway *et al*. (1982). The most unexpected correlation was between school size and suspensions: it is often suggested that larger schools create an impersonal atmosphere which leads to disaffection, disorder and suspension. The figures show exactly the opposite although this may be partly a result of there being two types of school in the sample: those taking pupils at age eleven (larger schools) and those taking pupils at thirteen (slightly smaller schools). Schools with a higher proportion of older pupils might reasonably be expected to have a higher level of disaffection to cope with.

It is one of the arguments of this book that fewer suspensions and less disorder follow from the decentralization of authority and distribution of power within schools. Studies of industrial organizations have suggested that increased size can have precisely these results (Pugh and Hickson quoted in Dunkerley and Salaman, 1980). There is anecdotal support for this being a difference between large and small schools which perhaps helps them keep their rates of suspension down. When supervising teacher-training students in large schools, one scarcely ever meets the headteacher and almost never needs to: the responsibility for students, as for many other features of the school's life, having been delegated. This is not the case in small schools where there is a tendency for the headteacher to be directly involved in all aspects of the daily routine.

Table 2.2 Comparable schools

	Roll	Poor attendance	Free meals	Susp.	Susp/frees %
School A 11–18	840	3.6	9.1	3.7	39.8
School B 11–18	1,040	3.1	9.7	0.2	2.0
School C 13–18	900	38.0	55.0	0.8	1.5
School D 13–18	1,100	41.0	30.0	3.9	13.0

Table 2.2 shows four sample schools. Schools A and B are suburban comprehensives, comparable in all respects except that one has a suspension rate eighteen times higher than the other. Schools C and D serve poorer urban areas yet the school in the least favoured situation has a suspension rate only one-fifth of the other. The standard if crude way of allowing for domestic disadvantage is to use the schools' percentage of pupils qualifying for free meals. Surveys have shown free meals to be a measure of catchment deprivation comparable to census records of social class and headteachers' estimates of social and economic disadvantage. In the city under investigation the proportion of pupils taking free meals varied from under 4 per cent to nearly 60 per cent with a mean of 21 per cent. There are two ways of combining these figures in order to judge how well schools are managing to contain their number of suspensions: one is to draw a scatterplot (see Figure 2.1). By inserting the mean values for suspension and free meals, it is possible to identify four groups of schools. Two of these groups are of particular interest: group A comprises schools whose free-meals rates are above average but whose suspension rates are nevertheless low; group B comprises those schools whose free meals rates are low but whose suspension rates are above average. It seems reasonable to suppose that school X is managing very well in potentially difficult circumstances; school Y, on the other hand, seems

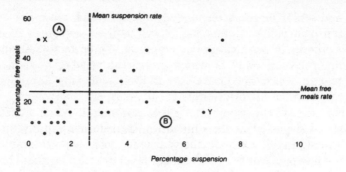

Figure 2.1 Scatterplot of free meals against suspension rate

to have an unnecessarily high rate of suspensions despite its favoured catchment.

The second method of comparison is to use a simple formula. In my survey, schools whose suspension rate was less than one tenth of their free-meal rate were doing better than average. However the validity of such a formula depends upon many factors which are not easily measurable: local variations in recording suspensions; the local average rates; the actual take-up of, as well as the changes in entitlement to, free meals. (Full details are given in a journal article, McManus, 1987: 262.) Table 2.3 shows four schools ranged in order of suspension rate and apparently, therefore, of effectiveness in this respect. When free meals are taken into account the order of effectiveness is reversed.

Table 2.3 What is a high suspension rate?

	Free meals%	Suspension %	Susp/frees%
School P	39.1	4.0	10
School Q	24.1	3.0	12
School R	9.7	1.4	14
School S	3.7	0.8	21

Having found a fair way of comparing schools, and a method of identifying schools with very high and very low suspension rates, the task was to identify the positive and negative factors at work. It is not easy to discover how a school's stated policies are applied in practice. For example, all schools have group tutors and some sort of system for dealing with disciplinary problems. Almost all schools claim that the form tutor is the key person in the system and that they try to ensure that group tutors retain responsibility for a class during its four or five years in the school. Most schools provide comprehensive policy statements on their pastoral and disciplinary organization. I found that, when presented with examples, heads and senior teachers responded in ways which were not congruent with their own policy documents. It was in their responses to examples that differences in practical policy emerged. Three factors seemed to be most important: the way in which group tutors were used in practice; the extent to which preventive rather than punishing approaches were employed; and the list of offences earning suspension.

In some schools the group tutor's role is nominal. When a crisis occurs, he or she is bypassed as the difficulties are referred rapidly up through the hierarchy. In other schools the year team act as a considerable barrier, either holding pupils at the year-teacher level or referring them back down to group tutors. Two examples were presented to heads: if a teacher has persistent difficulty with a pupil in class, what does he or she do? If a teacher discovers a serious incident out of class, what does he or she do? In almost all schools difficulties within class are referred first to the head of department and difficulties out of class to the head of year. It is what happens next that appears to be crucial (Figure 2.2 shows the possibilities). Schools with lower than expected suspension rates tended to give the group tutor a more significant and responsible role. There was an expectation that problems would be dealt with at the lowest level in the school's hierarchy. The group tutor was regarded as significant and important and decisions were not taken without consulting and involving them: in some schools the year team actively resisted attempts to refer pupils to higher authority. Schools with higher than expected suspension rates tended to have a rapid referral system where even the head of department or head of year might be left out of decision making. In these schools pupils could find themselves outside the head's or deputy's door for such everyday trivialities as dropping litter. Not surprisingly, these senior staff sometimes felt overwhelmed by a seemingly ever-rising tide of disorder and disruption. Delegation, or sharing, might have lifted their burden and reduced the number of pupils being rejected by their schools.

In schools where there was a positive and preventive approach to troublesome behaviour there was a lower than expected rate of suspension. Some schools had a special area or set of rooms where pupils causing

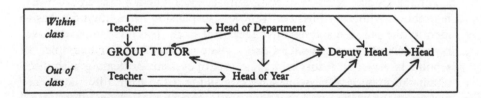

Figure 2.2 Referral routes for discipline problems

difficulties could be taught by particularly expert staff and then supported on their return to the ordinary timetable; others had integrated their support teachers into ordinary classes. This usually involved teachers in considerable planning for what was in effect a specialized form of team-teaching. It was not simply regarded as adding a remedial teacher to an ordinary class: the lead role in lessons was exchanged or shared and in some cases rendered unnecessary through careful preparation of resources and self-programming learning materials. Whether the support was wholly or largely within the ordinary class, there was an emphasis on tackling the problem in its original context: teachers were not encouraged to refer pupils to specialist staff in the expectation that responsibility for these pupils was being transferred. Working together was an effective and practically-relevant type of staff-development and training. Teachers could support one-another as well as the pupils: whatever the difficulties, teachers were sure of a colleague's support in discipline, teaching and the maintenance of personal esteem. All the pupils benefit, irrespective of their needs, from this integration of the pastoral and academic curriculum. It has costs in terms of staffing levels and the additional time teachers need to spend in planning.

The extra noise caused by more activity, discussion among pupils and between them and their teachers is also a discouraging factor. No school thought these costs outweighed the benefits. In contrast, schools with higher than expected suspension rates tended to respond to problems after the event. If they had units, they tended to be regarded as a punishment and there was not the emphasis on supporting return to the ordinary classes. Teachers came to believe that their responsibility ended once the pupil was referred. In extreme cases, troublesome pupils were exiled in an empty classroom and supervised by a rota of teachers; some were made to work outside the head's door. Not surprisingly, few pupils with serious problems responded positively to this punitive treatment.

Schools with lower than expected suspension rates had a restrictive policy in respect of suspension and used it only for serious cases of bullying and intimidation. There were attempts to prevent decisions being made in the heat of a crisis and the procedure was deliberately slowed down to give time for reflection. Interestingly, a pupil's past history was not allowed to unduly influence decisions about guilt and innocence. Some schools were also concerned to prevent pupils manipulating the system in order to be released from school: where it was suspected the pupil and his or her family welcomed suspension, alternatives were looked for. Schools with higher than expected suspension rates tended to have a list of suspension-worthy offences. After bullying, the most common offences for which pupils were suspended were verbal abuse to staff and disruption of lessons. Some schools automatically suspended in certain circumstances: for example, being caught smoking three times or setting off a fire-alarm. Some reasons for suspension seemed bizarre but were not: one school suspended pupils who failed to use the proper crossing point on a nearby dual carriageway notorious for fatal accidents. Other reasons seemed bizarre and perhaps they were. One pupil had been suspended for leading a pupils' strike against the teachers' strike: discovering the gap between practice and precept can be a punishing, if educational, experience.

Three other factors emerged, but less strongly. There tended to be lower than expected suspension rates where unruly classes would be reorganized, exchanging pupils with other classes; where teachers in difficulty would receive help in their classes, by being teamed with an experienced teacher; and where headteachers believed the social and non-academic side of school life was worth spending funds on. Asked if they would use school money to support a trip to the coast, some said there would have to be an educational input but others responded along the lines of 'money well spent' or 'how wonderful'. These factors may be clues to other aspects of school climate that I found difficult to measure. For example, pupils can be exchanged and classes reorganized only in schools where groups are of similar ability: such fundamental strategies are not possible where there is relatively rigid streaming, or setting is widespread. It may therefore be the relatively non-competitive atmosphere that is contributing to fewer suspensions, and the freedom to reorganize classes is a symptom of this. To support teachers in difficulty by teaming them with experienced colleagues indicates a degree of openness and collegiality that may itself reduce stress, and help the staff as a whole cope in difficult situations. The relationship of each of the six factors to schools' having higher or lower than expected suspension rates is given in Figure 2.3.

Each of the factors identified may seem trivial in itself but the figures

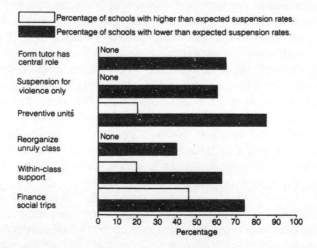

Figure 2.3 Suspension rates and school policies

indicate that modifying policies in line with these findings could reduce a school's suspension rate by about half. Taken together they indicate a significant difference in atmosphere between schools. In those where few pupils are excluded there is a greater degree of shared responsibility, a willingness to face up to and prepare for difficulties that arise, and a determination to accommodate and cope with the vagaries of adolescent demeanour.

Distributing authority to tutors lends support to the view that giving people responsibility makes them act responsibly. Perhaps the effect is more fundamental. Schutz (1972) distinguishes between consociate and contemporaneous knowledge of others. To know a person as a contemporary is to know them only as a member of a category of persons; to know them as a consociate is to know them as an individual in the way that members of a family know each other. Empowering tutors gives them the incentive to get to know their pupils as consociates. Tutors who know that their views will be listened to and given weight will see some purpose in seeking to understand their pupils – however unacceptable their behaviour. It may be thought that some pupils' behaviour is so unacceptable that it is beyond the reach of even the most well-disposed teacher, but there is evidence that this is rarely so. I have yet to meet a case where there was not at least one teacher prepared to speak on behalf of a troublesome pupil: and it is a common experience, in the adult sphere of deviance, to find apparently balanced (and often distinguished) people eager to plead on behalf of persons known to them but guilty of distasteful crimes. David Goode's chapter of Barton and Tomlinson (1982) provides support for the view that no human person is beyond our understanding. He describes a number of cases where severely impaired persons, whose disabilities engendered horror in strangers, were nevertheless known, liked and communicated with by parents, nurses or companions. When pupils realize that their tutor has real power to represent their point of view, however idiosyncratic, then genuine communication can take place. Teachers and pupils can get to know one another as individuals and not merely as typical members of groups, imperfectly understood and possibly distrusted. In such low-key and unglamorous ways as this can real democracy and understanding enter schools.

Harmonic or synchronized?

> The school is threatened because it is autocratic and it is autocratic because it is threatened. (Willard Waller)

This section generalizes the findings on school policies and in so doing tries to account for variations in schools' exclusion rates. The discussion relies on two theoretical ideas: the concepts of mechanical and organic solidarity introduced by Durkheim in a classic work (1893/1933), and the concepts of classification and frame described by Bernstein (1971). Durkheim argued that social cohesion depended upon one or other of two types of solidarity and that the nature of the law in a society served as a barometer of solidarity type. A school's declared policies and written documents are imperfect indicators since schools do not always act in accordance with their stated policies. There is normally a gap between word and deed. A school's rate of referral for permanent exclusion is the equivalent of the law's actual disposals and may be taken as a reasonably reliable indicator of its true threshold of tolerance.

Mechanical solidarity, which Durkheim found to be prevalent in what were then thought of as primitive societies, is 'born of resemblances . . . and directly links the individual with society'. He called it mechanical because it was analogous to the links between 'molecules of inorganic bodies'. The division of labour was undeveloped, beliefs and sentiments largely shared by all members of the group. Cohesion was strong where ideas and tendencies common to all members of the group were stronger and more numerous than individual ideas. In the terms used by Mead (1934), each person's 'Me' eclipses his or her 'I'. In this type of society individuality does not develop and the collective conscience acting within us envelops our personal conscience. As individuals depend upon the collective they 'become dependent upon the central authority in which it is incarnated'. In such a society law was essentially repressive: as social cohesion took its source from similarity, individuals were relatively dispensable.

Organic solidarity arose from the division of labour and depended not upon resemblances but upon differences among individuals. The term organic was used because it was analogous to the links between the different organs of higher mammals. The unity and capacity for action was as great as the individuation of the parts more marked. Members of society depended upon one another because they depended upon one another's specialisms. Solidarity of this type derived its strength from individuality; law was characteristically restitutive; in Mead's terms, each person's 'I' was greater than his or her 'Me'.

Durkheim proposed these two types as analytical tools and was not suggesting that they could be found in their pure form in reality. He proposed to take the ratio of repressive to restitutive law – criminal to civil – as a measure of the importance of the collective conscience to social cohesion. Punishment served to maintain cohesion in mechanical societies and only secondarily, if at all, to deter or correct. 'Inversely, commensurate with the development of individual types and the specialisation of tasks, the proportion between the two types of law ought to become reversed.' The concepts of mechanical and organic solidarity may be adapted and applied to schools. The argument will be that schools with high suspension rates exhibit the characteristics of mechanical solidarity and that those with low suspension rates exhibit the characteristics of organic solidarity.

Durkheim's ideas can be expressed in terms of Bernstein's concepts of classification and frame. In Bernstein's (1971) paper classification refers to the degree of insulation between curriculum contents: the strength of the boundaries between subject disciplines. Here I shall use classification to refer to the strength of the boundaries between individual actions, the degree of discreteness of individual acts, the certainty about the meaning of acts. Where classification is strong there will tend to be agreement about the significance of pupil behaviours. Where classification is weak there may be hesitation and uncertainty about the meaning of pupil behaviours: they will be individuated and pupils' histories may be searched for mitigating evidence. For example, with strong classification verbal abuse to a teacher will signify the same irrespective of the pupil and the circumstances: it will admit of no other interpretation but will be a piece of behaviour that could be entered on a behavioural questionnaire. Where classification is weak verbal abuse may be interpreted in many ways: it will be seen as an act having many possible meanings rather than an example of a questionnaire category. It may be taken as an insult; it may be seen as an insecure pupil's strategy to win approval from a peer-group; from a pupil with a history of domestic ill-treatment verbal abuse may be seen as a way of testing the sincerity of a teacher who has shown interest and concern. Analyses of the sort described by Dreikurs (1957) and Balson (1982), and used in Chapter 4, imply weak classification. Where classification is strong such reflection appears as indulgence: for example, swearing is swearing and there is no excuse for it.

In Bernstein's (1971) paper framing refers to the degree of control teacher and pupil have over what may be taught: the strength of the boundary between that which is permitted and that which is not. I wish to use framing to refer to the strength of the boundary between behaviours which the school regards as containable and those which it does not. Where framing is strong there will be a number of behaviours which earn suspension and a reluctance to make exceptions. Where framing is weak there will be fewer, and a willingness to allow the uncertain line to be crossed and recrossed before a pupil is finally excluded. Where there is strong framing, deviant behaviour is seen only as an impediment to the teacher's proper task; where framing is weak, coping with deviant behaviour is included in a teacher's professional responsibilities and is not seen as merely grit in the machine.

Figure 2.4 shows the four school types which result from combinations of weak and strong framing and classification. The harmonized type most fully exhibits organic solidarity and the synchronized type, mechanical solidarity. Both may be relatively stable but the synchronized type is

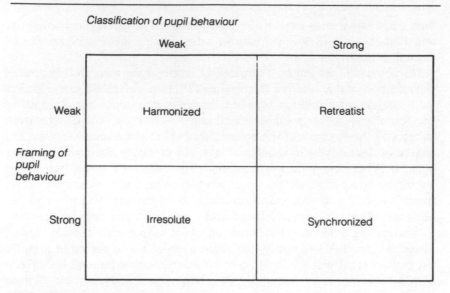

Figure 2.4 School type matrix

perhaps more vulnerable to change. For example, relatively inflexible standards and brittle distinctions would be threatened by increasing diversity in pupil intakes. The flexible and assimilative ethos of the harmonized type may allow it to accommodate change without danger.

Synchronized schools will have rules on such things as dress, hair-styles and deportment. The range of offences meriting exclusion will be wide and include many offences against collective norms; offences against persons will tend to be described in a collective-referenced vocabulary as will reasons given for exclusion. Authority will tend to be centralized and referral to it relatively swift: responsibility will be vertically distributed. As the school seeks to achieve behavioural uniformity it is likely that some segments will be perceived as threatening and there may be a corresponding anxiety about any possible increase in the diversity of the intake. For example, a rise in the number of pupils with special needs following the integrationist tendencies of the 1981 Education Act. There will be a moralistic and judgemental view of deviance and more vigorous attempts to suppress it. A pupil's record or school history may be used to re-define an otherwise trivial act as more threatening, and subversive motives may be attributed.

Harmonized schools will tend to have few rules on dress and they will be loosely interpreted. Offences earning exclusion will be few, and such as there are will be offences against persons. Authority will be laterally distributed: power and responsibility shared; teachers will have considerable discretion in their dealings with pupils and the headteacher will not normally be directly referred to in disciplinary matters. Such sharing may reduce the gap between the formal and informal systems within the school's organizational structure. Staff will have greater discretion to be flexible, to permit a degree of non-compliance in the longer-term interests of co-operation, respect and goodwill. Reasons for exclusion will tend to employ a person-related vocabulary. Since the school accepts a wide range of individual differences in demeanour there will be no areas where subversive groups are perceived to be sedimented. A pragmatic and utilitarian approach will predominate over a moralistic and judgemental attitude and there will be a correspondingly relaxed attitude to increasing diversity of intake. There should be evidence of positive and energetic attempts to repair breaches in relationships between pupils and teachers before any pupil is excluded. Where a pupil's history or record is referred to it will tend to be as mitigating rather than incriminating evidence.

These types are in effect opposing extremes of a scale: it is not suggested that any schools are actually like this in reality. They are similar to the incorporative/coercive school types proposed by Reynolds and Sullivan (1979). Moving from the macro- (or meso-) level of school organization to the micro-level of individual interaction, they are paralleled in Jorden's concepts of insulative/provocative teachers (see Hargreaves et al., 1975: 260–1). For example, there should be a higher proportion of deviance-insulative teachers in schools of the harmonized type. A school might therefore be typed as harmonized or synchronized by discovering the stated policies in respect of behaviour and by assessing the teachers in respect of their degree of deviance-insulativeness or deviance-provocativeness.

The grid generates two other types which might be regarded as intermediate forms but will not be used here. It may be that in that labelled retreatist, much is permitted but not approved of. For example, in the case of a synchronized type's staff losing the power to control aspects of their pupils' behaviour but continuing to believe they ought to do so. Were they to adopt the individualized view of pupil action found in the harmonized type, they would arrive at a more comfortable perspective and be able to negotiate. In the irresolute type there might be a realistic perception of pupil behaviour but a lingering attachment, perhaps ritualistic, to unsustainable norms and standards in respect of what a school should accommodate. A wider professional view of a school's responsibilities would resolve their conflict and reduce their stress. Suspension rates should be high, if somewhat arbitrary, in the irresolute type but may be low in the retreatist type at the cost of considerable internal disorder.

Typing teachers according to a dominant perspective, and schools according to a dominant ethos, can be too gross an over-simplification of reality. Referring to school types conceals the fact that schools as such do not have rules, policies and attitudes. Individual members of schools create and maintain rules and thereby influence the overall atmosphere or ethos according to their individual power and commitment. Furthermore, teachers themselves do not use a consistent perspective: in one situation, provoked; in another, insulated. Simple dichotomies give clarity at the expense of validity; attempts to increase validity result in cumbersome typologies which confuse rather than clarify. Compare, for example, Hammersley's (1986) complex teacher-perspectives scheme with simpler typologies such as Esland's (described and discussed in Woods, 1983).

Contrasting case studies

The argument will be illustrated by describing two schools – one of the harmonized type which will be called St Matthew's, and one of the synchronized type which will be called St Luke's. These two examples, the policies and pupils described, are constructed from data gathered from several schools through interviews and questionnaires. We move, as Schostak (1986) puts it, away from soft statistics towards hard social facts; but St Luke's and St Matthew's are real only in the sense that the characteristics of people and places in novels are real, and they serve some of the same purposes: protecting real people and highlighting only those aspects that are relevant to this book. This technique has been used by some writers in attempts to evaluate educational innovations and will be discussed in Chapter 7. Senior teachers or heads were interviewed about their policies towards disruption and suspension and other members of staff were asked for their reactions to common disciplinary incidents. Similar incidents are presented for discussion in Exercise 2 at the end of Chapter 3. All the strategies offered by teachers aimed at achieving some degree of co-operation but some responses were direct and confrontational whereas others seemed more impassive and disarming: particular teachers varied from situation to situation in which sort of approach they said they would use. For each example the strategy offered was assessed as either confrontational or disarming – these terms being adopted in preference to those used by Hargreaves and Reynolds. A confrontational strategy is one where the teacher's response is autocratic and unbending: demands are made and compliance through domination is aimed at. A disarming strategy is one where the teacher's response is less direct and more dispassionate: the teacher is unruffled and seeks to maintain order through mollifying and humouring. The questionnaire responses were categorized by two people and only those upon which there was agreement were counted. It was clear that few teachers approached every incident with the same perspective and most varied their strategies in different situations: of fifty teachers replying, only three were assessed as confrontational, and only one disarming, in all five situations. On the whole, teachers tended to confront problems directly. Even in schools exhibiting the highest degree of organic solidarity, and closest to the harmonized type, most responses were confrontational.

St Matthew's serves an area of poor housing and high unemployment: two-thirds of the pupils qualify for free meals, but its suspension rate is almost the lowest in the district. The headteacher describes the school's policy as follows:

> To be suspended from this school there would have to be not just
> one but a whole catalogue of serious offences and the catalogue
> would have to include a number of attacks, or at least swipes at staff,
> teachers hurt in prising pupils apart and so on. The final straw in one
> case was a very vicious attack on another pupil; in another, a girl
> thumped a teacher four times – she was protecting another pupil.
> In both cases there had been a series of offences before that and we
> would have to think carefully before having them back. Before we
> exclude a pupil the staff have to feel that we have tried everything
> and not been any help to the child. We have the usual list of
> detentions, report cards, attachment to senior staff and contracts
> between pupil and school. We try to mend situations before
> excluding. After an incident we try to give teacher and pupil time to
> reflect. There are no instant decisions. Staff might think about what
> had happened and think, yes, well, that's maybe provoked by me.
> We would not take the pupil's part against the teacher, we would
> arrange for the teacher and pupil to speak somewhere quietly. Not
> all the staff agree with this approach, it is not a unanimous view.
> Some say we might act more swiftly, but not many.
>
> My argument is that we must make special allowances for pupils
> who are socially disabled. Some pupils have physical disabilities and
> so we excuse them from some activities, let them be late for some
> lessons, for example. We have to accept that those whose
> relationships with others are disabled need special consideration too.
> One thing we have tried is to allow pupils to withdraw from situations
> which they feel are threatening their temperamental equilibrium: they
> are told that if they know they are going to blow up and do something
> they will regret, they should withdraw from the situation: either count
> up to ten or leave the classroom. I have given some extremely unstable
> pupils notes authorizing them to do this. It helps to keep the pupil in
> the school community and it is rather a skilful way of colonizing and
> making legitimate the flight-reaction many people have in situations
> where they cannot cope. In this school, walking out of a class and
> away from potential conflict can be a way of avoiding disruption. In
> most other schools it would make matters worse and itself become
> the target of punishment. It is seldom abused: most pupils go to the

agreed place rather than wandering the school shouting abuse through doors. That can happen though.

We are prepared to go to great lengths to keep hold of a disturbed pupil. We will accept a very basic minimum of co-operation as a negotiating baseline. We feel that if we can get them to school and keep them there we have a chance of improving them. If we exclude, we are not just admitting defeat but passing our responsibility for a pupil on to someone else. There is even less chance of success for others because the pupil is carrying the badge of failure already. We are always trying to find new ways, we try everything before even considering suspension. You've got to be prepared for things to fail, you've got to accept failure. It is like diagnosing faults on a car that will not start. You learn to resist your first impulse, which is usually to kick it. It is just as ridiculous to kick the pupil out of the door. You have to see a difficult pupil as a problem to solve not as a personally insulting challenge. Sometimes a crisis can be a turning point for the better: an opportunity for a teacher and pupil to form a more rewarding relationship. The pupil would see that they had upset someone and perhaps do something to make amends.

We are a very democratic institution: we believe in sharing the power and authority. To all intents and purposes the year heads are headteachers. I would never overrule them. They have a lot of autonomy, they have to have as there isn't always time for consultation, but they would try to consult the year team. I might not know of a suspension immediately, or as a matter of course: they might inform me later. I see delegation as a means of staff-development and education. If a teacher made frequent referrals to me I would see that the teacher was kept on the case, let them see what work was involved. In general I don't touch discipline. If I had a problem with a pupil I would refer it to the pupil's tutor. I do not think it would be proper for me to be judge and jury in my own case.

We have few rules written down and I cannot think of any off hand. They tend to lead to silly situations: we have requests not rules. For example, we have no rules about uniform but we ask the pupils to dress reasonably. If a pupil came to school in wholly unsuitable clothing then we would certainly not send them home or show them up in front of others. The pupil's tutor might compliment them on the outfit but point out that it was not suitable for school. They would have shown it off to friends and to us and not got into trouble. They would usually leave it at home the next day.

There are no full school assemblies but occasionally year groups assemble together. From time to time pupils, parents and staff meet for a sort of celebration evening. It is a bit like a speech day but it is individualized and non-competitive. Parents see individual teachers and may receive one of our awards. We have a very wide curriculum and pupils of all sorts of abilities manage to get an award for something or other.

St Luke's, on the other hand, has a very high suspension rate but very few pupils qualify for free meals. The school is pleasantly situated, popular, has a good reputation and is proud of its high standards. The head does not think the suspension rate is unnecessarily high and puts the school's policy as follows:

Some pupils make it impossible for their teachers to teach. For example, we had one pupil who broke our rules from almost the day he came here. In his first year he broke the uniform rules on eight occasions: these included wearing the wrong jumper, having no tie, and coming to school dressed in a jean suit and wearing a hat in school. In the end we had to suspend him when he came to school with a shaved head. It may seem a minor matter in itself, but we feel we have to get compliance in the small things or we find ourselves in battle over things that should never be challenged by pupils. Defeat on the issue of uniform will lead, domino style, to defeat in total.

We have a formal system of referral. A pupil would have to go through several tiers before getting to me. However, there are usually one or two pupils referred directly to me every day and if I do not get a satisfactory response from them I might well suspend them. I regard the school's discipline as my province and would certainly not want every class tutor involved. That would threaten standards. We do place a high priority on personal and social education, however. Tutors remain with the same class as it travels up through the year groups but they are not involved in matters that are properly the head's responsibility.

I am aware that our suspension rate is thought to be high; but we do have some very difficult groups of pupils. There are some pupils for whom there is no alternative to suspension now that the cane has gone. I am thinking of older boys, probably in the bottom half of the ability band, aiming for a low GCSE grade or none at all. Of course we take a pupil's record into account: for example, if a boy was badly behaved in a lesson, and he had a history of bad behaviour, then he would be quite likely to be suspended for it. Another boy might get a reprimand. We do not let troublesome pupils take up time that properly belongs to others. Some situations are calmed down by having the pupil stand outside my door. I do not think the staff would be very impressed if I held meetings and called in a counsellor or something of that sort.

The teachers at both St Luke's and St Matthew's are generally inclined to confront disciplinary problems directly: their confrontational responses outnumber their disarming ones. However, less than half of the responses from St Matthew's staff are confrontational and more than a third are disarming. In St Luke's case, two thirds of responses are confrontational and only a fifth are disarming. This suggests that one school has a wider and more flexible range of strategies than the other. In addition, St Luke's staff are twice as likely to say they would refer problems to senior staff and much less likely to express doubts or add qualifications to their answers.

In the harmonized type, like St Matthew's, suspension tends to be restricted to violence, group tutors have more significance and responsibility, and within-school exclusion units tend to be preventive rather than punitive; there is a diminished tendency to see particular categories of pupil as more productive of problems than others; a pupil's history, if used at all, has a mitigatory rather than an aggravating influence on the responses to their behaviour. The meaning of suspension itself is also different: in schools of the synchronized type, like St Luke's, it is a punishment and even an abandonment. In St Matthew's it forms part of the school's reparative policy: pupils are taken home rather than sent and there is an attempt to avoid the impression that suspension is a final break.

Conclusion

Some assumptions are implicit in the argument so far. First, that teachers' strategies and school organization affect pupil behaviour and not the other way round. Second, there is an underlying implication that harmonized schools are superior to synchronized: values intrude here as it may be said they do in Reynolds' (1985) notion of coercion/incorporation and Hargreaves' (1967) description of insulative/provocative teachers.

My particular interest is in factors affecting rates of suspension and methods of reducing those rates, for there is evidence that suspension itself is associated with later offending, irrespective of the severity of the reason for it. For example, in England, school reports influence magistrates' sentencing policies and suspendees are twice as likely to receive custodial sentences; in Scotland, all the suspendees in a sample of 678 offenders were referred to Hearings (Graham 1988). Suspendees may be simply more serious offenders but in a London survey, most excluded pupils claimed their behaviour was no worse than some of their friends who escaped exclusion (Mortimore et al., 1983). This does not clear up the matter however, for troublesome pupils are at least as inclined to blame others for their problems as anyone else. It seems reasonable to conclude, however, that schools which can hold on to their clients are more likely to keep them from a criminal career. It may be not just failure at school, but the school's response to that failure that is significant for pupils' future careers: delinquency is 'at least partly contingent upon rejecting or being rejected by the school' (Graham, 1988). There may be no simple one-directional cause. Teachers may feel constrained to be confrontational or disarming: they may feel that they are reacting to circumstances (rather than initiating them) by the pressure of pupil behaviour or parental and societal demands. Even infant pupils are able to constrain teachers' roles in classrooms (Bruner, 1980). Some pupils probably feel similarly caught up in situations which seem to leave them no alternative. It may be the case that confrontational strategies are less likely to lead to higher suspension rates in schools with favoured catchments. A policy may be ineffective in some circumstances and effective in others. Reid *et al.* (1987: 35) warn against applying generalizations to all schools and note the 'hints in the literature – little else – that some schools do particularly well for low-ability pupils but not for high-ability pupils'. This cautions against the uncritical adoption of policies seen to be favourable in another environment: teachers' strategies are, and I would add ought to be, individually motivated, interpersonally adapted and situationally adjusted (Woods, 1980b). The evidence discussed here suggests that change is needed at both the organizational and personal level. Chief among the former is that group tutors and year teams need allocations of both time and responsibility and need to be encouraged to use their autonomy to work co-operatively with difficult pupils. To make this latter possible some teachers will need to increase their understanding of, and ability to analyze and cope with, pupils' motives and strategies.

Personal histories of excluded pupils

In this section I shall discuss data on some typical pupils who were thought to be beyond the reach of ordinary schools. These pupils had been excluded from secondary and senior special schools and in some cases from schools for the maladjusted and units for excluded pupils. These cases are therefore extreme ones. That the pupils are largely unremarkable in their behaviour, certainly in comparison with other troublesome pupils, is further support for the argument that where there is the will to cope with problem pupils, teachers can do so.

My first major post working with excluded pupils required me to find and visit them at home in order to arrange home-tuition or attendance at my special centre. Before setting out to meet my new clients I looked at their files from which I expected to learn all about them. Invariably they were little help and it soon became clear that reports were not the simple records of events and explanations that I had naïvely expected. A similar problem confronted Garfinkel (1967) in trying to discover the selection criteria employed to choose applicants for hospital treatment. He found records to be so poorly completed that they were useless for his research project and he was led to ask why it was that the records at his disposal were so uniformly bad. He concluded that the hospital staff did not see the time involved as justified, and that the marginal utility of additional information was nil in circumstances where the use to which it might be put was unknown. Reporting carried risks to personal careers. For clinic staff, the chief function of the records appeared to be to provide evidence of the proper fulfilment of a therapeutic contract. They were compiled as insurance against the possible need to portray the clinical relationship as having been in accord with public expectations:

> Speaking euphemistically, between clinic persons and their clients and between the clinic and its environing groups the exchange of information is something less than a free market.

Cicourel (1968), studying police reports on suspected offenders, found them to be constructed in such a way as to justify police interference, locate the suspect in a legal context and map the event in legally relevant categories. Appropriate 'prior information' was used to support statements, including past record and family problems. Reports and records are not straightforward, actuarial accounts, they are compiled for various reasons and always with an eye on their possible audiences – parents, colleagues, superiors. Even after the Education Act 1981 it is rarely possible to draw up a statement of a pupil's special educational needs without having regard to the resources likely to be available, the reactions of the various parties to the document, and the need to protect the pupil's teachers and school from appearing to be ineffective or unconcerned.

The reports I received had usually been assembled after a crisis and when the reporting institution had already decided that the pupil was beyond their control. Psychologists have noted that some schools refer to them, not for advice about a pupil, but after a decision that the pupil must be moved has already been reached (see Welton's Bedford Way Paper No. 12, 1982). Often, teachers had not filled in the official forms fully, preferring instead to write statements in their own way. It was not uncommon to find a folder with up to fifty headings but almost all of them blank: the primary school report on one pupil included brief biographical details, a reading age, and the words 'Don't let him out of your sight'. In the records the principal concern seemed to be to show that the school had done all in its power with the pupil. All had tried everything they knew about. A scent of failure hangs about any admission of inability to control a pupil, and this is particularly the case where the referring institution is itself meant to be a specialist resource for difficult pupils. One example shows the exasperation: 'I can assure you that everything possible has been done. We have tried to educate him in the normal way but he has made it impossible for his teachers to teach. We can no longer accept responsibility . . . disasterous days lie ahead.' Some reports evidenced the reluctance to admit that a pupil is being suspended or expelled: 'It is not that we do not want him. It is not that at all. The problem is that this school is not suitable for him.' At another case meeting a teacher said 'We're sorry to do it, we don't want to lose him.' All the members of the staff present agreed that they did not want to lose him. Nevertheless, he was excluded the following day and sent to me.

Teachers were uncomfortable about expressing dislike of a pupil. The passive tense was used: 'Not a very likeable character'. Hargreaves *et al.* (1975) quotes a number of teachers at length and an extract from one shows a similar discomfort:

> I must confess that I can't like him, you know . . . I like them all really, even the ones who hate and irritate me, I do like them.

Nash (1973) suggests a taboo is in operation and Becker (1952) quotes a teacher who evidences guilt at his own harsh words: 'They're a bunch of bums, I might as well say it.' Some referred to a pupil's personal appearance as unattractive, unhealthy or odd-looking: 'unprepossessing appearance – Gollum like'. Hoghughi (1978) writes about the unattractive appearance of so many of his pupils and suggests that this may have set in train a series of hostile reactions of dislike and avoidance. Stott (1982) makes a similar point. Attractiveness depends to some extent upon health, personal care and self-esteem, but it is far from an objective quality that some pupils may simply lack. Goode (in Barton and Tomlinson, 1982) describes his work with Breta, a massively disabled girl whose drooping gait and excessive salivation had led one of her teachers to compare her to a slug. Her mother viewed her differently but, aware of others' opinions, told Goode, apologetically: 'I know you won't understand this but we think Breta's beautiful really'. During his time in the home Goode came to understand Breta as a person with likes, dislikes, expectations, routines and 'a beauty that was visible to the heart rather than the eye'. The lesson to be learnt here is that familiarity is needed: the opportunity to become acquainted with pupils as persons, not merely by description as they pass from one treatment agency to another.

Explanations and speculations on the causes of a pupil's behaviour, where they are offered, invariably do not refer to matters within the school. Home background or, more rarely, personal psychopathology are blamed. One school had compiled exceptionally comprehensive and detailed reports on a troublesome pupil – gathering, in the process, reports from the fourteen teachers who contributed to his timetable. Only one phrase in the collection referred to scholastic abilities or interests: '. . . a nearly complete lack of scientific awareness'. I did not notice at the time, nor did anyone else, that having fourteen teachers might have been one of this pupil's handicaps. There was much description and speculation about the pupil's home background – there had been inconsistencies in his upbringing, mother was said to be ineffectual, father had been in prison, a neighbour was being paid to look after the boy. Attributing school problems to home background, and sometimes to inaccurate perceptions of it, is common among teachers (see for example, Nash, 1973; Sharp and Green, 1975). The most sweeping example comes from a writer whose sympathy and dedication to working with difficult pupils was undeniable:

> I have come to the conclusion that where the parents seem quite normal it is only because we do not know enough about them.
> (Wills, 1967)

It has become customary to advise teachers to pay no heed to background factors and to concern themselves only with the rewards and punishments of the immediate classroom environment. Certainly, background information can engender a climate of despair, a feeling of powerlessness, and the abandonment of effort and responsibility. Yet it is well established that troublesome pupils do tend to come disproportionately from unhappy or unstable homes (Furlong, 1985: 199). Hoghughi (1978) found only 5 per cent of the children in his assessment centre to have stable families. Chronic rows, divorce, alcoholism and psychiatric disturbance characterized most of the rest. The home situations of the pupils in my unit were varied: some were dirty and bare beyond belief; others were comfortable and well appointed. All the families had some degree of difficulty and some were in tragic states of disorder. Most blamed the schools for their children's problems. Some seemed to be excessively indulgent of their children while others were openly hostile, comparing them unfavourably with their siblings. Discussions with parents showed, however, that scarcely one had deliberately treated their child cruelly, permissively or inconsistently. The damage had been unintended. Parents had found themselves helpless in the face of seemingly uncontrollable and growing difficulties, with their efforts to regain control seeming to make matters worse. Teachers often feel the same way. In Chapter 4 we will see how this information can be used positively as a source of strength.

Sometimes referring institutions found themselves in a dilemma. To have a pupil moved they had to show that he or she was ungovernable, but in so doing they ran the risk of making the pupil appear unacceptable to the target special school or unit. This is another of the hidden functions teachers had to have in mind when compiling reports. This feature has been present from the early days. Wills (1945) writes:

> We usually find when a boy has been with us for a little while that there are other symptoms not mentioned by the referral agency.

In Wills' experience these other symptoms frequently included bed wetting and soiling as well as temper tantrums and 'dirty habits'. In one bizarre case a special school had transferred a pupil to an ordinary school after reporting on the telephone that he was not maladjusted as had been thought. When the boy's new school received the records, sure enough they stated that he was 'not maladjusted'. The report continued: 'He is a delinquent and must now face the consequences of his actions.' Not surprisingly he did not remain long in his new school and was sent to me. I visited his original placement to discuss him. When I mentioned his name the teacher held both hands to his head as if shutting out a painful noise and uttered a long groan. Theatrical, but unambiguous however; and we shall see in Chapter 4 how such responses are an important clue to the nature of the pupil's problems.

That special schools and units, like some ordinary schools, find some pupils unacceptable is not evidence of irresponsibility. Centres were not opting for pupils who were in any general sense easier to cope with. For example, one unit tried to refuse pupils who were 'psychiatric problems, or low IQ'. This centre expressed a preference for tough pupils who were straightforwardly violent, and it managed them very well. In a survey of units for disruptive pupils, HMI (DES, 1978) quoted heads of centres who saw the need for 'control over the composition of the group'. Some recalled their early days when they had taken every school's most difficult pupils – their nominal purpose. They had found the work more congenial, and themselves more effective, with some sorts of problem rather than others. They now wanted the right to select and reject.

In an ordinary school, which had set up a support system for troublesome pupils, a similar phenomenon was observed. A pupil was eventually excluded partly because he had not conformed to the school's view of a troublesome pupil's appropriate role. A personal counsellor had been made available which the pupil had made use of but not in the appropriate way: 'He comes here four or five times a day on some pretext or other. He does not discuss his problems with the counsellor or respond to the support systems – rather, he takes advantage of them.' Here we see limits, unintentionally hidden from the pupil, on how counselling may be used: some reasons for visits are defined as pretexts or as taking advantage of the system. A possible complicating factor might be that some pupils do not readily discuss relationships, nor are they coded to operate on them (see an early paper of Bernstein in Halsey *et al.*, 1961). Another example comes from the children's ward of a mental hospital: 'We have a very free regime here, we believe in letting them act out'. This free regime had unstated limitations however, for the pupil under discussion was said to have taken advantage of it, and to be more suitably placed with me. Bastide (1972), discussing the history of mental disorder, sums up this phenomenon as follows:

. . . society plays as great a part as the sick person himself, who, to be recognised as sick has to make his behaviour conform to the behaviour traditionally expected of the madman.

None of the pupils referred to above were utterly beyond reach. Most of the time most of them worked at much the same sort of materials they had failed to settle to elsewhere. In a small unit they, and I, were free from the many pressures of an ordinary high school. One of my pupils said he preferred to be in a school where 'there was not too much people.' It is undoubtedly easier to stay cool and disarming when critical audiences of colleagues and conforming pupils are absent. It is easy to arrange what Reynolds calls a truce and others regard as 'simply a pretentious term for teachers not bothering anymore' (Musgrove, 1979).

HMI (DES, 1978) consider the possibility that small units enable the development of personal relationships, a freer atmosphere and greater flexibility. This may be close to suggesting that behavioural units can be a soft option for both pupils and staff. There are no compelling reasons to believe that the favourable aspects of small units cannot be reproduced in ordinary schools. Examples of effective high schools have already been described. We have also noted the difficulty in finding agreement upon what sort of behaviour is so serious as to necessitate permanent exclusion from school. This is not to say that no such behaviour exists, but only that it is exceedingly rare, and certainly insufficient to justify a large and growing behavioural unit sector. From only a handful in 1973 there are now several hundred and possibly as many as 1,000 (DES, 1978; *Where?* May, 1980; Graham, 1988). Proliferation of units and assessment centres, increases the uncertainty for some pupils. What from the administrative point of view is a series of specialized assessments, trial placements and treatments is subjectively experienced by the pupils as a career of rejection. Hoghughi (1978) notes that circulating pupils in this way can only increase their feelings of confusion and rejection; he mentions a pupil who had been in almost twenty placements. There is also an inherent illogicality in trying to re-adjust pupils by removing them from that to which they are not adjusted. The existence of separate provision is itself a discouragement to schools to find ways of accommodating their difficult pupils. The more complex the education system is as a whole, in respect of types of institution, the more likely it is that each institution will be able to specialize. Ordinary schools may find it easier to reject unwanted pupils rather than cope with them and each special unit will find it easier to specialize too: only the withdrawn, or only the dull and violent, or only the intelligent truants. All will be able to become more restrictive and increasingly closed to the full range and variety of pupils to the long-term detriment of comprehensive education in all its senses.

Three tests have been proposed for behaviour that is certain to be universally regarded as abnormal in all cultures and at all times: gross unpredictability; permanently inaccessible to communication; and consistent lack of minimum control of impulses (Kluckhohn quoted in Bastide, 1972). Whatever allowance is made for interpretation and ambiguity, few pupils in any type of school or unit cross these barriers. Inaccessibility to communication partly depends upon the skill and persistence of the other party. Whether a person is grossly unpredictable or lacks impulse control (which is another way of describing unpredictability) is also dependent upon the observer. In any case, everyone's behaviour is strictly speaking unpredictable (incomprehensible is closer to what is meant here). Looking too closely and for too short a time, as in physics, makes events look random and inexplicable: viewed in context and over time, patterns and explanations emerge. In support of this it is worth noting that in all the cases discussed there was always at least one teacher who found the pupil amenable. Sometimes it was a confident, almost arrogant, statement: 'He was all right for me.' Others seemed to be genuinely puzzled: 'I could never understand it. Every staff meeting there was somebody saying what a horrendous character she was but she was no trouble in here. She was all right for me.' Hargreaves *et al.* (1975) observed this phenomenon and noted its significance for understanding pupil deviance:

> Given that the conduct of the same class varies enormously with different teachers any explanation which rests exclusively at the pupil level must be deficient.

Whole classes vary in their behaviour from 'hungry half-starved wolves . . . [to] . . . docile lambs' (Wittrock, 1986: 409). Where there is the willingness, reflected in organizational flexibility and personal professionalism, schools can cope with troublesome pupils. There is no good reason for despair in ordinary classrooms.

Exercise 1: What type are you?

This exercise is derived from the work discussed in this chapter. It may therefore not be of interest to schools who have no reason to be concerned about the issues raised in it. The purpose is to explore how helpful it is, if helpful at all, to apply theoretical types to one's own situation. The first two tasks are necessarily crude but they serve, by bringing some elegant ideas down to earth, as a stimulus to discussion. First, look at the ten statements below and decide whether you agree with them or not. Second, tick those behaviours from the list that you think would seriously threaten your teaching or control. Third, spend a few minutes looking at the summary of types and strategies, before sharing your thoughts in groups of three or four. Do not feel constrained to hide any reservations about this exercise you may have: they indicate the complexity of the task of teaching and the need for a critical approach.

Opinions on troublesome pupils

1. They like fair, firm and clear rules.
2. They are determined not to conform to rules.
3. They work when teachers organize properly.
4. Improvements do not last, they do not change.
5. If I punish them, I let them 'save face'.
6. They should not be in the classroom, refer them.
7. I like them all really, share a joke.
8. Basically they are not interested in work.
9. I think they are all potentially winnable.
10. I show who the boss is, warn then punish.

Pupil behaviours

Arriving late	Talking when teacher talking
Tapping other pupils	Packing up early, as if to leave
Asking to go to toilet repeatedly	Unauthorized drawing on book
Missing lesson, absconding	Taking pupil's property
Smoking in toilets	Failing to bring omework
Rude remarks under breath	Unruly on way to school
Pushing past teacher	Taking teacher's property
Refusing to do set work	Graffiti on corridor wall
Playing with matches in class	Damaging classroom fittings
Running on corridor or stairs	Bizarre clothing/make-up
Cheeky/joky remarks to teacher	Rocking on chair defiantly
Talking when meant to be writing	Hitting teacher
Keeping coat on in class	Fighting in yard
Open abuse to teacher	Threatening teacher
Fighting others in class	Swearing at pupil in class
Chasing round room	Attempting smoking in class
Setting off fire-alarm	Refusing punishment
Throwing pencil across room	Leaving class early

Comments on exercise

For the first task, insulative or disarming teachers would probably agree with the odd numbers and disagree with the even ones. Most people find difficulty deciding without having a particular pupil, event and situation in mind. This illustrates the point made about the validity of strategies as opposed to styles. In the second task, about half the items are ticked on average. A low score might indicate that you are unflappable, or that you have iron discipline: again, more needs to be known about the particular circumstances.

Teacher style/strategy and school ethos/climate

Deviance-insulative (Hargreaves et al., 1975) exemplified by:	*Deviance-provocative* exemplified by:
Allowing face-saving and avoiding confrontations	Contest view of interaction, ultimatums/confrontations
Avoiding differential treatment	Neglect and denigration of deviants
Optimistic, defence of deviants	Expects trouble, punishes inconsistently
Belief that they really want to work, encourages any sign of progress	Pupils don't want to work, apparent improvement is deceit or cover for hostility
Informal relationships, respect, humour, sympathy	No outside contacts, ready referral to authority
leads to (?):	leads to (?):
Incorporative ethos (Reynolds, 1985) exemplified by:	*Coercive ethos* exemplified by:
Minimum institutional control or 'truce'	High level of control and punishment
Hesitation in enforcing rules likely to cause rebellion	Strict enforcement
Participation by both pupils and parents	Low pupil and parent participation
Underestimation of degree of social deprivation (optimistic)	Overestimation of degree of social deprivation (pessimism)
High expectations of pupils' ability	Underestimation of pupils' ability
Disarming strategy leads to:	*Confrontational strategy* leads to:
Harmonious atmosphere	Synchronized atmosphere
where teachers are	where teachers are
composed	autocratic
impassive	unbending
dispassionate	dominant
serene	formal
unruffled	stressed
shatterproof	brittle
and	and
many parts are played and many tunes are possible (minuets, modern jazz)	there is only one tune and we keep in step or we do not march at all

Chapter three

Teacher qualities and classroom management skills

The teacher skills and qualities said to be required by teachers of trouble-some pupils are often those that any teacher might need. The classroom management focus of the materials in Chisholm *et al*. (1984) is an example. Research upon which such programmes may be based is reported in Fontana (1985), Wragg (1984), and Walter Doyle's chapter of Wittrock (1986). This contrasts with the view, once common, that education was not a priority with troublesome children. For example, in a standard text on the education of maladjusted children, Laslett (1977) wrote that 'educational needs are not foremost' and described schools for the mal-adjusted as 'a preparation for learning elsewhere'. A later work however (Laslett and Smith, 1984) is a comprehensive and concise guide to teaching skills appropriate for all pupils and includes advice on coping with more serious problems in the classroom. Wills (1967), a pioneer of residential maladjustment therapy came to the view that perhaps he had 'underrated the importance of the education factor'. Brennan (1979) takes the edu-cational requirements for granted in a heavily critical report. HMI (DES, 1978) commented upon the inevitably restricted curriculum of disruptive centres: at the time of their report, these centres were increasing in number and it was becoming possible for some pupils to spend the whole of their school lives in them. Warnock (DES, 1978) drew attention to the recognition of educational failure as a factor in maladjustment and noted that, although some still perceive a conflict between education and ther-apy, schools increasingly emphasize the quality of the education they provide. Warnock found it necessary to justify the provision of education for the full range of pupils with disabilities and it is easy to underestimate the magnitude of this achievement: education in the ordinary sense, not therapy and treatment, is now taken for granted.

Robertson (1981) emphasizes, among an abundance of ideas and sugges-tions, the importance of the teacher presenting as an authority figure. It is easy to criticize this particular aspect as being irrelevant to the situation in schools: perhaps this is so, or ought to be so, and in secondary education unsubtle forms of control are usually less effective. However, it is worth noting some remarks by Kohl in this respect. A liberal advocate of openness and democracy he nevertheless found the need to assert his authority from time to time:

> In one short week I went from informal Herb, with an open collar and sweater, to Mr Kohl with a suit and tie, a very controlled manner and an unnatural, stern look. My students had taught me that I had to establish my authority before I could teach them anything. (Kohl, 1986: 38)

Hoghughi (1978) proposes a demanding list of qualities for those working with troublesome children: teachers must be stable, compassionate, sensitive, intelligent, resilient, mature and, ominously, physically fit. Laslett (1977) prescribes predicability and reliability but with exposure to less tolerant outsiders too. Wills (1967), with characteristic elegance says 'to live with maladjusted children you must be able to live without them and indeed without anyone – a whole complete person entirely sufficient unto yourself.' Hewett and Blake, reviewing the literature in Travers (1973), suggest that teachers of troublesome pupils do not need to assume a unique professional role: 'A competent teacher is a competent teacher whether working with disturbed or normal children'. This is true in so far as all teachers must be teachers of groups, able to cope with the unpredictable demands, the overlapping activities and the dynamics of maintaining public order in classrooms. Classroom management skills, by definition, primarily encompass the task of orderly management but that is not co-terminous with the task of managing disorder. Class management is an essential basis, but controlling and helping troublesome pupils requires other skills and insights which will be described in Chapter 4.

Basic classroom management skills

There are fundamental difficulties in trying to describe classroom teaching skills. These difficulties are related to those encountered in attempts to teach, or persuade others to teach, using behavioural objectives. The act of teaching is something more than the sum of its parts, and attempts to define it closely seem doomed to destroy that which they would describe. To a considerable extent human activities are beyond complete description: accounts, tape-recordings and films cannot capture the amount and complexity of events; some things are missed, changed or destroyed in the act of data-gathering. In the example given by Reid (1986), watching a video of a football match is not the same as being there. In addition, observers have attempted to quantify the complexity of teaching: for example, Jackson (1968) estimated more than 500 interactions in a typical teacher's day.

Teaching is rarely apprehended as the putting of skills into practice.

When a lesson is going well it may be experienced as an energetic blend of interaction and involvement, varying pace and tempo, new insights and explanations, and unexpected outcomes. Teaching skills are difficult to get a purchase on because they are dynamic rather than mechanistic in character (Eisner, 1982). The skills used in a successful lesson, and the objectives achieved, are easier to think about after the event. This does not contradict the argument that a description of teaching skills cannot completely capture the reality of classroom life. Reflecting on the characteristics of a good lesson can help identify techniques for use in future encounters: this is a long way from claiming that the success of future lessons can be guaranteed if certain skills (or objectives, for that matter) are used. This chapter and the three following should be read with this caution in mind.

These chapters constitute the substance of the in-service work that I hope teachers will be able to replicate in their own schools. In translating a course that was conducted in seminar rooms and teachers' own schools into a textbook some things are inevitably lost. I have tried to resist the temptation to write just another academic thesis although many references are given here that appeared only in supplementary handouts to the course. There is a convention, which Eisner (1985: 158) alerts us to, that 'the less expressive a description is, the truer it appears to be. Yet if there is an absence of emotional or qualitative content, the description risks leaving out more of what is important in the classroom.' As far as possible the text is faithful to the in-service courses on which it is based and the intention is to convey something of their atmosphere.

It often appears that experienced teachers have trouble-free lessons, not through knowing how to cope with troublesome behaviour, but because it simply does not seem to arise in their classrooms. The skills of classroom management become part of a taken-for-granted procedure and often neither the practitioner nor the inexperienced observer is able to identify them. The ability to control pupils is regarded as so vital a part of a teacher's personal identity that many continue to suffer in the isolation of their classrooms rather than admit weakness and seek advice. When advice is sought, it is seldom easy to give without conveying personal criticism. Part of this problem is the tendency for teachers to be accustomed to working unobserved and to feel uncomfortable if called upon to work in teams.

Hargreaves (1980) remarks that many teachers regard their teaching as an activity in some respects comparable to sex: being watched interferes with the performance. Watching teachers in difficulty is certainly embarrassing, and it is difficult to know how to offer advice without implying insult, as this observer's note shows:

The lesson is now out of control totally and I am embarrassed. The quiz goes on – some boys are singing. It is hopeless and embarrassing. Mr Wolfe asks me, Are they always like this when you're in? The answer must be no. (Delamont and Galton, 1986)

The aim of this section is to describe and discuss the teacher skills that have been observed to be associated with freedom from pupil disruption in expert teachers' classrooms. The skills discussed are listed in a summary at the end of the chapter and constitute a relatively objective agenda for teachers to use in helping less experienced colleagues improve their classroom control.

Lessons conducted in the traditional style often fall into phases to which varying rules and expectations are attached. Hargreaves *et al.* (1975) noted an entry phase, settling down, the lesson proper which included teachers' exposition and pupils' work, clearing up and finally exit. The amount of movement and pupil talk varies from phase to phase and some pupils seem to have more difficulty than others in adjusting to this. It is therefore necessary to give explicit directions and clear warnings when a change of phase is imminent. These warnings have been called 'flags' (Marland, 1975) and 'switch signals' (Hargreaves *et al.*, 1975). Some of the signals and cues observed by Evertson and Emmer (1982) included a real switch signal: 'moving to a specific area of the room, ringing a bell, or turning on the overhead projector'. If the lesson is planned, or the teacher can see its unfolding form if it is extempore, then it is relatively easy to make changes within the lesson clear and to prepare the pupils for them. For example: 'In two minutes we will stop and read the first paragraph.' The amount of class time occupied by transitions has been estimated at up to 15 per cent with the associated finding that these are peak times for misbehaviour to occur. Despite the common belief, external interruptions from visitors are responsible for only 10 per cent of classroom distractions (Wittrock, 1986: 406).

The traditional form of lesson, the recitation or question and answer type, is by its very nature vulnerable to disruption. Ironically, it is a form of teaching that was intended to put voice and life in place of the deadness of print. Stowe, an early teacher trainer of the 1840s, called it 'picturing out': he described how the teacher was to engage the attention of the class by interrogation, suggestion and ellipsis – which would nowadays be called the cloze procedure (see Curtis, 1963: 216). A basically similar style of teaching in America appears to have evolved from a different activity: having individuals recite lessons privately to the teacher (Hamilton quoted in Wittrock, 1986: 403). The teacher conducts an inquisition, attempting to involve the whole class and keep silent the non-attending parts of it. Observations of such lessons, for example Barnes (1969), indicate that questions are typically closed, that is admitting only of the answers in the teacher's mind, thus limiting and constraining the range of contributions from pupils. Although recitation has the appearance of a joint teacher and pupil search for understanding, in reality the teachers hold most of the cards and the pupils are reduced to guessing them. What masquerades as an inquiry after meaning and truth may become a game of 'guess the word I'm thinking of.' An example of learning degenerating into a guessing game in a primary school is analyzed in MacLure and French (1980). Teachers give information, elicit answers, direct who shall speak, decide whether an answer is acceptable or not, and evaluate publicly both the answer and the pupil's effort. Pupils are limited to seeking permission to speak and reacting or replying if called upon. Perhaps some procedure of this sort is inevitable in crowded classrooms where teachers' knowledge has to be shared in some sort of interactive way: few school teachers consider straightforward lecturing to be appropriate or possible.

Approximately one third of classroom time is said to be occupied in this way and in general observers note a high degree of pupil involvement as compared with other classroom activities. Where the questions are closed and admit of only limited answers, participation is limited to the more able pupils; where the emphasis is on ideas and opinions, and almost all answers are acceptable, lower ability pupils take a greater part and some of the more able tend to withdraw (see Doyle's review in Wittrock, 1986: 402–5). Class discussion sessions in which all answers are apparently accepted have been noted in infant schools (MacLure and French, in Woods, 1980a). However, although teachers seemed to accept all answers, this was only a surface feature of their remarks to the class, and the authors show that pupils' logically derived responses were in fact rejected in favour of the single answer in the teacher's mind. There is no doubt that the whole-class recitation method generates a considerable number of easily breakable rules. A pupil need only speak to a neighbour upon the topic under inquiry to create a disruptive event. Mehan (1979) notes that the rules of turn-taking, and the ways of displaying knowledge which are appropriate to the classroom community, may remain implicit. Some pupils need these rules and expectations making explicit.

The traditional teacher control of the classroom does not necessarily evaporate in open, resource-based environments. Whatever the limitations and difficulties of recitation as a classroom strategy the traditional teacher presence is still necessary from time to time. Edwards and Furlong (1978) reported on a school organized along open, resource-based lines where pupils had fewer restraints and more opportunity to follow their own learning paths. To some extent they were able to create their own 'local' curriculum, to work at their own pace, and to have a wider range of their knowledge and interests valued. Nevertheless, the authors observed no marked reduction in teacher control of knowledge – booklets were a substitute for teacher talk – and teachers retained some of their directive role, though in response to pupils' demands rather than on their own initiative. Where possible, therefore, it may be strategically appropriate to avoid the recitation (or teacher versus the class) style. To use a varied menu of learning and teaching styles is the first step towards pre-empting control problems in the classroom.

Early encounters

Control is normally easier to establish if the teacher is in position ready to receive the class. It is not an auspicious start to have to calm an already disorderly group. Rutter *et al.* (1979) reported that where teachers were waiting for classes and able to supervise their entry there was less school disorder. Research reported in Wragg (1984) showed that experienced teachers, when compared with students, were more likely to greet the pupils, occupy a central position in the room, wait for silence before speaking, issue directions authoritatively and use eye contact. They did not rely on voice alone to convey their requirements: posture and expression were relaxed and confident. Goffman (1959) has observed that impressions given off, as distinct from those deliberately given, are normally taken as a more accurate guide to a person's inner state. Naturally, if a troublesome class is expected there is a temptation to cut short an unpleasant encounter by arriving late. Similarly, one is more likely to find oneself shouting and less confident about taking a position forward of the desk while looking pupils in the eye. Many years ago a teachers' newspaper published a cartoon showing a teacher standing in front of a class, arms folded, impassive. The pupils are depicted in a state of disorder: paper aircraft and chair legs fill the air; cobwebs stretch from the teacher to the walls and ceiling and the caption is: 'I'm still waiting.' It takes courage to try non-verbal control skills and few teachers are completely free of the fear that they too may find themselves still waiting.

Laslett and Smith (1984) convey the briskness associated with effective teachers in their summary of the entry rules as greeting, seating, starting. They and Marland (1975) point out that a straightforward start to lessons, with something that occupies pupils in their desks, allows the teacher to cope with interruptions and late-comers. Where this advice seems uncongenial or inappropriate, perhaps where pupils are engaged in group projects, interruptions can still be prevented from becoming disruptions. For example, late arrivals can be briskly and amiably greeted and directed to the topic, without shifting one's attention from the rest of the class. There is no need to express annoyance or begin an interrogation: any necessary enquiries can be conducted later.

One way of proceeding with classes that are already out of hand is to draw up a short list of rules and make some sort of bargain with the class. This is especially effective with primary age pupils. When asked to suggest three rules for the class, both teachers and pupils tend to express them in negative terms. For example: no shouting; no wandering about; no spoiling other people's work. It is more effective to express the rules positively so that the pupils know what they have to do rather than not do. The three rules mentioned would therefore be written up on the board as follows: we must talk in quiet voices; we must stay in our own places; we must be helpful and polite to each other. Having established some simple and achievable rules in this way the teacher may then offer a reward. This can be tangible or not according to the particular circumstances: some classes are happy just to show they can keep bargains. In a primary school, a teacher might say something like this: 'I will look around the class every few minutes – that will be about twenty times this lesson. If everyone is obeying our rules on at least half of those occasions then there will be extra story time this afternoon.' The required success rate must be set at a realistic level that is likely to be achieved: the target can always be raised on future occasions – it is a bad idea to be too ambitious and begin with failure. Bull and Solity (1987) note the importance of stressing to the class the natural consequences of keeping the rules; this makes it easier to gradually withdraw the artificial system when a co-operative and productive atmosphere is established. A similar procedure was found to reduce disruptive behaviour in a study of two secondary school classes (McNamara, in Johnstone and Munn, 1987).

It may be the case, difficult to prove, that some populations of pupils are more amenable to these techniques than others. Rutter remarked that it was very difficult to be a good teacher in some schools. Calderhead (1987) reports on an experiment to discover the influence of the class on teachers – in this case two trainees. One who appeared to have established order of a precarious kind through a good deal of shouting and threatening was exchanged with another who kept control using a quiet voice and positive, rewarding behaviour. The students altered their behaviour so that the former became quieter and the latter began to coerce and shout. This is, however, no reason to surrender a skills approach: if pupils are such powerful constraints upon teacher behaviour then it can never be too early to begin re-educating them.

Wragg's team reported that experienced teachers tried to present a brisk, hard image on first meeting a new class: they would be resistant to enquiries, keep their 'mystery' or perhaps play on their eccentricities if these were known, respected or feared. Many used their first lessons to explain their rules which related to territory, property, work, talking and safety. However, Fontana (1985) warns that teachers should limit their continuous talk to no more than one-and-a-half minutes for each year of the average class age. Many teachers convey their extensive ownership of the classroom by specifying how pupils must use and keep neat their books, materials and desks (Evertson and Emmer, 1982). Rules were precisely stated and continually reiterated. This does not necessarily lead to confrontational situations if, once established, teachers are prepared to allow them to be discussed. For example, in one behavioural unit I visited the chief rule in operation was: 'We don't lay a finger on you and you don't lay a finger on us'. I witnessed a discussion on this rule arising from a complaint by a pupil who claimed to have been poked in the chest by a teacher. The group decided by vote that being poked in the chest did not infringe the rule; a pupil who had flapped his hat in a teacher's face, however, was found guilty and ordered to apologize. Whether this sort of discussion is genuinely free varies according to each situation. Wragg noted that some teachers would allow rules to arise in discussion, but it was clear that rules were not negotiable and the discussion was little more than a way of involving the pupils in the exercise. On this theme, Delamont (1976) reports Torode's observations on teachers' use of the consensual 'we'. Too much can be made of such refinements, however, and it is not necessarily the case that all aspects of a successfully dominant style can be simply transplanted. Where the first lesson was related to the curriculum it tended to be simple and undramatic. In contrast to these intentions, students aimed to be friendly, approachable and to identify with the pupils. Rules would come out naturally 'as problems arose'.

Students often intended to begin their encounters with something interesting and active, though many chose a less risky start on the day. In one class a student chose to demonstrate a chemical reaction which simulated a volcano: an event which came to symbolize the lesson. In contrast, effective classroom managers tend to begin with activities that have 'a simple, whole-class instructional structure, and the work was familiar, enjoyable and easy to accomplish' (Evertson and Emmer, summarized in Wittrock, 1986). Often, the teaching of the rules and procedures was the substantive lesson.

Evertson and Emmer (1981, 1982) found significant differences between more and less effective teachers in their behaviour at the start of the school year. They conclude, as others have (Ball, in Woods 1980b; Doyle in Wittrock, 1986) that the beginning of the year is crucial for establishing effective classroom procedures and advise that planning should be done before school starts. Effective teachers had 'a better behavioural map of the classroom and what was required for students to function within it'. This map would not omit the basic precautions mentioned by Fontana (1985): no dead tape-decks, illegible visual aids or stiff glue. The teachers of younger pupils placed more emphasis on teaching their rules and for all teachers the time spent on this activity varied from a few minutes to over forty minutes. Time did not appear as significant, however: effective teachers were more explicit and more likely to give copies of the rules or have pupils write them in their books. In addition: 'More effective managers tended to have more workable systems of rules, and they taught their rules and procedures systematically and thoroughly' (Evertson and

Emmer, 1982: 486). This seems to be stating the obvious and in some respects all observational studies are vulnerable to this charge: effective teachers are found to do the things that effective teachers do. In this study they were more vigilant, tended to use more eye contact, responded quickly to inappropriate behaviour, checked and gave feedback on work, maintained contact with the full class and set appropriate tasks which were clearly explained. They kept better track of progress and had 'stronger and more detailed accountability systems'. They were better predictors of pupils' concerns and difficulties and were able to see the classroom 'through the eyes of their students'. Doyle too reported that effective teachers maintained vigilance over the whole class and kept individual contacts brief (Wittrock, 1986: 402).

It is possible that those teachers typed as less effective are merely those unfortunate in their classes. Evertson and Emmer dismiss this possibility with the claim that classes did not differ in misbehaviour levels during the first week. However, the graph they give in support of this shows that less effective teachers had almost 30 per cent more 'unsanctioned off-task behaviour' during the first week of term (4.5 per cent compared to 3.5 per cent): this difference was not, however, statistically significant. Even if no differences in initial behaviour are noticed this does not mean that classes are similar in their potential for disruption. Teachers often find there is a honeymoon period before groups and individuals settle down or 'find their feet': this has been documented (for example, Ball, 1981; Beynon, 1985; Wragg, 1984). The concept of effective management shares a ragged border with effective teaching, professionalism and common-sense. Some ineffective teachers returned no marked work to pupils during the first three weeks of term. Another instructed a low ability English class to 'Write an essay from the perspective of an inanimate object'; this would be a difficult if not inherently impossible task for anyone but, 'the problem was compounded by an unclear explanation of the term, perspective'. In Wittrock (1986: 398–401), Gump estimated that 65 per cent of pupils' time is spent working at their own desks; Rosenshine reported that pupil attention was lowest in deskwork activities, especially when these were frequent; Silverstein and Kounin found deviance during deskwork to be four times as high as in teacher-directed, whole-class activities.

These findings clearly underline the importance of interesting and appropriate work but they also suggest that the rules bounding deskwork activities may need review. Deskwork is usually conducted individually and teachers find themselves periodically calling for silence. Classmates who help each other find themselves accused of copying or cheating. If co-operation were a more frequent requirement in deskwork, there would be fewer rules to break, less disciplinary intervention and possibly more learning.

The main part of the lesson

Giving the pupils an outline of the lesson's planned form helps to minimize interruptions and expressions of surprise at a later and possibly more vulnerable time. Similarly, to start with some deskwork ensures that all the pupils have the books and materials they will need for the lesson. This is particularly important with disorderly and forgetful groups. It is sometimes difficult to maintain a fresh and vigorous demeanour with topics repeated from year to year but some extra reading, or re-sequencing the material can help. Laslett and Smith (1984) refer to the Henson and Higgins view that pupil motivation can be engendered by taking an interest in pupils, knowing their names and treating them courteously. This involves being generous with praise and Laslett and Smith suggest preparing a number of synonyms for such tired words as good and nice. Bull and Solity (1987) advise 'full praise statements': gain attention, show approval, specify the progress, point out its benefits, and challenge them to do better. Balson (1982), however, distinguishes between praise and encouragement: certainly, older pupils do not always respond gratefully to praise and this advice must be used with discretion. It is equally important to convey enthusiasm for the lesson topic and thereby communicate to the class that it is something worth taking an interest in.

Partington and Hinchcliffe (1979) noted that effective class managers prepared effectively and extensively: as well as the content, they planned for organizational matters such as movement, time, and the tasks of particular pupils. To make a brisk beginning, explaining the relationship of the lesson's work to the course or to pupils' present concerns and future interests, is preferable to wrangles about the last lesson's leftovers or missing homework. These can be attended to later when they do not keep uninvolved pupils waiting. A variety of activities and tasks is more likely to engage the pupils than a monotonous period of listening or writing. Gannaway (1984) found that pupils were less likely to co-operate in lessons, especially ones judged boring, if there was too much writing. Some pupils regard writing as the only activity that counts as work and resent lessons where no writing is done at all. Teachers need judgement in this matter.

Attempts to introduce new learning methods and groupings sometimes collapse into disorder because pupils are unused to autonomy and unclear about what is expected of them. They may pester the teacher with questions or occupy their time in unwanted activities, hoping that some other group will come up with an answer that they can reproduce. Where pupils are set to solve problems in pairs or groups it is necessary for the task to be explicit. It may even be necessary to specify a number of words, or the headings for lists under which appropriate results may fall. Pupils sometimes fail to co-operate in open-ended paired work because the teachers' evaluation criteria have previously indicated that only some results are valued. This repeats one of the problems encountered with whole class question and answer sessions where questions which appear to be open to several answers are in fact closed and admit of only one answer which is decided by the teacher. Where the task set is open and therefore to some extent ambiguous it is necessary for teachers to reduce the risk of pupils incurring negative evaluations, that is low marks and criticism. Failure to take account of pupils' perception of the teacher's evaluation criteria may result in pupils declining to co-operate: they may pester the teacher for the answers or turn their attention to something safer. Wrong answers may be pupils' attempts to transform tasks into something they can achieve or they may be a clue to the pupils' perception of the teacher's requirements (Posner, 1980).

Doyle and Carter (1986) analyse classroom tasks in terms of their degree of ambiguity and risk. They observed pupils pressing a teacher for additional guidance with a written assignment until they had transformed the work into something easier than the teacher had intended. She also made available extra marks in an apparent attempt to meet the pupils' anxieties. This opens the possibility that teachers might systematically present easier, low-level work to keep pupils occupied and reduce management problems. HMI often complain that pupils are not set sufficiently demanding work. For example, in Education Observed No 2 (DES, 1984):

> Usually expectations are too low . . . almost invariably the tasks which are set are too closely directed by the teacher . . . pupils need to be encouraged, and expected, to take more responsibility for their work.

The work by Doyle and Carter suggests that it is not low expectations that are the primary cause, but the demands of crowd control in busy classrooms. Three solutions seem possible: teachers might use control and management techniques that are strong enough to withstand the disruption that high level academic tasks seem to involve; methods of group working might be adopted which free the teacher from a barrage of pupil questions; and associated with this, a noisy and talkative class would no longer have to be seen as evidence of poor teaching. Doyle quotes work suggesting that, in open activities, teachers' talk is more positive and related to learning rather than control; and that group work, when carefully structured and rewarded and where individuals are accountable for performance, has positive effects on 'achievement . . . race relations and mutual concern' (Wittrock, 1986: 400). Denscombe's paper (in Woods, 1980b) suggested that noise is overrated as an efficiency indicator but described, in an open classroom environment, pupils using subtle strategies of friendliness in order to take rests from work. However, if Doyle and Carter are correct, many busy and well-ordered classes are far from completely engaged in worthwhile learning.

Caspari (1976: 20) shows how a teacher's presuppositions about how supposedly open-ended tasks should be completed caused her to overlook valuable and revealing contributions from pupils: expecting a descriptive essay, she failed to see the value in an imaginative and fantastic account. Mercer and Edwards (1971) use the concept of 'educational ground rules' which are the hidden or implicit cognitive frameworks to which pupils must have access in order to successfully complete tasks. These may be related to particular modes of expression or presentation integral to the nature of a topic: for example, the conventional way of presenting a letter or describing an experimental observation. They may be idiosyncratic: for example, 'creative writing' or the insistence on hands being raised before contributions will be listened to. Many of the taken-for-granted requirements and ways of presenting classroom tasks are more inaccessible to some pupils than others. Martin (1976) has drawn attention to the distance between written expression and ordinary talk and others have pointed out how important talk is to thinking (for example, Barnes, 1969; Driver, 1983).

Sybil Marshall's (1963) classic essay on primary education demonstrated the importance of talk in learning. Classroom writing tasks that can be accomplished to the satisfaction of the teacher in language that is close to the pupils' present speech are more likely to engage the pupils' co-operation. Martin believes that written tasks of this sort 'would free the writer to think in writing and to learn through using written language in the same way that he already uses talk'. Some teachers may find this inappropriate because of the gulf between the pupils' spoken language and the requirements of the topic. In such cases this draws attention to the need for particular types of expression to be taught: it is an error to assume that its lack is an indicator of missing ability. Some pupils will already have had access to elaborated literary styles of presentation; others need them making explicit.

Some of the disaffection experienced in classrooms is partly caused by pupils having differential access to attention and understanding. Keddie (1971) believed her small scale study, carried out in a secondary school humanities department, showed that teachers preferred middle class conformity to working class independent mindedness. Attempts by working class pupils to relate the curriculum to their own experience of life was graded as only 'C' ability. It must certainly be the case that some teachers are so immersed in their material, or so unfamiliar with it, that they are unwilling to be diverted from their lesson plan – or the textbook. This can hinder learning in both open, discovery-learning environments as well as in formal recitation.

A similar study in a craft department (Tickle, 1984) showed that some craft teachers' implicit criteria prevented some pupils engaging in high-level work. Those pupils who were believed to be less able actually got

55

more teacher time but their tasks were more closely directed and they were presented with less challenging assignments and problems. Tickle suggests that, despite teacher claims to value creativity, they acted as if a facility in basic craft skills was a condition precedent to it. Some pupils in such situations must necessarily feel frustrated and undervalued. Some studies have shown that apparently free, open, discovery work is more closely constrained than teachers claim. Atkinson and Delamont (1977) describe an example from secondary school science and an interesting comparison with the training of doctors on hospital wards. The suggestion is that this phenomenon helps teachers resolve a dilemma: the need to communicate knowledge and the ideological belief that pupils must direct their own learning if it is to be of significance. Many teachers have been introduced during their training to the views of Rogers (1961) who asserts that significant learning cannot be taught but only facilitated. Sharpe and Green (1975) show that, in a progressive primary school, pupil choice can lead to some pupils receiving less teacher interaction than others: specifically, working class children were said to remain known to teachers only as types (contemporaries) but middle class children became teacher consociates – known to them as well as if they were family members. Hargreaves (1978) is a theoretical analysis of classroom coping strategies as learned responses to material, ideological and societal contraints upon teachers. To be aware of these influences and their possibly hidden effects upon pupils is a partial aid to avoiding boredom, disengagement and disruption.

One of the most widely applied studies of teacher behaviour in orderly classrooms was carried out by Kounin (1970). A particularly valuable skill, which he termed 'withitness', consisted in giving the pupils the impression that the teacher had 'eyes in the back of her head'. Some years earlier, Dreikurs, whose work is used in Chapter 4, wrote: 'One requirement of all good group leaders – including teachers – is the ability to see everything that goes on in the group at any given time' (1957: 50). Brophy and Evertson (1976) use the term monitoring; Marland (1975) calls it the lighthouse effect. Successful teachers, in respect of classroom order, frequently scan the class and regularly make remarks, which Kounin said must be timely and accurate, to show that they are missing nothing, even when they do not otherwise intervene in inattentive behaviour.

Specifically, teachers watch the behaviour of groups in order to keep the momentum of activities moving. It is necessary to remain vigilant when the pupils have been set a piece of deskwork: in some classes, distracted pupils may look up to find the teacher apparently counting them. Regular marking and giving feedback have the same effect. Copeland had some success with a computer system designed to stimulate the attentiveness and overlapping demands of the classroom. The trainee was required to 'conduct a question–answer session . . . while monitoring the order of turn talking, the accuracy of answers, and another student who is supposed to be engaged in a seatwork task' (Wittrock, 1986: 425). Teachers need to maintain this classroom awareness when dealing with one individual or a group. This may be done by speaking to one pupil while looking at another or by helping an individual using a 'public' voice if the help or directions are appropriate. An expert class manager can question, explain, organize, mark, discipline, listen all at the same time – and while attending to a note from the headteacher. A teacher's day may be short in hours, but long in minutes.

Kounin indicated other teacher skills to which he gave idiosyncratic terms. 'Thrusts and dangles' contributed to classroom disorder: teachers should not interrupt pupil work precipitously and neither should they leave issues incomplete and unresolved. Teachers who stayed on one issue long after they had lost pupil attention were 'overdwelling'. Those whose foresight was so hazy as to produce confusion in the pupils were sometimes engaging in 'flip-flops'. This involved starting a new activity and then returning without warning to the one just abandoned: for example, 'maths books away, take out your readers, how many people got number fifteen right?' All these sorts of teacher behaviour interrupted the smooth flow of the lesson: the resulting loss of momentum contributed to a disorderly atmosphere.

Physical location in the classroom is a part of the teacher's non-verbal communication with the class and may also influence attention and behaviour. If possible, pupil desks should be arranged across the narrow length: a closer relationship is created with fewer opportunities for disengagement to develop, out of range and out of sight, into distraction (Grunsell, 1985). Studies have shown that pupils behave better and complete more work when seated in rows – though this may be because discussion and mutual help are defined as misbehaviour rather than work. Further, pupils seated in the front and centre of the room are said to be more attentive, although to some extent this could be where attentive pupils choose to sit. However, some experimental evidence suggests that in general it is helpful to insist on potentially inattentive pupils occupying a central position (see Wittrock, 1986: 402). To stand in front of the teacher's desk, rather than behind, indicates a potential mobility and possible territory invasion that helps to keep pupils' eyes upon the teacher. Evertson and Emmer (1982) noted that some of their less effective teachers 'did not circulate among the students during seatwork and thus diminished their ability to observe accurately'. Ironically, less effective teachers were observed to be more likely to leave the classroom (Wittrock, 1986: 410).

Responding to trouble

The first response to incipient disturbance need not be a verbal rebuke or comment. A stare, averting eyes sideways (not submissively down) if the stare is returned in an uncomfortable or defiant manner by the pupil, can sometimes prevent an escalation of the unwanted activity. Adopting an authoritative stance, for example folding one's arms, or moving closer to a disruptive pupil, invading his or her territory, are other possible ways of regaining control without drawing public attention. Sometimes an invitation to respond to a question serves a similar low key purpose and, with younger pupils, a touch on the shoulder perhaps. For the same reason (avoiding too public a profile early in a potential conflict) it is best to make corrective statements short: nagging, threats, interrogation and recitation of past misdemeanours should be avoided.

It is easy to underestimate the need to make requirements explicit and to target remarks by using names, specifying both the unwanted behaviour and the desired activity. Social class styles of adult/pupil interaction may sometimes be a factor here. King (1978) in extensive observations in infant schools noted examples of a middle class 'oblique' mode of disciplining pupils: 'someone's being silly'. This may not be correctly decoded by some errant pupils. Reasons given for telling pupils to desist may be more readily accepted if they refer to the needs of the activity, and their congruence with precedent and routine, rather than personal preference. Torode, in Stubbs and Delamont (1976), reports on the speech used by a Mr Cramond in enforcing his rules. He refers to 'the order of events' thus confirming a shared system of rules and expectations. This protected the teacher from challenge by relieving him of responsibility for rules which he referred to as if they had a reality independent of personal preference. An extension of this technique is to focus on correcting the behaviour rather than criticizing the individual: this allows all parties to maintain a degree of objectivity and coolness towards the interaction, avoiding attacks on pupils' personal esteem. Caspari (1976) notes how difficult it is, even in marking work, to prevent some pupils taking correction as personal criticism: separating one's view of a person from one's view of their behaviour is much more difficult. It is similarly inappropriate to compare pupils to siblings as this, too, personalizes the unwanted activity when it is best distanced and discarded.

Kounin's research did not show clearly whether a ripple effect, his term for pupils falling into line after one of their number has been corrected, always occurred. Probably only the successful correction of pupils who have status in the pupils' eyes has this wider effect. Comparisons are similarly unlikely to be effective where a low status pupil is the comparison: Walter is a poor model for Denis the Menace. Fontana (1985) suggests drawing attention to suitable models, rather than making comparisons. Pupils may sometimes object that an individual is receiving unfairly indulgent treatment when a teacher decides to ignore rather than challenge an unstable pupil. If this differential tolerance is acknowledged, and a suitable reason given, most pupils will accept the situation: adolescents are particularly aware of their individuality and will accept unequal treatment when the reasonable circumstances are explained. Doyle (in Wittrock, 1986: 412) notes that some teachers take account of pupils' responses in deciding which rules to strictly enforce and which to regard more flexibly: in some circumstances, informality can give the teacher considerable discretion and 'power as a rule arbiter'. At the other extreme, few pupils will accept that mass punishment of a whole class or group is reasonable.

Allowing the natural consequences of misbehaviour to take their course is usually the easiest and most agreeable method of punishment. For example, homework preparation is not done so the lesson is missed, walls are defaced so they must be washed after school. Evertson and Emmer (1982) say there is no need for 'praise machines'. Co-operation in class results in positive consequences: for example, completing tasks and being allowed to answer. Punishment is probably more effective where it is supervised by a person who knows the pupil well and is respected by the pupil. Where the teacher knows that a pupil is unamenable, and intervention will result in aggravation of the situation, it is still necessary to show in a neutral way that the behaviour has been noticed and is unwanted. From time to time, overseers must overlook. Laslett and Smith (1984) make a useful distinction between 'planned ignoring' and 'just hoping the nuisance will go away'. To correct only the pupils on the fringes of disruption, pretending not to have noticed the central character, will not normally enhance the teacher's classroom status. Doyle (in Wittrock, 1986) reports that good classroom managers 'tended to push the curriculum and talk about work rather than misbehaviour'. The less successful focused on misbehaviour to the extent that work ceased, while their more effective colleagues found the working atmosphere carried the burden of control. One unsuccessful teacher, who managed to keep pupils on task for only a quarter of the time, rebuked pupils nearly 1,000 times in one day.

Loud public rebukes can be effective when they are rare and unexpected; but they communicate weakness where they are a regular feature of a teacher's classroom. Soft and private reprimands, preferably in the absence of an audience, are more likely to be effective: 'a soft answer turneth away wrath'. Numerous public rebukes can disturb the class to the extent that the teacher increases the disruption that he or she seeks to diminish. An effective intervention is 'abrupt, short and does not invite further comment or discussion from the student' (Wittrock, 1986: 421). A relaxed posture, a voice pitched low, an absence of gesticulation or poking help to keep confrontational situations calm. A teacher in a unit for excluded pupils, who happened to be addicted to chocolate, sometimes contrived to unwrap and eat a bar when faced with particularly violent and dangerous situations. Eating is something we do when feeling unstressed, this helped define the situation as unthreatening, and helped to soothe troubled feelings. An unwanted confrontation can sometimes be halted by simply stating the conditions under which co-operative relations can be resumed: explicitly state the peace terms and withdraw from the interaction. Where a pupil has to be removed from the room, it helps persuade the pupil that the teacher is rejecting the behaviour and not the person if the pupil is led to the door rather than ordered out. At the same time some simple condition that must be satisfied for re-entry can be repeatedly emphasized: the rejoining of the group, on what may be privileged terms, is thus uppermost in the exchange – rejection, and the reason for it, is minimized. This style of control helps maintain a cool demeanour and avoids alarming and exciting other pupils, whose continued need for attention must not be neglected. If, in the course of dealing with an incident, the teacher falsely accuses the pupil, a generous or even extravagant apology can be both calming and evidence of the teacher's invulnerability and confidence.

Clearing up and exit

The completion stages of a lesson or individual learning session sometimes require planning and preparation in their own right. Often the most difficult pupils are the first to finish work (to their own satisfaction) and this should be planned for. With disaffected groups, an orderly and coherent end to a lesson can leave a general impression of having achieved something worthwhile: this feeling is not confined to the pupils. More effective schools in Rutter *et al.* (1979) tended not to have lessons finishing too early. Laslett and Smith (1984) note that 'hard-won control is most frequently lost and learning wasted at the end of lessons'. In so far as one lesson's end is another lesson's start, professional responsibility and staffroom harmony depend upon good management in the concluding phase. As the end of a lesson approaches and release for both parties is at hand, the teacher may find less difficulty in gaining attention. It is unwise to use this period for a recitation of the errors of the past session, perhaps mixed with demands for silence, backed by threats of instant detention. The opportunity is best used to summarize and draw together the themes of the lesson's work and perhaps relate them to the intended programme for the next meeting. Review what has been achieved as if all had achieved it: experience shows that even in the most disorderly and chaotic classes, a majority of the pupils are engaged on task for most of the time. It does not depart so far from reality therefore for the teacher to take a positive view and to define the situation as a success. An orderly dismissal, with a relaxed and smiling teacher, helps to minimize problems and is a better prelude to the next meeting than an atmosphere of recrimination and threats. Particularly uncooperative pupils may be held back for a brief word as the class leaves.

Sockett discussing a possible professional code for teachers in Gordon (1983) lists six items relating to classroom practice. He suggests that teachers should always be properly prepared before classes begin; they should ensure that pupils are always productively engaged; they should not frequently discipline any particular individual during teaching; they should concentrate on their pupils' successes and praise them generously; they should set and mark work regularly and speedily; they should have high expectations of their pupils and manifest them constantly; and they should be punctual. These are, as Sockett himself says, conventional and common-sense prescriptions. As with much classroom management advice, some of this may seem to be too trivial to require specifying and as likely to lower the status of teaching as to raise it. One does not suppose the BMA includes punctuality in the professional code of doctors – perhaps it is as well, for they seldom are. The impression of simplicity and triviality is a false one. Rules and prescriptions vary in their significance according to the context: for example, punctuality does have a juvenile and trivial aspect in everyday life, perhaps reviving childhood memories of reluctant compliance. In teaching, however, it is part of a professional relationship with colleagues as well as pupils: this context makes imperatives of many seeming trivialities. The summary at the end of this chapter, which is in the form of fifty tips, should be read with this caution in mind.

Research on classroom management yields much information helpful to experienced teachers who wish to work with less effective colleagues. Those intending to use it in this way should note Laslett and Smith's (1984) advice on helping colleagues. One should listen with empathy, keep confidences, try to offer practical advice, reassure the teacher that asking for help does not imply incompetence, and avoid punishing a request for advice by involving the teacher in extra labours. Research is also not without value to those who already feel confident of their classroom competence. Doyle (in Wideen and Andrews, 1987) suggests that such data should not be used uncritically as a list of rules to apply. Experienced teachers use research as activators or modifiers of their existing planning, filtering it through existing schemas and integrating it into their practice. A further suggestion of Doyle's is to use research to identify more encompassing instructional functions.

This takes us back to the problem raised earlier: much of the advice is appropriate only in some contexts, and much of it seems obvious and trivial. Some of the skills identified are of a clearly more general level than others. For example, using names, making eye-contact, standing in a central position and issuing authoritative statements are all lower level activities that might be encompassed in the higher level skill of gaining pupils' attention. Gaining pupils' attention is a more general teacher skill necessary in all teaching contexts, whereas the skills encompassed by it may be merely contingent: there are many ways of gaining attention. This goes some way towards explaining the disagreements among teachers about what skills betoken an effective teacher. If the skills identified are low level, there will be much disagreement just as there is in moral debates about low level rules. For example, there can never be agreement about whether it is wrong to tell lies or not: faced with a murderer asking after one's friend, we have to defer to precepts of more general application. Doyle suggests three candidates for the role of instructional functions: coverage, as measured by such things as the opportunity to learn, pacing, and the match between class activity and curriculum documents; explicitness, which must be neither too little nor too much for the task; and accountability, which includes the monitoring activities by which many students are motivated. Exercise 3 is an opportunity to begin what Doyle terms 'practical reasoning' in respect of classroom management skills.

Teaching skills for traditional classroom management

Early encounters

1. Get there first, introduce yourself, supervise entry.
2. Occupy centre stage, make directive statements, plenty of eye contact.
3. Give impressions as well as instructions: voice tone and pitch, facial expression, posture, use of space, proximity – relaxed and confident.
4. Scan class to get attention, mid-sentence stop and wait, stare.
5. Demeanour brisk, hard, resist queries, keep mystery.
6. Part or whole of first lesson: content simple, undramatic, not too exciting, perhaps on rules, safety, management.
7. State rules or draw them out in 'discussion' – work, property, talking, movement. Use consensual 'we'.
8. Discover and use names.

The main part of the lesson

9. Give the lesson a clear form and state it.
10. Make a businesslike start: leave last lesson's leftovers or inquisitions on missing work till later.
11. Starting with a little deskwork helps to settle restless classes and organizes books and equipment.
12. A fresh and vigorous approach engages pupil attention: personal study or observing a colleague may revive a jaded topic.
13. Preparation should include time and materials as well as the content of the topic.
14. Organize and plan movements (who, what, why, where, when),

give warnings of changes in activities, remind pupils of any changes in rules.

15. Show how content is related to pupils' present concerns or future interests and connect it with their existing knowledge and attainments.

16. Vary the activities and learning styles: watching, listening, writing, making and question/answer sessions as well as work in pairs and groups.

17. Beware of unequally distributing your attention, questions, evaluations: be flexible enough to value unexpected contributions.

18. Some groups need explicit instructions for relatively unstructured or pupil-directed tasks: specific questions, lists and set times for each component.

19. Keep a roving eye: show that everything is noticed even if intervention is avoided.

20. Do not let an individual or group monopolize your attention: mark, explain, organize, discipline, read and listen all at once.

21. Keep the momentum: vary the pace without confusing halts.

22. Do not stay on one issue too long: use telepathy.

23. Mark, praise, encourage, give feedback or evidence of careful monitoring regularly.

24. Do not interrupt the flow of a lesson unnecessarily: keep things suddenly remembered or noticed till later.

25. Do not leave an activity and then return to it abruptly after starting another.

26. Be aware of your use of space: at front, across narrow length, potentially mobile for exposition; at rear or moving for pupil work.

Responding to disruption

27. Try to nip trouble in the bud using eyes, gesture, proximity, territory invasion, touch or an invitation to contribute to the lesson.

28. Use pupil's name, specify unwanted behaviour and the target activity.

29. Give task related reasons for disapproval rather than stating personal preference.

30. Make corrective statements short: avoid nagging, threats and interrogation.

31. Do not recite past misdemeanours.

32. Do not make unfavourable comparisons with siblings, and use only models that the pupil respects.

33. Correct the action not the actor: infer approval of the individual while correcting the behaviour.
34. Try to let natural consequences be the punishment and have a respected person responsible for their supervision.
35. Avoid mass punishment of a class or group.
36. Do not be an inflexible ruler: pupils usually understand the need for exceptions if reasons are given.
37. Where a child is unamenable to your control, show in a cool, dispassionate way that you are aware and disapprove.
38. A hard stare, averting eyes sideways if necessary, can be more effective than a verbal rebuke.
39. Focus on the principal in any disturbance: do not pick on supporters – they will fall into line if the chief agent of the disorder is controlled.
40. In a confrontation, keep voice low, arms still. posture relaxed and avoid poking.
41. Soft and private reprimands are sometimes more effective than loud public rebukes (Proverbs 15:1).
42. Break off arguments with peace terms clearly and simply specified.
43. Where a child must be ejected, lead out while repeating some concrete and achievable conditions for re-entry.
44. Do not neglect the class when dealing with a difficult pupil.
45. Give generous apologies for mistakes: imply your authority is invulnerable to error.

Clearing up and exit

46. Prepare and organize the ending of a lesson: it may not happen naturally – plan and leave time for it.
47. Be prepared for the most difficult pupils to finish their work ahead of the class.
48. Review what has been achieved and relate it to future plans.
49. The departure of the class allows an opportunity for a brief word with those who have not co-operated.
50. An orderly dismissal, with a relaxed and smiling teacher, minimizes problems and is a good prelude to the next meeting.

Exercise 2: basic trials

The group should divide into pairs or threes for this exercise, each taking one or more examples for discussion. Groups larger than three may prevent some members from contributing as fully as they wish. Ten minutes is usually ample time for small group discussions before sharing ideas with the whole group. In reality, of course, decisions are usually required in a considerably shorter time than this. For each incident, decide what action should be taken and what further information you would like, or other factors you would take into account. The principal task, however, is to decide on the appropriate action and to be able to justify it by reference to experience, reason or other evidence. There are no certain answers but there are some things to avoid and some strategies likely to be more successful than others. The course leader should have read the comments on this exercise in order to ensure that the full group discussion is usefully conducted.

1. In a busy corridor at change of lesson time. A pupil has apparently just kicked an orange along the corridor. You have told her to pick it up but she does not move or speak.
2. On duty at break time you see a crowd gathering. Two sturdy boys are facing each other and a fight seems imminent.
3. As the class enters your room, one of the pupils says in a loud voice that she is doing no work for such a boring teacher as yourself. She slumps in her seat with folded arms.
4. During your exposition in the early part of the lesson there is a sudden outburst of laughter from a group. Other pupils turn in their direction and look at you as the laughter spreads.
5. Although you and the class are waiting to begin the lesson, two pupils continue their conversation as if oblivious to your presence. They continue chatting, ignoring your call for attention.
6. You enter a classroom to find the whole class in turmoil and completely out of control. You consider calling one out to the front but fear it will be (accurately) described as victimization.

Comments on the 'basic trials' exercise

In general, the more varied the experience of the group, and the higher its level of expertise, the more its members' decisions will have provisos and reservations attached. Such groups are also more likely to feel further information is necessary before a decision can be taken. In severe cases of indecision this phenomenon should be pointed out – it will doubtless be well received – and teachers asked to relate the case to their present groups to narrow the range of solutions considered. When these cases are presented to inexperienced student-teachers there is a greater readiness to offer a general solution, often described as if no alternative was in principle possible. This indicates that: experienced teachers do have a professional knowledge that is not merely common sense; thoughtful reflection is a factor in professional expertise. This difference between the experts and the beginners is reflected in studies reported by Berliner in his chapter in Calderhead (1987). When shown films or slides of classroom scenes, teachers saw complex activities where beginners saw only surface features. Suggestions from teachers and, for comparison, students are given below.

1. 'Try to deal with it when the audience has gone – if it's change of lesson time, that should be possible.'

    'Pick it up yourself and say something like: that's a bit of luck, I don't fancy school lunch today.'

    'It would depend on who had done the kicking and whether I was sure – I would be able to estimate their intentions and know what to do. It would probably be too trivial to get into a row about defiance over.'

    A popular solution from the inexperienced: order the pupil to go to the head, and if they refused take their arm and lead them or go and fetch the head yourself.

2. 'I think you would have to intervene at once but in a light way. I'd ask who was paying them, no sensible person gets themselves bashed for free – I might get rid of the crowd by pretending to take a collection.'

    'You have to be careful not to rush up with a blue light flashing – if there's a weaker one he might take the opportunity to get a quick one in as rescue is at hand, and so you might actually cause a fight to start that might have been avoided.'

    'I might hurry slowly if they were equally matched and it wasn't too serious – let them have a brief punch – I find they're easier to separate then because honour's satisfied and they are both a bit hurt.'

    'It would depend on the pupils and when it was – I usually find a sharp shout stops them.'

    'If it was something silly I'd shout: give 'em room. If it was more dangerous I would get there as fast as possible.'

    Inexperienced students usually see no alternative to instant reaction to what is always assumed to be a very serious situation.

3. 'No one's going to admit they have this, but when it happens I say: fine, school's supposed to be boring, I spent last night working to get this lesson as boring as this dear, I take my job very seriously.'

    'I would say, okay, join in when you like – I might not take any notice at all – I'd make some brisk remark and leave it at that.'

    'It would depend which class it was. I usually say: look, you think it's boring but I've been doing this lesson for twenty-five years – just think how bored I am with it.'

'I would avoid feeling challenged and probably ignore it in most cases – secondary pupils are always bored whatever you do.'

Most students assume that the pupil's remark is intended as a serious comment: they would explain the importance of their subject.

4. 'This is usually because you've said something that means something rude to the pupils, just shut them up and carry on.'

'With little ones it's usually that someone's made a noise – best to ignore it.'

'It reminds me of the music hall comedians' rule: unexpected bursts of laughter – check flies.'

The inexperienced would make the pupils come out and tell the joke to the class in order to silence them.

5. 'It depends whether it is deliberate or not – some kids do get involved and don't notice. I might say to the class: shush, these two are talking and I can't hear.'

'I would probably pull a chair up if it was some kids I know and say, do go on, how interesting.'

Students are generally at a loss in this particularly tricky situation, sometimes referred to in the literature as 'third-partying'. One of the most inappropriate suggestions made was to threaten that, for every minute they continued talking, the whole class would be kept in for five minutes at the end of the lesson. This idea did not come from a mathematician.

6. 'I wouldn't bother about being called unfair – I'd just say I always pick on someone with some sense when I want a job done.'

'I would apologize, in a very loud voice, for keeping them waiting – that usually causes enough puzzlement to produce enough quiet to make a start.'

'You can just go in and shout any name, tell them to come out to the front, they all want to know what's going on so they go quiet and you've got them.'

Beginners would usually shout until they got silence. The most interesting suggestion ever offered was from a student who would 'just speak to the quiet ones'.

Exercise 3: Discovering general teaching functions

This is a ground-breaking activity in that little work has been done in this area and original insights are therefore possible. It is also difficult so, unlike other tasks in this book, it is preceded by some comments. The purpose is to clarify the relevance and application of classroom management skills to your own circumstances: discovering which general principles are important will clarify the role of particulars and help prevent disagreement about items which are functionally equivalent. This exercise will help you think more systematically about the familiar classroom scene, alert you to the ambiguities of classroom-management rules, and give you insights and confidence in your classroom practice. The fifty tips presented as a summary to this chapter are distributed for convenience into the lesson-phases identified by Hargreaves *et al.* (1975). You are asked to redistribute them, adding any you think are missing, by grouping them into clusters which can be encompassed in more general teaching functions. There are many ways of using the list of teacher skills: the one outlined here is probably a good way of sorting out ideas and clearing up disagreements.

The first thing to do is to clarify two meanings of the term, general. General can mean that something is prevalent or generally applicable. For example, teachers generally spend their first lessons explaining their classroom rules. General can also mean something abstract, high-level, or inclusive. For example, a general teacher skill is to get attention. Note that general (prevalent) skills can be quite low-level and specific; general (inclusive) skills, by definition, are higher level – and probably prevalent too.

Groups of three or four should spend about thirty minutes on this activity. Begin by deciding which skills are prevalent in your particular school: in many cases it will be easier to list those that are not applicable to your circumstances. Keep a note of disagreements. The next step is to try to group the skills into generally inclusive groups. You could begin with those skills which are not applicable to your school, or those on which there was disagreement. The three categories proposed as starters by Doyle (coverage, explicitness and accountability) may be helpful but there must be others. You should find that disagreements disappear when low-level skills are grouped into higher, inclusive categories. For example, a teacher who begins lessons by calling for order is not in contention with one who begins by waiting silently: both are using forms of attention-getting. Your group work is complete when you have resolved, or at least understood, disagreements and decided on some general inclusive categories into which specific skills fall. If a category you believe to be a generally inclusive one seems to include nothing but itself, then it is probably low-level and applicable only to limited contexts; if a category seems to include everything, it is too inclusive and should be divided. (Two absurd examples would be, respectively, distributing pencils and surviving.) Beware of taking the generally applicable nature of a skill for granted. For example, in the Evertson and Emmer (1982) research, eye-contact was found to be less important in maths than in English; and Japanese pupils are said to remain attentive without lifting their gaze from their desks (Martin Monk, *TES*, 17.6.88: 20).

Ideally, participants should have had some days to think about the list of skills before the meeting. After the group meetings, compare results in plenary session. The plenary session will be easier to keep on task if someone marks up group results on a board.

Chapter four

Pupil perspectives, motives, and strategies

Some research on pupils has attempted to uncover their views and opinions rather than treating them as objects whose attributes can be measured. Finlayson and Loughran (1975) found that top stream boys perceived their teachers to be less authoritarian in their behaviour towards them than was the case with the perceptions of lower stream boys. In comparisons between schools, teachers in low delinquency schools were perceived to be less hostile in their behaviour towards pupils than their colleagues in high delinquency schools. If pupils think teachers are hostile towards them, this would clearly influence pupil co-operation. Even if the pupils are mistaken, there are implications in these findings for how teachers present their discipline requirements. If the connection between disruption and domestic upheaval is accepted, then it is important for teachers to avoid confirming the pupils in their antagonism towards others. Some pupils will be working off their ill-feelings towards adults in the relatively safe surroundings of the school. Not surprisingly, they may engender teacher hostility by their behaviour. Whatever the case, it is arguably our professional responsibility to understand what may be happening and take the first steps towards breaking out of the cycle.

Many studies find pupils of all ages and dispositions to be in general agreement about how teachers should behave. Teachers must keep order, explain things clearly, have interesting lessons, treat pupils with respect, be fair and friendly and have a sense of humour. Teachers who have favourites or who show pupils up in front of their peers are strongly disapproved of. A summary of several enquiries is included in Docking (1980: 108–9).

I have found pupils excluded from school to have similarly conventional views and often blame the weakness or unfairness of their teachers for their own predicament. This may be pupils seeking to come to terms with their behaviour by blaming others or it may be simply a clash of views: what some pupils call 'having a laugh' is what some teachers call unacceptable insolence. Others, whose reasons for their behaviour are related to their domestic troubles or obligations, may cover these shaming facts by blaming teachers. Tattum (1982) refers to the neutralizing effect of pupils' explanations in helping them account for their misbehaviour. Teachers who had not interested them and who had picked on them unfairly deserved to be treated with disrespect.

Werthman (1963) took delinquents' justifications of their behaviour at face value and Marsh (1978) found pupils judged and repaid teachers who transgressed their standards by not knowing pupils' names or being too soft and not teaching anything. Woods (1980a) is a useful collection of papers on pupils' strategies, the dynamics of friendship groups and pupils' attempts to negotiate space for themselves amidst the competing pressures upon them. In most respects, pupils appear to be relatively conservative, particularly in their expectations of teachers. Davies (1984), in a study of difficult girls, suggests that they had more rigid moral standards than average and were less tolerant of teachers who deviated from their requirements. They were said to be annoyed by teachers who set a poor example, were rude, arrogant or who insulted the girls' 'reputation'. Schostak (1986) quotes Empson's remark that the criminal is 'the judge of the society that judges him'. Davies' girls, in close agreement with pupils in other studies, expected their teachers to have knowledge, to teach it, and to be able to keep control without over-reacting 'when there was no need'.

Taking pupils' perspectives seriously is itself an important development, irrespective of the utility of the information gathered. It requires teachers to understand that on the public stage of the classroom, private intentions are vulnerable to interpretations not intended (Schostak, 1986). The work in this chapter, particularly the analyses of Dreikurs (1957) and Balson (1982), depend upon accepting pupils' perspectives and motives and seeking to satisfy the legitimate concerns that they expose. Studies seem to find that pupils have a rational basis for their behaviour: this is partly a consequence of researchers setting out to find one, but the evidence seems to be that pupils are capable of trying to be objective and rational when given the opportunity. To accept this as fact is to move a long way from the once popular view that difficult pupils had something wrong with them and that to be cured of it they needed to be removed for specialist treatment. Pring (1976), describing his difficulties with a group of inattentive and disorderly fourth-formers, asked himself, not what was wrong with them, but what was it to educate these pupils who, in spite of their behaviour, had '. . . minds that questioned, puzzled, doubted, drew conclusions . . .' He continues: 'They were already engaged in some form of mental life (even Deborah) and it was that that made them educable.'

This argument is taken a stage further by Cronk (1987) who attempted to achieve understanding and co-operation with a chronically disorderly class. She argues that pupils can be trusted to be concerned with teachers' interests and that misunderstanding is at the root of antagonism in schools.

She attempted, with some success, to banish it from her classroom. This involved both accepting the pupils' point of view and getting them to accept her own position in the school, bounded as it was by colleagues' expectations and other constraints. The solution to the problem of conflict is to convince pupils, through an accepting relationship, that they are persons of value: both teachers and pupils need to acknowledge each other as persons and not seek refuge in the categories of (authoritarian) teacher or (intransigent) pupil. This may seem to be a circuitous route to getting pupils to comply with the traditional teacher role that pupils seem to expect. And it still leaves the problem encountered by Herbert Kohl (1986): is it essential to establish control first and become flexible later? Or can friendly negotiations be conducted from the outset? And how honest have they been if the outcome is always compliance on the teacher's terms? The process of reaching this result is not unimportant. It may be impossible to be fully and genuinely democratic in the classroom, but we do not avoid trying to be. Accepting pupils' points of view, revealing one's own feelings and dilemmas, sharing concerns and aspirations, all imply genuine efforts at openness, communication and understanding: not a bad basis for classroom co-operation.

Testing teachers and discovering rules

Pupils' classroom behaviour can be taken under two major headings: discovering and testing teachers' rules, resolution and ability to maintain order; and displaying, developing and defending personal identity. Most pupils also wish to establish and maintain a place in their chosen friendship or peer group which may or may not be one that is approved of by their teachers. From time to time pupils, like any other workers, seek a little light relief from the inescapable tedium and tension of daily life: they like to 'have a laugh' and they prefer their teachers to have a sense of humour too. The particularly difficult motives of pupils who may be in an extreme state of distress and confusion will be discussed separately. Motives may be in conflict. For example, a pupil may wish to develop and display a personal identity as a bright pupil, pleasing to adults. He or she may also wish to retain an acceptable status in a classroom group where over-zealous, compliant pupils are rejected as 'swots and creeps'. Apparently incomprehensible behaviour may thus be witnessed from time to time. A successful and academically ambitious pupil may be caught in a piece of extravagant misbehaviour by which he or she intends to demonstrate to classmates an enjoyment of, and affinity with, their irreverence for school-ing. For example, a bright primary school girl put a drawing pin on her teacher's chair, explaining that she feared that other pupils thought of her as a 'goody-goody', which of course she was. For an example of this in a prestigious grammar school see Lacey's (1970) discussion of Sherman, a top pupil who balanced his achievements with mischief.

How pupils perform under each of these headings will depend upon their beliefs, expectations and attitudes. Their accumulated experience of dealings with adults, and in particular their parents or guardians, will to a large extent set the context for their first encounters with teachers. For some pupils classroom disruption is no more than a temporary strategy adopted to break the tedium of a boring lesson or to punish an incompetent or humiliating teacher. Their misbehaviour is transient, of no wider or deeper significance, readily abandoned and easily controlled. Other pupils perceive the classroom as an extension of a harsh, unjust, unpredictable and unforgiving world: a world of stress, poverty, indifference or cruelty that most of us are fortunate enough never to have encountered. For such pupils school offers a relatively safe environment for the exploration of their distrust, apprehensions, anger and insecurity. Their classroom disruption and disaffection may appear even in the most exciting and well conducted lessons. It is difficult to bear and apparently impossible to eradicate whatever the level of care and encouragement given. Its significance and source of energy are largely from without the classroom. This is not to say that such behaviour is a straightforward, determined effect of domestic environment: this behaviour is part of an active strategy. It is not determined in a mechanistic sense, and it is this that allows the teacher some purchase upon it.

Pupils of all ages want to know what rules are in operation in any given situation. The less specific and convincing the teacher, the more the pupils will explore the boundaries of what they suspect to be permissible. As we saw in Chapter 3, it is not enough to state rules and expectations verbally: tone of voice, expression and demeanour are among the non-verbal communications by which pupils assess whether teacher means it and whether he or she has the determination and ability to control their wayward experiments. Pupils, like adults, form expectations of others in the light of their appearance and perhaps their reputation. They may be pleased to discover that they were correct in their prediction or disappointed and troublesome if the teacher turns out to be unexpectedly permissive or unaccountably strict. A pupil interviewed in a unit for disruptive teenagers blamed his present placement on the fact that he had not had 'big enough teachers'. The boy was of small build and physically unprepossessing so we may assume he was speaking metaphorically.

Teacher testing is particularly prevalent at the start of the school year. And equally prevalent at the same time are teachers' attempts to make rules and expectations clear and to make them stick. For a long time this particular teacher activity remained invisible to university researchers and writers, partly because higher education takes a longer summer break than schools do and partly because teachers are reluctant to be observed 'licking the pupils into shape'. This has had unfortunate consequences for the training of teachers.

One of the studies reported by Wragg (1984) is of a trainee science teacher who had observed the regular class teacher conducting orderly lessons whilst lounging on the desk, making quips and flirting with the girls. The student attempted a similarly relaxed performance when his turn came only to find it received with outraged indiscipline. The student had not observed, and had not been informed about, the extensive rule setting that this relaxed teacher had engaged in earlier in the term. The majority of secondary school science teachers choose rules and safety procedures for the first lesson of the year. The implicit message is here congruent with the explicit one: the teacher decides what is allowed and what is not: the pupil is expected to comply.

To recognize these skirmishes as merely teacher tests is usually all that is necessary to prevent them escalating into hostility. Teachers who perceive them as personal attacks on their authority and competence, or who explicitly identify them as stupidity, risk prolonging and aggravating the behaviour. From one point of view, pupils are not so much challenging the teacher's authority as trying to discover its form and extent in each particular case: they rebel in order to find out what rules they must conform to. McDermott claims that some low-ability pupils used misbehaviour in order to 'draw the teacher back to their group so that reading instruction could continue' (Wittrock, 1986: 420). Forms of misbehaviour which are often taken as tests of the teacher's authority may also have a beneficial function. For example, Delamont and Galton (1986) note that for some pupils, fighting is an essential part of sorting out peer-group relationships. It may be that in more liberal schools, pupils' increased area of discretion requires more of these sorting activites. 'Rough-housing' may help to produce an orderly school. Whether this is so or not, there is no doubt that to accept these testing encounters as part of the ordinary routine is to cut away their power to offend: pupils find not an opponent but an understanding and indestructible adult with whom they are content.

Teacher testing takes many forms. A powerful negotiating counter on the pupils' side is the level of noise in the classroom – a matter over which they have considerable control. The closed classrooms so prevalent in primary schools, and to a greater extent in secondary schools, are an organizational feature largely responsible for creating the noise weapon. Noise is one of the few features of classrooms that can be detected from without: above a minimal level it betokens indiscipline and disorder. As Nash (1973) noted, keeping pupils quiet is part of the teacher's job. It is no help to cite evidence that pupil talk is essential to learning in a wide range of subjects, including science where practical activity might be thought a suitable substitute for talk (for example, Barnes, 1969 and Driver, 1983). The significance of noise in classrooms is extensively treated in Denscombe (1985) and in his chapter of the book edited by Woods (1980b).

Not all pupils need to be actively engaged in testing behaviour and many members of a class may owe much valuable information to the active service of a few. Ball (1981) noted that the fate of those explorative pupils who elected to test the boundaries influenced the behaviour of others in the class. A noisy dispute between two pupils may be serving as a test. Teachers who seek to pacify and mediate in such public arguments may unintentionally and implicitly display their ignorance of pupils' more subtle forms of warfare. The appropriate tactic is to briskly silence the parties, perhaps with an offer to settle the dispute for them in their own time after the lesson. Teachers who did not lose their tempers, did not ignore the tests, and did not show confusion were more effective in establishing control (Ball, 1981).

Verbal disputes may take a stylized and alarming form as in 'sounding/woofing' imported from American youth culture, though Doyle says it is not widespread (Wittrock, 1986: 418). Beynon (1985) observed this type of misbehaviour and noted that a smiling 'victim' indicated a teacher-testing tactic was in progress. Verbal tests include requests for readily available information or the offer of counterfeit or absurd answers. Non-verbal tests often take the form of outdoor clothing and hats if the encounter takes place indoors. Other strategies include an over-literal response to instructions, a walk that is too fast or too slow, an inappropriately relaxed or stiff posture and extravagant yawns and displays of tiredness. Werthman (1963) is an interesting early description of some of these tactics employed by American teenagers. The wise teacher will expect to be tested by pupils in early encounters and he or she will therefore be neither disappointed nor dismayed. It is important not to identify testing behaviour wrongly: it is not so trivial that it can be ignored but is not so serious that it merits excessively vigorous suppression. Pupil mythology contains stories of teachers who were easily baited and driven into rages in which they sometimes injured themselves. The best tactic is to appear unsurprised and to react in a calm, clear and unconfused manner. Early encounters between secondary school teachers and their classes have been illuminatively researched by Beynon (1985). The topic is also treated by Ball in his chapter of the book edited by Woods (1980a). Pupils expect teachers to keep order and to make curricular demands upon them. They expect teachers to be worthy of their attention and respect and to be able to withstand their probing and provocation.

Displaying, developing, and defending personal identity

Becoming an autonomous person involves rejecting some characteristics and adopting others. Parents, teachers, brothers, sisters and friends may all be rejected and new affiliations experimented with as adolescents attempt to carve out what they are and what they are not. The eager compliance that many young children display, gradually – and sometimes not so gradually – gives way to the stubborn independence, reluctance and defiance of the teenage years. This is seldom a straightforward progression. Caspari (1976: 22) notes that 'at one time they want to be looked after like very young children, at other times they oppose whatever those in authority say'. Reconciling the need to choose an individual path with the limitations imposed by family, school and society is not an easy task. Few accomplish it without trauma. It is necessary to accept that deviant behaviour is a normal part of growing up and a part of becoming a person in one's own right. A population of compulsive rule-followers is an unwanted, appalling and sinister alternative. Adolescent pupils are known to particularly resent rules about and criticism of personal features such as dress and hairstyles and teachers are wise to be flexible in these matters (Werthman, 1963; Reynolds and Sullivan in Gillham, 1981). The growth of individuality involves sensitivity to perceived attacks on personal morals and dignity as well as a wish to have some autonomy (Marsh, 1978; Corrigan, 1979; Davies, 1984).

An interesting difference in the possibly differing approaches of boys and girls to impending adulthood is mentioned by Stott (1982). He quotes a survey which showed that whereas boys who ran away from home tended to involve themselves in petty crime, girls did not. The suggestion is that boys run away in order to accomplish illegal purposes but girls run away in order to resolve personal problems. Girls seem to face the fact that they must one day separate from their parents, perhaps to create a new family, earlier than boys. Unable to cope with the uncertainty in respect of time, and the need to prepare for a break from parents to whom they still need close attachment, some choose to make a break immediately. For them, the certainty of instant separation is preferable to the continuation of what they come to perceive as a jeopardized relationship. When young people go beyond acceptable limits it is therefore important to show that although the behaviour is disapproved of the teacher still values the individual. The inappropriate act must be corrected without rejecting or attacking the pupil's self-image. Some confused and troublesome pupils complain that teachers do not recognize them as the sort of person that they really are, deep down below the surface hostility.

It is part of Cronk's (1987) philosophical argument that conflict between persons, and specifically between secondary school pupils and teachers, is a consequence of misunderstanding: that is, a failure to communicate with each other and to understand intentions and feelings as well as the constraints under which each is acting. On a related theme Sharpe and Green (1975) quote the distinction between knowing someone as a contemporary and as a consociate. Put simply, this is the difference between recognizing someone as a member of a category of persons, and knowing someone as if they were a member of one's own family: the difference between noticing a black child, a middle class child or a disruptive child and meeting Peter or Jane. Where the category is feared or distrusted by the teacher, or simply mysterious to them, there is little hope of under-standing and every possibility that ignorance will grow into hostility. Fam-iliarity is more likely to breed understanding than contempt: hence the phenomenon of 'going native' and coming to share and reinterpret the world from the perspective that was originally the object of dispassionate study. The plain conclusion to be drawn is that there needs to be space and time in schools for teachers and pupils to meet and get to know one another. This may be through regular timetabled contact at times which allow informal communication; it may be through a whole week shared on a field trip or holiday. Timed arrangements may not be essential: where teachers have responsibility for, and discretion over, the treatment of their pupils, both parties will see the benefit of understanding one another. If the school provides the purpose and incentive, the time may look after itself. It may be objected that teachers cannot take account of individual pupil needs but are constrained to treat all equally regardless of individual development: accusations of unfairness have to be avoided. At least with adolescents, this objection is not difficult to counter. Teenagers who are trying to become independent can be persuaded that different treatment is appropriate from time to time.

Concerning exceptional children

Some pupils have a limited number of inflexible strategies in their interac-tions with others. They may comply, ignore or fight, and assume that other people's behaviour always fits one of these categories (Horney quoted in Laslett, 1977). Experience of adults has led them to adopt rigid and restricted views of adult behaviour: they may be reluctant to accept that anyone can be genuinely concerned about them. This attitude is sometimes a strong compound of two elements: that other people are heartless, ruthless and untrustworthy; and that they themselves are defective and worthless individuals. Adult attempts at making a friendly relationship and showing kindness may be construed as weakness, want of intellect or deception. Sometimes such children give evidence of their perspective in gross misunderstandings: a smile may be interpreted as a challenge to fight or as a sign of someone's contempt. Teachers who work with difficult children are not unaccustomed to having their normal, relaxed facial expressions misconstrued. They may be greeted first thing on a frosty, winter morning with 'What's up with you? You're in a bad mood aren't you'. This hypothesis can sometimes be self-fulfilling.

Stott (1982) believes hostility to adults is usually an extension of hostility to parents. This does not necessarily betoken parental fecklessness or cruelty. Hostility is often a reaction to a fear of being abandoned or removed: such fears can be engendered through circumstances under no-one's control. In some cases the child's fears result from misperception due to a physical or intellectual impairment. Parental perfection is unattainable and parents may fail to live up to their children's expectations through illness, poverty or other misfortune.

Stott (1982) stresses that children need a secure attachment to a loyal, dependable, caring parent figure. Deprived of a permanent, secure attachment a child seems to prefer the certainty of abandonment to the uncertainty of unpredictable adults: like a jilted lover who seeks revenge upon, or destruction of, the lost one. Generalizing from experience, some pupils may hypothesise that all adults are similarly unreliable and seek to avoid any kind of attachment. One consequence of this is that those teachers who feel and show most concern may receive the most hostility though it be interspersed with trust. Stott describes examples of family situations conducive to the development of behaviour likely to be described as maladjusted. First, the preferred parent may be lost through divorce or death and the remaining parent proves an inadequate replacement: a father may die and the mother take to drink, for example. Second, the preferred parent may be undependable through tiredness, lack of interest or weariness induced by a tiresome baby: those infants who wake at dawn and do not require sleep again until late evening, and then only fitfully, try the patience of even the most comfortable and well-disposed parents. Third, there are situations of potential loss where a parent threatens to have a child put into care or sent to live with a relative: often this threat has massive credibility, for some family circumstances lead occasionally and unpredictably to such separations. The fourth situation is one of potential loss: this may be through a parental illness requiring periodic hospital treatment; it may be through occasional imprisonment or flight from creditors; it may be because parental rows persuade a child that family break-up is imminent.

Hostility then may be viewed optimistically as the aggressive search for that which is lost. Laslett (1977) discusses the distinction between deprivation and privation. Those who have suffered privation have never known a warm, human relationship, either through sensory disability or the lack of appropriate parenting. They may become withdrawn for they cannot seek that which they do not know they have lost. Deprived children, on the other hand, have experienced the loss of a valued relationship and aggressively search for a replacement. Interestingly, teachers often unwittingly identify this motive in accusing troublesome pupils of behaving as if the world owes them something: from one point of view this behaviour, exasperating though it is, can be seen as a sign of potential progress. Hostile children may be expressing disappointment at finding adults to be less than they wish them to be. From a practical point of view, it matters not at all if such an estimation is incorrect. To believe that improvement is possible is to act towards the pupil in an encouraging way and to help to bring improvement about. A possibility defined as real may turn out to be real in its outcome.

Some pupils seek refuge from reminders of wretched memories in extreme behaviour: they may have periods of complete frenzy, climb dangerous scaffolding, or wander fairgrounds or city centres in search of distraction. Stott (1982) terms this wild, excitement-seeking, behaviour 'avoidance compulsion' – its purpose, however dimly appreciated by the child, is to blot out present reminders of past traumas. To avoid reminders of experiences that have wounded in the past is a form of self-defence in a literal sense. It may be the prospect of meeting a teacher who is particularly valued by the pupil, and who therefore revives fears associated with past relationships which became painful or were destroyed. Even the architectural features of a particular room may trigger turbulent feelings associated with a past trauma. A milder but more disruptive way of distracting oneself is to hum, whistle, or make repetitive groaning noises in the classroom. Such behaviour is less intensely annoying if it is interpreted as a desperate attempt to remove discomfort.

Balson (1982) does not refer to this pupil strategy but it is possible to use one's own feelings, as he suggests, to help identify it. For example, in Chapter 2 I described a teacher whose response to a pupil's name elicited an avoidance-compulsion behaviour from the teacher. This pupil had a fear of new people and situations which he disguised as insolent disobedience. On trips to museums, for instance, he would defiantly and abusively refuse to get out of my car. He tried to get himself sent home from my unit by inciting other boys, and nearly succeeded when he bribed one to stand on a wall exposing himself to passing traffic. When this failed, he began arriving earlier than me, pulling the door handle off, and blocking the lock with putty. This continued until we agreed a truce one morning, just before 7 a.m. He was the only surviving baby born to a tragic couple: perhaps obsessive sheltering had something to do with his fears. In ordinary school, and a school for the maladjusted, he created mayhem, was suspected of arson, and was impossible to communicate with. He was not, as many thought, a delinquent but might have been transformed into one by being put in custody. Now in his twenties, he has never taken a job, has somehow found a wife, and is an unexceptional parent: not a success story, but better than might have been expected. An ordinary school would have needed two things in order to cope with him: sufficient and suitable teachers and the courage to give at least some discretion in dealing with him. In other words, schools need staff with the skills and understandings, but flexibility and liberty are required in the organization.

Children who have grown up accustomed to being let down by adults may repeatedly and severely test teachers who seek to help them. Periods of peace and progress may be broken by violent and distressing confrontations. Often a recent recruit to a school's staff is the person who seems to make progress with a difficult pupil and to have finally caused the pupil to settle down. But from the pupil's point of view, the situation is by no means stable. Past experience has taught them to expect disappointment: they must test to see whether 'interest is genuine and permanent' (Stott, 1982). Confronted with a teacher who appears to be friendly, the pupil may be confused. He or she may suspect deception. He or she may be prone to loss of control and may wonder whether the new ally on the teaching staff can withstand such a crisis. The pupil may seek relief from uncertainty by staging a scene or relapsing into disruptive behaviour. It is at this point, when the teacher's reserves of patience and optimism are stretched, that continued patience and optimism are vital to the disturbing pupil's progress.

It is well to remember that only the apparently genuine merits testing and to take the crisis as an unskilled and socially inept method of indicating provisional approval. It may not feel like one but to be the subject of such a test is a compliment to the teacher's ability to shake the pupil's misanthropic convictions. A teacher who is willing to invest in such an unpromising relationship must accept the possibility of loss and be determined enough to begin again. A pupil may steal money from the teacher as well as trust. In one case a girl confronted a teacher who had expended much effort upon her, including taking her home and taking her out with her own daughters of the same age. The girl climbed on to a table and dived to the floor at the teacher's feet injuring her head. In these circumstances it is not easy to see any purpose to continuing evidently wasted efforts. This is what the pupil expects but may not hope for. To be able to carry on after such incidents, to prove to the pupil that whatever happens they will still be accepted, is to be able to take control and exercise influence at a time when the circumstances are most opportune for change. The pupil least expects to be accepted after such crises: a teacher who is still welcoming, and possibly still smiling, may make a dramatic impact on a disturbed pupil's shell of fear and hostility.

Pupils who carry burdens of past troubles often find difficulty communicating feelings of regret in a way that is easily recognized. It is important that their self-initiated attempts at restitution are not thwarted. Wills (1945) thought that punishment removed the pupil's need to learn how to repair damaged relationships. They may try to make amends for actions they regret in ways that may create a fresh offence. This camouflaged reparation may take the form of attacking another pupil they judge to have offended the teacher; they may insist on finishing a piece of work, previously praised by the teacher, at an inconvenient time; or they may choose to strip the bookshelves in order to tidy them and in the process prevent the rest of the class from using the books or carrying on with their work. In circumstances where the pupil's activity must be stopped, a positive form of words indicating recognition and acceptance together with postponement is advisable. The most dramatic example I have encountered was on a visit to the elegant gardens of a stately mansion. A pupil who had behaved outrageously on the bus journey chose to make amends by ripping plants from the carefully classified arrays and presenting a bouquet to her teacher. The flowers said one thing to the teacher, another to the gardener.

Pupils may sometimes be the agent of their parents' motives. Some parents may believe their interests are served by having a problem child at school. Certainly those who were humiliated or failed by their own schooling may take satisfaction in having a child who illustrates their conviction that teachers are ineffectual. Those seeking vicarious revenge range through the social class spectrum – from straightforward criminal to 'militant muesli'. In other more tragic cases, a parent may hope to hold together a crumbling relationship or marriage by magnifying and encouraging problem behaviour in a child – perhaps to convince the errant partner that their child needs both of them. Related to this are those cases where a child is not permitted to think well of a parent who has deserted: the remaining parent's bitterness being a source of confusion in a school environment where loving two parents is implied in activities, talk and reading.

Delamont and Galton (1986) remarked on how the idealized, stereotypical family with defined roles penetrates and permeates school life. There are those children whose parent is unable to come to terms with the death of a partner. We must minimize the hazards for a pupil unable to think well of both parents, as others do (Hanko, 1985). Many pupils in these situations are unable or do not know how to express their confusion in school; and their frequently abstracted attitude may lead to their being typed unhelpfully. Hanko (1986) contains casework examples and Schostak (1986) speaks eloquently for such pupils: 'There is an aspect to being alive that is non-transferable, unutterable, opaque and alone. Pain cannot be shared – self licks its own wounds.'

By the time serious behavioural problems have developed, for example, where a child substitutes a coping strategy of withdrawal for one of aggression, the original event may be long past. The past can live on in the present through its effects and its memory. Teachers may find that they are presented with emotions and feelings that rightfully belong to another person, another time, another place. Dyke (1987) suggests that to recognize that one is acting as a focus for projections 'can enormously assist the teacher in resisting being overwhelmed by these feelings'. The attitude of mistrust or hostility has to be viewed as the pupil's problem not the teacher's: how they choose to react, however, can help or handicap its solution; receiving hostility becomes a professional duty not a personal failing. In many cases of domestic disorder, poverty is the most obvious handicapping factor. Poverty acts upon children through their parents and some parents are more resilient than others. Teachers sometimes feel powerless when faced with situations that seem remediable only through massive injections of skilfully managed cash; but it is always possible to help a family to cope by helping a pupil to learn self-control. Domestic problems cannot be solved but teachers 'can go a long way towards alleviating them if they recognise they exist' (Chandler, quoted in Hanko, 1985: 62).

Sometimes there are no features in children's lives or domestic circumstances that seem relevant to their testing strategies or disturbing behaviour. In such cases the only possible conclusion seems to be that there is some biological or psychological pathology in need of chemistry not education. Sometimes this diagnosis is accompanied by the claim, only partly humorous, that the wrong child was brought home from the hospital: he or she does not even look like the others in the family and they have no behaviour problems. The pessimistic acceptance of a pathological cause is unwarranted. Children have to win attention in their families as elsewhere. For example, a child may be unable to gain parents' attention and rewards as a quiet and studious person if that role is already occupied by a sibling. The busier the parents, the harder the offspring must battle for a scarce commodity: some children learn to use tantrums, some extreme greediness or selfishness, others use sickness and pains. They may find that merely being more noisy or less sociable is effective. Some develop food fads, which change if they are ineffective attention winners: Stott (1982) claims that institutional children do not use this strategy for this reason. He gives examples of pupils who used learning failure to win the attention of parents: dyslexia, like knowledge, can be power. Those children who try a succession of such strategies only confirm the adult's opinion that they are truly maladjusted.

It is not suggested that any information schools may have on domestic circumstances and history is for intervention or remedy by teachers. Caspari, for example, points to the unreliability of domestic information and says that it is in any case 'only of limited use in the day-to-day relationship between teacher and children in the classroom' (1976: 2). She then goes on to say that such information 'will of course increase (the teacher's) understanding of the child's behaviour and will influence his reaction towards the child . . .' This is not a slight benefit, however. There is value in understanding how a pupil's behaviour in school is related to an inextricably, tangled network of interactions, past and present and possible. Knowledge helps to prevent unintentionally reproducing the domestic traumas in school. All teachers recognize, for example, that care must be taken when pupils are bereaved.

There are many other situations that can be unintentionally evoked: for example, the accidental re-enactment of rejection, abandonment or restriction that is the domestic cause of a pupil's distress (Hanko, 1985). It is also not the case that the families of troublesome pupils are necessarily feckless: for example, some children lack a relationship with a dependable adult, not because the adult is not there, but because unsuspected deafness has interfered with communication. The effort to understand how children have experienced and responded to their home lives should also counter the pessimistic determinism that often accompanies discussion of pupils' homes. Home conditions are not a determinant irrelevant to teachers' concerns. The assumptions, expectations and attitudes that pupils carry into school are rooted in their experience and influence the strategies they adopt in encounters with teachers. Recognizing this we may feel inspired to disappoint the pupil's pessimism and remain open and friendly – willing to accept the pupil's feelings. It is part of our professional role to receive and cope with emotions and confusions. This includes those that belong to past relationships or to troubles elsewhere.

Children's behaviour is usefully viewed as an active response to their experiences, not an unconscious causal result. As Bastide (1972) notes, problems from another time or place can affect the present only by being retrieved in the present: traumas are not single but double. If their behaviour is to be changed it is necessary to avoid reproducing or re-enacting the domestic stresses and attitudes that have contributed to their present difficulties. Resisting the automatic, combat-response that some pupil behaviour evokes is the first step in changing one's own behaviour and thereby improving pupil experience. The teacher's tactic must be to be patient and determined that the pupil will find his or her fears to be groundless. Understanding must be strong enough to withstand whatever havoc the pupil can create. The teacher must provide security and predictability: a splint in which a damaged self can heal. Banishment and reproach must be avoided, and even kind words may be unacceptable but acceptance can be communicated without words. Before troublesome pupils will risk facing up to themselves, they have to be sure they have found a teacher in whose company it is safe to fail.

Attention, power and revenge

In dealing with cunning persons, we must ever consider their ends to interpret their speeches; and it is good to say little to them, and that which they least look for. In all negotiations of difficulty, a man may not look to sow and reap at once; but must prepare business, and so ripen it by degrees (*Of Negotiating*, Francis Bacon, 1625).

A useful approach to troublesome children is to be found in Dreikurs (1957) whose ideas are developed in Balson (1982). This involves trying to identify and analyse pupils' motives and use this information to guide teacher responses and strategies. Far from concerning itself with surface behaviour this method recognizes that the same observed activity may signify radically different motives. For example, what appears to be attention-seeking behaviour may in reality be a struggle to defeat or have revenge upon the teacher. The correct identification of the pupil's motive is a condition precedent to effective action. Balson (1982) suggests that we should ask ourselves what the pupils' purposes are in their behaviour and not simply seek answers to the question 'Why?'

This is not merely a semantic distinction. To ask why a person acts in a particular manner often brings an answer in terms of causes external to that person. We often speak of pupils' home backgrounds as if they were inaccessible causes whose effects lie beyond control. By asking what purposes the pupils have we leave responsibility for action and the possibility of remedy with the pupils. Passive, deterministic pessimism is replaced by optimistic effort.

Dreikurs (1957) proposes four goals of disturbing behaviour which he relates to the child's experience in the family. Balson (1982: 92) says: 'All maladjustment has its origin in a basic loss of confidence.' Attention-seeking results where young children have done badly in the competition with siblings for parental attention: 'Children prefer being beaten to being ignored' (Balson, 1982: 13). Efforts to control the child result in struggles for power in which there can be no final victory for to win is to teach that power struggles are valuable and worthwhile. This struggle can develop, where parents are bent on victory at any price, into mutual revenge. A fourth goal, the display of inferiority, will not be considered in this book.

Dreikurs goes on to suggest that in pursuing these goals a child may be active or passive, and may use constructive or destructive methods. For example, there are four ways in which a pupil can be an attention-seeker in the classroom: an active and constructive way would be to be a 'teacher's pet', always attentive, willing and helpful; an active and destructive way would be to take the role of 'class clown'. A passive form of attention-seeking could be to become very pleasant but helpless, in need of constant attention, kindly given; a passive and destructive form could be stubborness.

The type of behaviour that cause teachers most concern is of the active-destructive type and Dreikurs suggests that a pupil may progress from being a nuisance, to a rebel and finally vicious. Improvement does not involve re-tracing these steps, for a pupil 'can become adequately adjusted if he can be convinced that he is liked and can be useful' (Dreikurs, 1957: 16). However, Stott (1982) warns that in a hostile pupil's route to improvement there may be a period of heavy attention-demanding: a vicious rebel might become a nuisance before abandoning disturbing behaviour altogether. The analysis is detailed but succinct and interested readers are recommended to go to the original text, which is rich in examples and cases.

Dreikurs points out that the same behaviour can serve different motives and each child may have different purposes from time to time. For example, being lazy can be an attention-seeking strategy; it can be a struggle for power with a teacher; it can be revenge upon an ambitious parent. The same child might seek revenge upon over-judgemental parents by being disruptive at school and disappointing them; he or she might try to get sympathetic attention at home by being passive, quiet and withdrawn. The inevitable clash of view between home and school on his or her behaviour would satisfy the child's wish for power. Two clues are available to us in identifying the pupil's motive and knowing how to respond. First, observing one's own feelings: if irritated, attention-seeking; if challenged, power; if outraged, revenge. The teacher's 'automatic reaction is generally in line with what the child wants her to do' (Dreikurs, 1957: 34). Second, observing the child's reaction to correction: if the behaviour stops momentarily, attention; if it continues, power; if it gets much worse, revenge.

Much difficult behaviour in classrooms is described as attention-seeking. If the child is using an unacceptable repertoire only to gain attention, then it is likely that the teacher will feel no more than mildly irritated. Balson suggests that the child is saying 'I'm special, attend to me'. Such behaviour is likely to stop when attention is given and resume as soon as the teacher turns to others in the class. The strategy most likely to succeed here is to be watchful and exploit opportunities to give attention to the attention-seeker when he or she is engaged on the proper tasks. As far as is possible the unwanted behaviour should be ignored or only partially attended to. For example, the child may be instructed to resume the proper seat and wait, but the teacher avoids eye-contact, giving only the minimal attention necessary to the delivery of the instruction. Dreikurs suggests giving attention but in unexpected ways: for example, instead of telling off someone who repeatedly falls of their chair, invite the class to stop work and watch. He suggests disclosing the pupil's motives to him or her in a non-accusatory style ('Could it be that you want to keep me busy . . . ?') and agreeing a fixed number of times for special attention ('Ten times enough? Okay, that's one'). Explicit rules are not possible of course, and Dreikurs notes 'each teacher must experiment . . . and establish her own technique' (Dreikurs, 1957: 53).

What appears to be, and is typed as, attention-seeking may in fact stem from different motives and produce stronger and more distressing feelings in the teacher. If the teacher feels the pupil's behaviour is a threat to his or her authority, and feels angrily impelled to force the child into line, then the pupil's motive is power. Both pupil and teacher are likely to be feeling that they must show the other that they cannot be dominated. Balson advises that the impulse to fight is best resisted, thus depriving the pupil of an opponent, and reducing the likelihood of such an unsuccessful pupil strategy being repeated. Dreikurs suggests encouraging a power-seeker to exercise it in legitimate ways: for example, help and protection for others, but discreetly supervised. Openly admitting that the teacher ultimately has no real power can also disarm the pupil.

To resist habitual impulses is not easy and extinguishing unwanted power-seeking behaviour in this way may take some considerable time. Any discomfort or uncertainty shown by the teacher rewards the pupil's efforts and gives the pleasure of victory without a struggle. Other pupils are unlikely to remain unaffected by these phenomena. To be convincing the teacher must genuinely feel unchallenged, so that without the need of speech, he or she communicates imperturbability. This is easier to achieve if we recognize the discouraged and 'frightened child behind all the manifestations of grandeur' (Dreikurs, 1957: 56). Dreikurs points out that children rarely understand 'the predicament in which the teacher finds herself as a result of her exposure to so many pressures' and advises giving the pupil a sense of significance by showing the pupil that he or she has the power to help. This is essentially the same argument that Cronk (1987) develops and illustrates.

A further escalation in motivational intensity is evidenced when the teacher feels more deeply hurt and unjustly treated. In such cases the child may be seeking revenge for some real or imagined hurt in the present or a past situation. The child is seeking to even the score and the offended teacher may feel urged to do likewise. This impulse must be resisted if the child is even to consider abandoning this strategy. Dreikurs observes that the support of other pupils, all that the teacher wins in struggles with revenge-seekers, can serve to further isolate the individual.

> It takes a great deal of stamina to convince the revengeful child . . .
> that he can be liked. Here the group can be an extraordinary help but
> it can also be a dangerous accomplice. (Dreikurs, 1957: 57)

Balson (1982) says: 'All misbehaviour reflects children's decisions about how they can most effectively belong to the group.' To continue work with pupils exhibiting such extreme behaviour requires a self-assurance and conviction well beyond the norm. To understand and perceive behaviour in the ways described by Balson and Dreikurs is a powerful support to the teacher's will. To become convinced that one understands the pupil's real feelings is to gain the power to produce real consequences for the pupil.

Each of these three motives – attention, power and revenge – may be evidenced by similar pieces of behaviour: lies, nagging, bullying, stubbornness, destruction of equipment are not in themselves evidence of one motive or another. It is necessary to examine one's feelings and to observe the effect of one's response in order to retrieve the pupil's motive. For example, suppose a primary school child refuses to join a line of pupils preparing to cross a dangerous road. If the teacher feels irritated and on taking the pupil's hand has no difficulty persuading him or her to comply, then the pupil's motive was to seek attention and no more than that. If the teacher feels challenged and on taking the pupil's hand has to use force to drag the pupil into line, then the motive was power. If the pupil is seeking revenge the teacher will approach with gloom and foreboding. On taking the pupil's hand the pupil will not only resist but also kick and struggle.

The action taken may in each case be identical – and in matters of safety or possible harm to others instant intervention is essential. This does not mean that the pupil will perceive all intervening teachers' actions as the same. The teacher who appreciates and empathizes with the pupil's perspective will inevitably communicate through tone of voice, facial expression and general demeanour that the pupil's distress, bitterness or confusion are understood and accepted even though the behaviour must be prevented. It is not the case that understanding and accepting a person's rational and reasonable basis for action necessitates permitting those actions.

When confronted by behaviour of this sort, which may or may not turn out to be attention-seeking, it is helpful to have a four point strategy in mind. First, the feelings and emotional reaction produced in the teacher by the pupil's behaviour are probably intentionally so produced. Second, the automatic impulse to respond in a habitual fashion, perhaps in kind, is a signal to pause and reflect on the pupil's motives and intentions. Third, the teacher's own feelings and impulses are a clue to the pupil's state of mind and may be a mirror image of them. Fourth, in order to deprive the pupil of success in his or her attempt at manipulating the teacher's reaction, the teacher must take control: this involves rejecting the normal impulse and dodging the pupil's snare, however painful the necessary agility. Such a strategy takes seconds to describe but will normally operate in a fraction of that time. It is not suggested that teachers who are responsible for pupils should respond to crises with passivity and a caricature of thought. Crises are to be accepted as inevitable increments of progress: the term does indicate a turning point and knowledgeably and carefully handled a crisis becomes a turning point from which progress follows (Hanko, 1985).

As with adolescents, the behaviour of young children is orientated towards others but although it is clear that infant and pre-school children depend upon adults it is sometimes not noticed that they depend upon their peers too. Aggressiveness in pre-school children is common and often results from attempts to join games that others are playing. Many young children have difficulty expressing their wishes to their peers. Those whose verbal skills are less developed, or whose experience of playing with others is limited, may push others or throw things in an attempt to attract attention and join the game. During a period of observation in a playgroup I observed a boy lying along a slide and preventing three other children from using it: the three had been following each other up the ladder and down the slide with a good deal of merriment and noise. A member of staff told him to move, and when he did not, she told him not to be naughty, and took him away. The trio resumed their game but before long were again blocked by the troublesome boy. This time they called out and a different adult came. She took the boy's hand and helped him up the ladder and down the slide; the other three joined in and the game become four children chasing up the ladder and down the slide. It is not difficult to imagine the boy's development if he always had his behaviour defined as naughty; and it is easy to see how much more helpful it is for the teacher to assume the best motive and respond to that. As children grow into the primary age range, some find that to be accepted as a friend they have to show that they can find their own friends elsewhere (Caspari, 1976: 17). Occasional rejection becomes part of the relationship (Davies in Woods, 1980a). To know this is to know how to respond to pupil disputes and also how to help them cope with them.

Manning and Herrman (in Cohen and Cohen, 1987) have identified some characteristic strategies of young children who have more than the average number of behaviour problems. The games of poorly adjusted children appear to have fewer roles in them than those of well-adjusted children. For example, children playing in the house might include visitors in the game as relatives or tradespeople; the troublesome child may refuse to allow anyone else in and restrict the game to only two. Difficult children are more rigid in their application of the rules of the game, less willing to accept ideas from other people or to suggest roles for anyone other than themselves. Problem children spend more time in the group than alone. Perhaps having few interests to occupy them when there is no room in a chosen game contributes to their stressed behaviour. In sharing, they risk losing control of any game they have gained entry to or started. These characteristics of very young children are similar to some of the school features associated with difficult behaviour in later years: easily broken rules and a restricted range of topics and ways of learning.

I have argued that pupils' disruptive behaviour may result from understandable perceptions, beliefs and intentions; and that understanding and accepting this insulates the teacher from personal hurt, permits the possibility of communication, and gains, however slowly, the pupils' attention and respect. Cronk (1987) argues powerfully for the view that pupils can be trusted to respect the interests of others and that disruption and disorder result from misunderstanding each other's intentions and personhood. She proposes open discussions where teachers and pupils can get to know one another as persons accepting and respecting each other's intentions and the constraints under which each operates. Her argument is philosophically complex but was tested in her attempt to teach, and get to know, a disorderly class. Her path to success with 3Y was littered with difficulties but mutual respect, understanding and calm were eventually achieved: a familiar result to teachers who choose to spend their working lives with disaffected children. In large schools opportunities for personal interaction of an honest and open kind may not occur automatically, but Cronk's experience shows that time can be allocated without disarranging or threatening organizational efficiency.

Focusing on the mental and emotional state of pupils does not lead to easily listed techniques or explicit guides to action. Caspari (1976: 3) cautions against expecting to acquire perfect understanding and points out that 'the wish to understand our children and ourselves in relationship to them has a profound effect on this relationship and on our ability to deal with troublesome children'. This approach, however, does benefit both pupil and teacher. It necessitates considering the pupil seriously as another thinking person and reflecting upon the pupil's point of view. To adopt this approach is to communicate to the pupil, not necessarily in words, that he or she is seen as significant, important and deserving time and effort to understand. Pupils learn that their surface behaviour, over which some fear they do not have complete control, will not be accepted as a complete reflection of their personal qualities and feelings.

Dreikurs (1957: 20) says that up to the age of ten, a child will show the characteristic 'recognition reflex' when informed about his or her goals, and give up the behaviour. Older people, who have 'an increasing power to rationalise and put up a front', will take longer to abandon their goals – though they too will recognize them. Dyke (1987) points out that there are times when to present an interpretation may not relieve the child: '. . . it may feel to him like someone prodding him on his sorest spot'.

Sometimes the correct identification of deep motives and intentions, or merely the attempt so to do by the teacher, can defuse a threatening situation and cause the pupil to abandon mutually unwanted behaviour. For example, in one incident in my unit: 'You can't come in here with that knife, you will frighten the pupils, and you frighten me'. Satisfied that he was not powerless, as he feared, the knife was redundant and surrendered. Pupils also learn that teachers' expectations of them are high. No doubt their spirits are lifted by this optimistic declaration of faith, which may appear all the more genuine for being implicitly and non-verbally communicated. Pupils learn, perhaps for the first time, that they are worthy of consideration, in both senses of the word.

A policy of understanding pupils has benefits for teachers but it also extends their professional responsibilities. Learning to analyse pupils' mental and emotional dispositions is necessarily learning to adopt a dispassionate and objective perspective. On learning of a pupil's fears we come to see behaviour in a different light (Hanko, 1985). Understanding is partial insulation from personal involvement of a painful and overwhelming kind. Teachers can understand why they are the focus of pupils' confused and misdirected feelings and not perceive such feelings as personal attacks. They can sidestep antagonism focusing their concern instead on pupils' deeper motives. They may also understand why some sorts of behaviour and attitude distress them more than others, for no-one is wholly exempt from inner conflicts and uncertainty. It becomes easier to see difficult behaviour as part of ordinary life and, for many pupils, a necessary manifestation of their present concerns.

Coping with conflict is seen, not as grit in a machine that would otherwise work smoothly, but as one part of teachers' professional responsibilities: an aspect of the job, not an impediment to it. So resolved it becomes as irrelevant to wish it away as it would be for dentists to complain of patients' tooth decay or police to blame their failure to catch burglars on the number of traffic offences they have to attend to (naturally, teachers are not the only professionals tempted to limit their responsibilities). This takes us back to the concept of the deviance-insulative teacher (Hargreaves, 1975) and the disarming strategies discussed in Chapter 2. The ideal teacher tries to be optimistic, defends, understands and allows for difficult pupils, avoids confrontation, respects pupils' dignity, and engages them informally in a sympathetic and sharing climate.

Exercise 4: identifying motives

For this exercise, members should divide into groups of two or three so as to allow all participants the opportunity to discuss the case or cases allocated to them. Fifteen minutes is usually enough time to spend in small groups, on these cases, before sharing ideas in plenary session.

The task is twofold: to identify the pupil's motives and to determine what action would be appropriate. Although there can never be certain answers, some reactions are usually avoided by teachers experienced in the management of difficult pupils. In some of the cases it is possible to speculatively identify a commendable motive; in others it is only understandable. It should be remembered that similar actions or interventions may be experienced in importantly different ways by the pupil. The teacher's feelings may be non-verbally communicated to the pupil: being restrained by someone who sympathizes with and accepts your perspective is not the same as being restrained by someone who believes you are simply evil. The course leader should read the comments following the exercise before the plenary discussion is conducted.

1. In a nursery/reception class a pupil repeatedly pushes a dolls' pram into a wall of plastic blocks that two others are trying to construct. The builders protest but the pram-pusher looks set to continue the demolition work.
2. In a primary school playground at break time, you see a boy of nine chasing some pupils round the yard with a large pointed wooden sword. Some seem frightened and the sword looks dangerous.
3. A secondary school pupil comes to your registration group wearing wholly unsuitable clothing which clearly contravenes the school's uniform regulations. These rules are generously drawn as the school serves an area of extreme poverty. The outfit is clearly newly purchased and looks as though its designer intended it to be worn on the beach.
4. A pupil in the class is a constant irritant. She scrapes her chair, drops things and is regularly at your desk asking for help or repetition of instructions already given.
5. One of your pupils is often late without reason. If challenged, a confident or arrogantly stated excuse is given and there is invariably a refusal to comply with instructions or follow the lesson.
6. A regular attender but nevertheless completely uncooperative pupil seems to spare no effort in being as unpleasant as possible to both pupils and staff. Sometimes found pretending to be asleep on top of cupboards or on chairs placed for visitors near the school entrance. Responds violently when checked by staff or challenged by pupils: steals or spoils other people's property.

Comments on Exercise 4

1. The common-sense, unsubtle and untutored response is to see this behaviour as naughtiness and even to confine the child to what is known in some nurseries as the 'naughty chair'. A more refined perspective chooses to see the demolition as merely an inexpert and socially inept attempt at interaction: a clumsy way of asking to play by a child who wants to join the game. The appropriate action is therefore to encourage all three children to co-operate in the project – and to stay to see that this happens – perhaps suggesting a purpose for the building that includes the pram.

   It may be that the demolition expert is in fact driven by a baser motive, and the strategy may need to be revised – for example the teacher may have to occupy the child constructively upon some other activity. To begin by assuming the former motive avoids the possibility of wrongly labelling the pupil and perhaps assisting the development of a disruptive self-image. Alternatively, a pupil intent on disruption may revise the strategy on being unexpectedly pleasantly treated. Even if the child has to be removed, the teacher can take care not to begin a cycle of scolding and response by saying something like: 'I know you want to play with the bricks, but there are too many children there at the moment.'

2. This case illustrates how important it is not to assume that consideration of pupils' motives necessitates inaction. In a situation of danger, instant intervention is the first and most essential action. The common-sense response would be to summon the pupil and confiscate the sword. The optimistically disposed teacher would similarly call the pupil but might accept the pupil's pride in his possession, one perhaps made in the school's workshop, and understand his wish to demonstrate its effectiveness: the weapon would be admired and shown to others. In such an atmosphere the pupil may well accept the dangers and willingly surrender the sword for safe keeping. Nothing is lost by beginning with this assumption and the end result, in respect of safety, is the same; but in the hands of a thoughtful teacher a high spirited pupil may escape receiving a negative evaluation. If the assumption is mistaken, and the pupil is intent on harm or revenge, then his reaction will be hostile and the sword will not be surrendered without a struggle. In this circumstance the teacher would have to remain controlled and cool, using only the minimum force necessary, while giving a calm and firm explanation: as far as is possible the urge to become embattled must be rejected if the analysis and advice of Balson (1982) is accepted.

3. In this situation the habitual response is along the lines of: the school has regulations; they have been breached; there is a referral procedure; it will be invoked and the pupil sent home to change. A more sensitive response, and having regard to the poverty in the locality, would again be to accept that the pupil wishes to demonstrate personal pride in new possessions. He or she wishes to show them off to friends. The pupil may also wish to show teachers a newly acquired adult taste in clothes. (The industrial and commercial interests that schools are encouraged to serve are here caught red-handed.) With this understanding the outfit may be favourably commented on, with the proviso that it is not entirely suitable for school, and must be replaced on the following day. The pupil's attempt at identity construction will not have been damaged. In many such cases some remnant of the inappropriate clothing may reappear on the following day: for example, many pupils attend the state's schools in their only pair of shoes and it is unlikely that they will all put school's requirements ahead of teenage fashion when making a purchase.

4. This case, and the two following, are the type often described as attention seeking but which Balson (1982) suggests may sometimes be more complex. If the restless behaviour makes the teacher feel irritated, and if it stops momentarily when attended to, then the child is most likely to be seeking attention only: the behaviour is the equivalent of saying: 'Look at me, give me some recognition.' The teacher typically feels wearily exasperated: 'Not you again.' As far as possible the behaviour should be ignored, or partially ignored: the pupil may be told to stop, or resume her seat, but in a detached way, eyes averted and denied full interaction with the teacher. The next step is to ensure that the pupil receives attention, and rewarding interaction, while properly engaged in the lesson at her desk. This is very difficult to achieve: when a time-consuming pupil is quietly engaged, teachers automatically turn their attention to the other pupils whose rights have been neglected.

   However, this is the most crucial time for an attention-seeking pupil and effort expended by the teacher at this point will usually be rewarded. Some teachers find that an occasional humorous role-reversal can help: they suggest pestering the pupil at her desk, peppering her with questions and enquiries. Punishment, which in these cases often functions as a reward for the unwanted behaviour, is usually ineffective and is in any event unhelpful to the youngster's personal development.

5. A clue to the pupil's intentions is invariably found by examining one's own feelings. Most teachers on reading this case feel challenged and impelled to exert their authority. Sometimes this is possible, through threats or cajolery, but if the pupil is motivated to demonstrate personal power then a struggle may ensue and serious confrontation becomes unavoidable. One way of avoiding this is to reject the impulse to become tangled in a battle of wills and not allow oneself to be manipulated into a confrontation. Appear unconcerned about the challenge whilst conveying disapproval of obviously inappropriate behaviour. Try to feel impassive, nonchalant, detached: this is what we are doing, take it or leave it.

   Where the lateness is persistent it cannot always be ignored merely because it is taken to be an instrument of a power struggle that we are seeking to sidestep. Lateness with older and more determined individuals is difficult to eradicate, and often springs from domestic responsibilities or upheaval. If punished by detention, lateness may become absence. Remember that there is a very high correlation between absenteeism and poverty. The most profitable approach may be for the pupil's personal or group tutor to negotiate an agreement and have the pupil regularly report to him or her.

6. This is an extreme case and few ordinary schools encounter persons as distressing and distressed as this. The behaviour could simply be an extravagant example of attention-seeking were it not for the violent responses elicited by pupils and teachers. Since the reaction goes further than a struggle for power, space and time it probably falls into the category Balson describes as revenge-seeking. The pupil is seeking redress for a real or imagined hurt, perhaps an event in the past or a continuing unfavourable circumstance. This may not have included the school and its population at the outset: they may have had feelings belonging to some other situation deposited upon them and in consequence of an understandable reaction have become part of the pupil's pool of adversity. Teachers who expend time and patience on such pupils often find the hostility hurtful.

One possible strategy, for a school that wishes to retain and make progress with such a pupil, is to reject the impulse to repay injustice: recrimination and counter-attack only prolong the cycle of hostility and malevolence. Convince yourself that other people's hostile attitude to you is not your problem but theirs: the proper response to this distress that they feel is sympathy – perhaps even pity. To respond to hostility with hostility produces a sort of defamatory badminton: if the resentful exchange is to stop, one party has to lay down the racquet and withdraw. The responsibility falls on the teacher as the dispassionate, cool and controlled professional. At every opportunity try to indicate that you understand the pupil's confusion and believe the surface hostility to be unrepresentative of them as they really are, deep down. One teacher in a unit for troublesome pupils told such disturbing persons that they were an ocean: on the surface, choppy waves and tumbling water but deep down all was still and cool and peaceful, but occasionally a big ugly fish would pop out and try to take your arm off. This sort of overdrawn imagery, an unexpected response in a conflict, can allow laughter to displace violence. As in all difficult cases, much progress depends upon the school making it possible for at least one teacher to get to know such a pupil thoroughly well.

Exercise 5: focus on one pupil

The purpose of this exercise is to apply the method of analysing pupils' goals to a particular individual. Teachers should have read, or have had explained to them, the work of Dreikurs and Balson described in this chapter and outlined in the questions below. Spend about ten minutes alone considering a troublesome pupil before discussing your thoughts in small groups.

1. What are your feelings about the pupil's behaviour – irritated, challenged, wounded?
2. How does the pupil respond to correction – momentarily stops, persists, gets much worse?
3. What motives therefore do you believe the pupil has – attention-seeking, power, revenge?
4. Following this, and from your knowledge of the pupil, do you now see his or her behaviour in a different light?
5. What new policies, or understandings, could be tried?

Chapter five

Controlling stress and confrontations

Our remedies oft in ourselves do lie,
Which we ascribe to heaven: the fated sky
Gives us free scope; only doth backward pull
Our slow designs when we ourselves are dull.
(*All's Well That Ends Well*, Act 1 scene 1)

Sources of stress

This book is to a considerable extent concerned with the prevention of
stress, specifically stress arising from difficulties with pupils. In this chapter
I shall describe ways of coping with troubles and confrontations that have
not been prevented, including problems that can arise between colleagues.
The stress of managing large groups of pupils with all their demands
and difficulties is sometimes compounded by uncertainties and unrealistic
expectations. Confronted by troublesome behaviour, teachers can never
be sure how much they themselves have contributed to the problem; and
most teachers probably suspect that the gap between perfection and what
they manage to achieve most days could be filled with extra effort on their
part. Other professions, which work with much less intractable material
than teachers do, are able to accept that failure is an inevitable part of
ordinary life. For example, general practitioners fail to correctly diagnose
half the asthmatic children who come to them (Research reported in *TES*,
5.8.88: 6). Naturally, when dealing with children, this sort of thing is to
be expected: but it is easy to imagine what the politicians and the papers
would say if teachers explained a 50 per cent failure rate in this way. The
common finding by HMI that one lesson in five is less than satisfactory is
regarded as a disgrace requiring tough action. Yet there can be few
professions or industries able to claim an 80 per cent satisfaction rate; and
none that face the complex and competing pressures that are the daily
routine of schools. The first task in coming to terms with reality is to
understand that perfection is unattainable. Of course, we all try to be

perfect, we do not deliberately try to fail, but to fret over not achieving that which cannot be achieved is to make failure ever more likely.

The inevitability of structural conflicts in teaching is implicit in the sociological work on teachers' general coping strategies. Andy Hargreaves (in Hammersley and Woods, 1984b) describes the constraints to which teachers must accommodate: such ideological conflicts as the contradiction between fostering individual development and preparing pupils to fit into an existing, and in some respects uncongenial society; and material considerations such as pupil behaviour in crowded classrooms, and the scarcity of resources. Woods (in Hammersley and Woods, 1984a) has described some strategies teachers use to manage perceived constraints. These include compromise and co-operation with pupils (negotiation and fraternization); keeping self and pupils occupied in predictable and manageable activities (ritual and routine, occupational therapy); and indifference, absenteeism, and staffroom cynicism (absence and removal, morale boosting). These accommodations made by teachers enable the school system to survive: even those which seem to defeat educational purposes may have a longer-term function. For example, in a time of high unemployment with resulting pupil disaffection, busy-ness, routine and compromise may prevent serious rebellion and organizational collapse. Bird *et al.* (1981) noted that the strategies of pupils too 'are usually those which enable a quiet life rather than a profitable and purposeful educational experience'. These writers demonstrate how an inefficient system could survive through the accommodations made by those who suffer under it: coping strategies are kisses of life from victims.

The principal causes of stress in teaching are generally found to be poor staff communication, disruptive and noisy pupil behaviour, poor working conditions, lack of time and too much work, and trying to uphold standards (Kyriacou and Sutcliffe, 1977, 1979; Galloway, 1985; Woodhouse *et al.*, 1985). There is a superficial congruence between some stressors arising from pupil behaviour and some of those involving colleagues. In the survey by Woodhouse *et al.* (1985), disruption of lessons was matched with administrative disruption; aggression appeared among both pupils and staff; truancy was matched by absenteeism; and inappropriate classroom talk was said to be the equivalent of communication breakdown in staff meetings. Teachers claimed, in response to a questionnaire, that their main coping strategies included trying to be consistent and honest, establishing a routine that keeps the pupils occupied, and trying to get things into perspective (Dewe, 1985). However, when Woodhouse *et al.* (1985: 121) asked teachers to keep diaries, punishment appeared in 74 per cent of incidents with pupils and in 33 per cent of incidents with staff. The authors comment that this automatic response, an attempt to regain control, is inefficient whatever its immediate benefits: 'The legacy of the punishing approach for the person using it was listed as damaged interpersonal relations, alienation, anxiety and personal suffering'. This takes us back to the arguments discussed in Chapter 1. The complexity of causes and meanings associated with stress in teachers, and the dependence on self-disclosure, make research findings no more than suggestive. For example, although there is said to be a correlation between low job satisfaction and high stress, one survey found that the more effective teachers reported higher levels of stress, possibly because they had the confidence to be honest (Kyriacou and Sutcliffe, 1979; Woodhouse *et al.*, 1985). This suggests an interesting conversation to have with oneself when feeling stressed: teachers who feel stressed are probably superior teachers; being so informed, they no longer feel stressed; not feeling stressed, they are not superior, but if not superior, they feel stressed, which suggests they are superior after all. And so on.

Caspari (1976; 41, 57) suggests that the teachers' fear that troublesome behaviour is partly their own responsibility can delay discussion and action until a dramatic and public crisis has been reached. Teachers delayed drawing attention to problems 'if they were afraid that the behaviour of the child might be a reaction to the behaviour of the teacher'.

Hargreaves (1982) has commented on the non-supportive relationships among many teachers leaving each to solve problems alone. To offer help is to 'suggest incompetence' and 'violate professional autonomy': 'Teachers bear their stress in painful isolation. It attacks the heart of the teacher, both physically and metaphorically.' Stress in teachers is known to lead to physical illness which itself becomes an additional burden (Kyriacou and Sutcliffe, 1977). Effects of this sort are clear evidence that a taboo prevents real problems being shared and tackled. It is as though personal difficulties cannot be taken seriously until they have become transformed into physical afflictions.

Bastide (1972) suggests that psychosomatic disorders represent the triumph of natural medicine: only disorders in the soma – ulcers, heart disease, cancer – command attention. For some teachers, difficulties in personal relationships, felt as personal guilt, are hidden away and re-presented as physiological trauma: the symptoms then come to be seen as the substantive problem; personal pathology protects organizational inefficiency, administrative injustice and collegiate indifference. Troubles in the classroom are contributed to by all the participants, including the teacher, but this is no reason to cover up. It is in the nature of things that some pupils and some teachers will find each other difficult to bear: specifically, teachers vary in the range and intensity of feelings they can cope with – between themselves and within themselves from day to day. As explained in Chapter 4, teachers should not always blame themselves if they are the target of a pupil's problems: to be selected to carry a troubled pupil's burdens is in many respects a compliment.

Learning to perceive school troubles in the ways suggested in this book is one way of reducing their intensity and power to hurt, and it makes possible the sharing of problems with colleagues, in consultation not competition. Stressed teachers cannot think objectively or effectively. A task's complexity can affect a person to the extent that the worry survives the original problem and the task itself becomes lost in a fog of anger and misery. Misperception transforms tasks into problems, which become more inclusive and refractory. For example, after a bad time with a disorderly class, teachers may begin to see it as symptomatic of 'what things are coming to' as well as their own hopeless entrapment in a job in which they no longer have faith. Instead of thinking about the specific, difficult lesson, they brood over what is now seen as personal failure, a wasted life, a hopeless future. Definitions of stress, like definitions of misbehaviour, recognize this combination of real-world problems and the personal perceptions of them. Some teachers see some matters in a more serious light than others do. As Mahoney (quoted in Hughes, 1988: 5) says, 'an individual responds – not to some real environment – but to a perceived environment'. In the productive decade of curricular innovation, the 1960s, some teachers in trial schools found the experience stressful; others welcomed the freedom brought by what Jenkins termed 'institutionalized chaos' (OU course E283); and, to the despair of innovators, some teachers took no notice at all.

Comprehensive definitions of stress include both halves of the equation: these are sometimes termed the engineering model and the psychological model. Briefly, stress is an unwanted and overwhelming feeling resulting from a person's perception of the demands of their situation. Stress results at the point where a person's perceptions, understandings and attitudes conflict with what they see as the demands and deprivations in which they have to work. Stress has been defined in an aphorism as anger turned inwards; for a full discussion and definition see Kyriacou and Sutcliffe (1978). Gray and Freeman (1988) dealing with stress in teaching distinguish the personal dimension from the organizational. Where physical and organizational circumstances are beyond our control, all that may be left to us is the modification of our perceptions and the re-adjustment of our expectations. This is no small thing. From one point of view, our perceptions can often be the only source of stress: in normal circumstances, whatever situations we find stressful, someone else will find them enjoyable or will be indifferent. Although it can be as difficult to alter our attitudes as it is to alter the external stressors, those that are our own are at least potentially under our control. This assumption underpins much of Chapter 4.

Writers on stress distinguish two personality types: type A people who are said to be ambitious, perfectionist, pressurized autocrats; type B people who are relaxed, detached, easy-going and phlegmatic. Type A people are more stressed than type B and the suggestion is that, to avoid being over-stressed, we should try to be like type B (see for example, Gray and Freeman, 1988: 55). These types are in many respects similar to the insulative and provocative teacher types discussed in Chapter 2. The difficulty with this model is not that it oversimplifies: constructing ideal types for comparative purposes has a long history in social science. Its major flaw is the assumption that people behave according to the same personality type in all situations. Indeed, when we encounter examples of people with varied lifestyles, this fact alone is often taken as evidence of mental instability: for example, philandering clergy and shop-lifting magistrates. A teacher may be perfectionist and autocratic in a drama class but relaxed and easy-going in written composition; and calm and unruffled with a disruptive pupil but snappy and intolerant with his or her own children. The concept of personality is not very helpful here: fixed personality traits are by definition relatively stable and resistant to change, for good or ill. The danger in discarding the concept of fixed personality traits is that persons are then seen as enslaved in the situation: individuals turn themselves 'into the kind of person the situation demands' (Lacey, 1977, commenting on Becker). For this reason it is important to realize that a situation's nature is to a considerable extent decided by us. In Chapter 2 related problems were discussed in respect of teacher types. The concept of strategy, a way of achieving a particular goal in a particular situation, is more useful than type. Where common elements are present in a person's strategies it may be possible to identify them as one of several personality types. In helping people to cope with stressful situations, however, the emphasis needs to be on strategy: personality type is felt as a given, fixed, objective entity; strategies are limited, local and changeable.

Responding to stress

In any situation take the first feelings of stress, powerlessness or despair as a signal that action is needed. It may help to see a cue, like a studio light, indicating the need to prepare oneself. Pausing in this way involves rejecting the unwanted feelings or the urge to become embattled in a confrontation. Teachers in general are said to have a tendency to over-react with pupils and under-react with colleagues. In either case, if the habitual response leads to stress it must first be rejected to clear the way for a more helpful strategy. Pausing and rejecting puts the threatened person in control: realizing that one has taken responsibility for one's actions is an encouraging indication that the control of stress is within one's power; it is not the same as feeling that responsibility is thrust upon us by external constraints. This feeling of power over oneself while under stress reverses the pressure: we feel less overwhelmed and more able to make the decisions: whether to react; in what way to react; how energetically to react. The urge to retreat or fly from the situation should diminish:

knowing we have control over our impulses removes the need to escape. As Miller puts it: 'If I can stop the roller coaster, I don't want to get off' (quoted in Woodhouse et al., 1985). Much of the procedure described so far is no more than old fashioned self-control, but like many traditional remedies it can be effective. For example, Hughes (1988) describes how talking oneself through problems (or 'engaging in self-statements') has been helpful in controlling a range of unwanted impulses: smoking, obesity, phobias, learning and behaviour difficulties. In some studies a 'turtle response' is advised which involves withdrawing, psychologically at least, and relaxing. This technique is not always possible in teaching situations.

Action can be of two broad types and elements of both are needed in most circumstances. We can pay attention to and seek to change those external stressors that displease us; or we can look inwards to our own particular attitudes. Those who are successful in taking control and accepting responsibility should be able to use it in their relations with others. Woodhouse et al. (1985) reported some success in encouraging teachers to take control of their own behaviour and change their behaviour at work. Stress resulting from the organizational arrangements of a school, or the actions or omissions of colleagues, may be countered by asserting oneself. Hall et al. (1984), in evaluating an in-service course, found that teachers saw assertiveness training as 'a potent learning opportunity'. Assertiveness requires essential issues to be identified and stripped of their extraneous personality factors: communication must be open, honest and direct with specific, clear statements. Assume an upright posture using full eye-contact whether standing or sitting. It may help to clasp your hands or fold your arms. Clearly state the facts and your feelings: for example: 'This class is too large, I do not wish to take it until it is halved'. Gray and Freeman (1988) advise identifying that part of the problem that is yours and concentrating on that. This means not being sidetracked into discussing other people's difficulties. For example, when told that there are not enough rooms/teachers to split the oversized class, do not suggest possibilities. These will invariably be rejected and you will swiftly find yourself drawn into discussing administrative problems over which you have no control. Of course, if you know there is an easy solution that has been overlooked then point it out. But if it is rejected, withdraw and stick to your own part of the problem. Repeat the facts and state your feelings and demands.

Beware of being drawn into discussing your reasons and if you do give them do not let them obscure the main issue. Gray and Freeman (1988) suggest offering to discuss reasons at some later time, and simply repeating your objection like a broken record if necessary. Criticisms and general statements are best questioned rather than replied to. For example: 'When you say unprofessional . . .' This may lead to their being abandoned and the focus returning to your problem. If it does not, return to the principal issue by reiterating your opening statement. Another red herring to watch for is the irrelevant reply to a demand. For example, having complained about the oversize class, the person in charge of the timetable might say: 'There are lots of oversize classes, and other teachers are not complaining.' This is of course an implied criticism of yourself, but do not respond with a catalogue of your contributions to the school. Make your original statement again but preface it with: 'I appreciate that but . . .' If you feel it is appropriate to adopt a more authoritative stance, use a stronger preface instead: 'I am not asking you that. This class is . . .' This latter opening might be inappropriate and hazardous when there is a large status gap. The general procedure therefore is to accept all responses, not to respond to them, and to continue repeating your problem. In stressful encounters it may be easier to keep your mind on the strategy if you determine to include the word 'No' in every statement you make. Then, even if you are sidetracked, introducing the 'No' reminds you to make your simple direct demand.

It is not uncommon to prepare for these assertive encounters only to be met with instant capitulation. Perhaps the added assurance is non-verbally communicated, and the adversary sees at once that resistance is useless. On the other hand there may be a flat refusal to talk, the phone may ring and be gratefully seized, you may have a class waiting, or your target may be practising the same assertion techniques. In these circumstances state that you will return later and withdraw. This prospect may produce the action you want or some concession, and if it does not, take up the issue again. Remember that even if you lose on one issue it is not a total loss: if you are in the right, you can be sure that other unjust burdens are now less likely to be put upon you. Finally, if you are reluctant to try assertion, or particularly timid, you can increase your determination to face up to a person by resolving to tackle a number of problems, perhaps in different spheres and with different people over the coming months, and planning this before you begin. Garfinkel (1967) found, in an experiment to encourage students to haggle over prices in shops, that those given several to do were less likely to back out at the last moment. They were surprisingly successful too.

The second type of action is personal and is appropriate to situations where there is no particular external factor that can be changed. For example, you may be depressed about teaching in general, your inability to interest pupils in a subject you value, the gap between your moral and social attitudes and those of your classes. In so far as these feelings result from exceptional personal standards, and not ineffectiveness as a teacher, this situation calls for a reorganization of priorities. Goals must be altered and ambitions which have become unrealistic must be abandoned. Some teachers hold an image of an ideal teacher which they believe they should attain. Perfection eludes all of us, of course, and recognizing this fact may remove one source of stress. Some teachers believe that only they have problems and meet each one with continuing dismay, as if they hoped that after surviving their last problem there would be no more. This too is an unrealistic perception of life. It is necessary to recognize that problems are part of everyone's daily routine: they should not be greeted with surprise but accepted; like the others they will pass in time, solved or not.

Some personally orientated strategies are sometimes dismissively termed, palliatives. These include having a moan in the staffroom or at home, sleeping on the problem, having a drink, or developing a time-consuming interest that occupies the thoughts through the day. This last can take the form of religious or political action: one person's palliative is another person's salvation – or election. Staffroom humour or cynicism seems to be widespread in secondary but not primary schools (Delamont and Galton, 1986; Woods, 1976). Palliatives are said to outnumber direct actions in the ratio of two to one (Dewe, 1985). However, the distinction between direct action (problem solving) and palliative (regulation of emotions) is not a certain one. Among the palliatives listed are many items that are arguably problem solving such as: talk to more experienced colleagues; indulge in self-analysis to sort out the problem; build up self-confidence. On the list of problem solving, direct actions are such things as: take short cuts on things you don't like; discipline the children; keep the children occupied. Dewe's conclusion, that organizational structures limit direct action, seems unsupported by his evidence. Nevertheless, palliatives may be the only appropriate strategy where more direct intervention proves futile or could jeopardize a teacher's career. The historical, literary and artistic world offers some consolations if not feasible possibilities. It is well known that many important historical characters, writers and humorists were partly driven to their achievements by personal unhappiness or domestic disorder. Transforming one's problems into heroism or literature may be unrealistic but it is possible to delight in the efforts of others. For example, the author of a weekly column in *Punch*, usually Michael Bywater, works off a quantity of personal stress through the colourful description of those who have wounded him: nail-faced managers, thick-legged, horse-faced racquet-bashers, and hateful, speech-less oafs who shout and reek.

In severe cases of tense depression, a straightforward relaxation exercise may help (Iwanicki referred to in Woodhouse *et al.*, 1985). A simple one is as follows: take deep breaths for two minutes or so, breathing in deeply while slowly counting to five, or more if you can; exhale slowly, counting again, and press the air right out of the lungs; tense the muscles, while imagining you are very cold, then relax and feel yourself becoming warm. In this state of relative calm it may help to imagine yourself managing the depressing or stressful situations more successfully. This is a form of talking oneself into coping: work reviewed in Hughes (1988: 8–10) suggests it may help sufferers to change their behaviour. The sceptical and observant may have noted that deep breathing, relaxation and daydreaming are very much the benefits associated with a brisk walk followed by a doze.

The acronym SCRAPP summarizes the coping strategies described so far. The first feelings of Stress are a Cue for action; the first step is to Reject the urge to become embattled, the anger, the depression, or the feeling of powerlessness; then Accept responsibility for your own behaviour, take control of yourself and decide whether and how energetically to react; finally consider Physical, direct action such as asserting yourself, or Personal self-orientated action such as discarding unrealistic ambitions, developing other interests, and relaxation exercises.

Confrontations

> For whosoever exalteth himself shall be abased; and he that humbleth himself shall be exalted. (Luke 14:11)

Coping in situations of confrontation and severe conflict is an extension of the earlier discussions on understanding pupil motives and controlling teacher reactions. This section concerns confrontations that the teacher has not provoked and does not wish for. It is assumed that everyone understands that unwanted confrontations can result from pupils being subjected to humiliation or sarcasm, and therefore such a style is best avoided. From time to time it may be judged desirable to confront a pupil and risk, or even hope for, a crisis: where a teacher has shown patience and tolerance over a considerable period, presenting a pupil with some harsh truths can provoke the sort of crisis that becomes a turning point in the pupil's efforts to reform. Laslett and Smith (1984: 87) suggest that occasional confrontations of this sort can benefit the pupil, the class and the teacher's management. This kind of confrontation is controlled and most effectively managed by a teacher who knows the pupil well and for whom the pupil has respect. The points which follow apply to situations where conflict is unlooked for and in danger of being uncontrolled.

Avoid being manipulated

The first sign of approaching trouble is the cue to be on guard against slipping into an habitual or automatic response. It is necessary for the teacher to accept responsibility for his or her actions and to accept that they are in control and able to avoid knee-jerk reactions: the serene, dispassionate professional, not a puppet of the pupil's capricious emotions. The warning signs include a feeling of personal hurt resulting from both one's positional authority as a teacher being attacked and one's attempt at reasonableness – there has invariably been one (Pik, in Cohen and Cohen, 1987). In the first stages of a conflict both the office and person are rejected: two blows which are often sufficient to preclude the possibility of the teacher retaining equanimity or recovering control. Confrontations always take place with at least one of three possible audiences in attendance whose effect on the actors is to heighten tension and drive judgement off the stage.

There is invariably an audience of pupils present. The teacher therefore feels constrained not to lose face and often feels that, for the sake of the others, there was no alternative but to stand firm irrespective of consequences. From the pupil's point of view, the presence of others hinders any inclination or opportunity to back down from a public act of defiance. If the audience can be removed, or the teacher is able to remove the pupil or allow a retreat, serious conflict is less likely. The two other possible audiences are often absent but are none the less influential. The teacher may feel contrained to stand his or her ground on principle, perhaps having in the past declared such principles to colleagues and friends. These people constitute a shadow audience constraining the teacher's actions. Wagner, in a chapter of Calderhead (1987), terms the conflicts resulting from 'self-imperated cognitions' as 'knots'. The suggested remedy for the problems that arise from refusing to see things as they are, but only as they should be is: stop being ruled by 'musts' and become determined to accept responsibility for choosing anew in each situation. There is an apparent contradiction in advising that one must not be ruled by musts, but a rule about rules has a different logical status to a rule about things. The pupil may have a parallel audience who similarly give him or her 'no other choice.'

The third possible audience consists of those persons who will inevitably appear on the scene if the conflict does not evaporate. For the teacher, this audience consists of colleagues and superiors; for the pupil, parents, and friends from other groups. All three audiences contribute to the fear, embarrassment and tension and put accurate perception and balanced judgement at risk. Pik (in Cohen and Cohen, 1987) includes the sadness teachers often feel in such unlooked for conflicts as another factor confusing wise judgement. To be aware of the effect of these audiences is the first step in understanding and controlling one's reactions. If the audience of pupils is to be encouraged to accept the reintegration of the pupil into the community, care must be taken to define the crisis in a way that makes this possible. For example, to say 'Helen is not herself today' is preferable to 'Helen will not be able to stay in this school if she does not improve'. The words and actions of a teacher who is highly regarded by pupils will influence the troubled pupil's view of self, and the class's view of him or her too. Future harmony depends on words being carefully chosen.

Identify the pupil's point of view

Unlikely as it may be, a time of acute stress is a time to try to step into the pupil's shoes and understand and possibly accept the reasonableness of their behaviour from their point of view. Another way of looking at the situation is to see the confrontation as the pupil's particular distress, not the teacher's. As Hanko (1985: 80) puts it, what others think about us is their problem; our reaction to this is ours. Wills (1967) tells a story about a Quaker who was the victim of a murderous hold-up on a lonely road. With a gun at his head there was good reason to be alarmed but his distress was directed elsewhere, for he said to the robber: 'Dear fellow, what has brought you to this?' It may be that the teacher has carelessly or unintentionally provoked an outburst and most teachers are able to accept this and restore calm with a placatory or apologetic statement. The attempt to grasp what is driving the pupil's action helps to distance the teacher from the feelings of personal hurt and professional incompetence. The pupil's feelings may be a mirror image of the teacher's and the latter may often be used to retrieve the former. The teacher may also reflect on the influence the pupil's audiences are having upon his or her behaviour and the possible reasons for the pupil investing so much in what may have begun as a trivial exchange or minor offence. Often, the open discussion of these audience effects can stop a confrontation situation developing. For some teachers, who habitually show patience and have good relations with a pupil, a sudden aggressive confrontation can be exceptionally distressing and undermine the teacher's confidence in his or her understanding. A distressed pupil may finally lose control when faced with a teacher who is, from the pupil's point of view, unusually kind: this contradiction, perhaps added to several lessons of failure and frustration, can be the trigger that causes the pupil to relinquish self-control. To be selected in this way may be seen as a compliment to one's importance in the pupil's eyes. To worry about it is inappropriate: just as it would be for a specialist surgeon to worry because all the most hopeless cases were pushing at the door.

Avoid ratchet statements

Ratchets turn only one way and any threat or remark that cannot be abandoned or withdrawn inevitably carries the dispute forward and raises its temperature. Threats of force or removal are particularly effective in bringing a crisis to a violent climax. There should always be some physical or interactional escape route for both pupil and teacher. Assaults upon teachers sometimes result from physical attempts to block doorways to escaping pupils. The feeling, and subsequent claim, that 'there was no alternative' is an example of the tyranny of 'musts' discussed by Wagner

(1987). There is always an alternative to every imperative – except this present one. Confrontations are times when hurtful things are said. Laslett and Smith (1984: 104) describe a case in which the teacher shouts insults and threats. These are difficult to withdraw and there is greater than normal danger that a pupil may store and live up to any deviant labels that have been applied. Some pupils even have difficulty separating corrections of their work from criticisms of themselves personally. Caspari (1976) gives examples of this. It is much more difficult to separate comments on one's behaviour from attacks upon oneself. The primary offence must be prevented from becoming the focus of later, secondary action as the pupil seeks to live up to the deviant designation (see Lemert, quoted in Hargreaves *et al.*, 1975: 5).

Accept or divert an attack

It sometimes costs nothing in terms of esteem or control simply to accept an insult or act of defiance. This is to apply one of the principles of judo to verbal contests: go with the opponent's force rather than resisting it and use it to unbalance them if possible. One teacher in a school for maladjusted pupils recalled how a pupil noticed the wedding ring on her finger and said 'I don't know how you ever got a fella, with a face like yours'. She admitted that such remarks can be hurtful but she was not wounded by it for as she said: 'I had long ago come to much the same conclusion myself, and I told the pupil so.' Kohl (1986) suggests diverting attention from the threat by giving misused objects a name. For example, as a chair is lifted ready to be thrown, 'Don't do that to Boris, he cannot stand heights.' Another example given in Robertson (1981) concerned a teacher who entered a classroom to find a pupil about to hit another with an iron bar taken from the gym: 'Right, pokers away, books out.' These examples are not merely evidence for the common belief that a sense of humour helps in a crisis: humorous judo is more than a facility for easy jokes. Turning the other cheek is a strategy with a long pedigree.

Try procrastination

A straightforward technique is simply to refuse to become embroiled at the particular moment chosen by the pupil. The dispute is postponed without surrendering any other issue. Kohl (1986) advises putting the burden of choice on the pupil: withdrawing from the struggle and leaving the pupil to decide when he or she is ready to resume co-operation. In this case, the teacher specifies what the pupil must do to mend the breach and then withdraws. There is no need to specify a time limit and the importance of the conflict may rapidly diminish: with luck, postponement becomes cancellation. Inflammatory or ratchet statements can sometimes be withdrawn in a graceful and humorous way by being put off till later. For example, teachers sometimes say 'I shall ask you once more and then . . .' – a threat follows. To be sure, the teacher will have to ask once more and no doubt the prospect of having to carry out an impossible threat, or abandon it, increases the tension by another notch. One way out is to add, having paused, an absurd date and time in the future when the pupil will be 'asked once more'.

Repair the relationship

Where a confrontation has occurred and does not end in a satisfactory way, the pupil should be seen alone before the next timetabled meeting takes place with its attentive audience waiting breathlessly to be entertained. A private face-to-face talk can be disarming – particularly if it begins with conciliatory remarks from the teacher. A closeness and openness is possible face-to-face that is often unachievable in classrooms: '. . . in the face-to-face situation, the other's subjectivity is available to me through the maximum of symptoms . . . no other form of social relating can reproduce the plenitude of symptoms of subjectivity present in the face-to-face situation' (Berger and Luckmann, 1971: 43). More succinctly: 'If thy brother shall trespass against thee, go tell him his fault between thee and him alone' (Matthew, 18:15).

People who are unsure of themselves find apologies embarrassing and shaming; those who have authority can sometimes use apologies to confirm and enhance it. It is therefore important for teachers to feel confident in their expertise and to understand that 'It is not demeaning to make an apology' (Laslett and Smith, 1984: 102). Some schools, determined to succeed with disturbing pupils, ensure that such meetings follow conflict, and may emphasize their importance by setting aside the headteacher's room for them. In rare cases the pupil will decline to co-operate but it is still possible for the teacher to indicate that the matter is closed by a light comment: one teacher suggested that it was always possible to offer a brief apology for an offensive remark if she had made one, or a self-deprecatory gesture and a wink and a smile in passing.

Confirming continued co-operation

Despite protestations to the contrary, and in the face of all the evidence, most confrontational pupils do not want to be rejected. Some may even be using confrontations to test, in a socially inept way, the reliability and sincerity of their teachers. They must therefore be assured that, despite what may have been said during the conflict, and irrespective of future behaviour, they are expected to continue following the same timetable at the same school with the same teachers. For many pupils this will be unexpected for they may frequently have been threatened with banishment from both home and school. It also reassures them that perhaps they have found someone they can trust to forgive them and with whom they are sure of a welcome even if they fail: till death us do part, if necessary.

Exercise 6: three stress cases

Participants should divide into groups of three or four. Each case needs at least fifteen minutes, so if time is short, distribute the cases among the groups and share results in the plenary session. In each case, discuss your feelings, how you would cope, and what action, if any, you would take. Note any recommendations that would need to be considered on a school-wide basis. There are no comments following these cases: participants need to consider how the advice in this chapter would apply if these incidents occurred in their own particular circumstances.

1. After persistent difficulties with an aggressive and difficult pupil in a largely co-operative class you order him out of the room. He refuses to leave so you go and fetch the deputy head who takes him away. After a few minutes he returns unabashed and resumes his seat. Shortly before the lesson ends the deputy enters and proceeds to tell off the entire class for their 'continual bad behaviour' in your lessons. Unspecified action is threatened if any more is heard from you about them. The deputy, clearly satisfied that this action has given you support in a forthright and helpful way, leaves the room. You have another class to go to.

2. You are behind with the end of term reports and have been pressed by the head for completion. You have the last period of the day free and intend working on them then and staying in school until you finish. Just before your free begins, a pupil brings a message from the deputy asking you to retain your present class until school ends as their next teacher has gone home with a sudden headache. The class is a tough and difficult one and you are exasperated after barely surviving a double period with them. You could bring up the whole matter of frees and absenteeism at the next staff meeting, though you know from experience that the missing teacher, who is often absent, will not be there.

3. A November morning. A cold wintry rain is sweeping the playground. Only the staff are in school as it is a training day but two pupils, poorly clad against the weather, are sheltering in the doorway. They did not remember or were absent and never received the instruction to stay at home, have travelled several miles, are wet through, and it is well known that neither will find anyone in at home. A senior teacher tells the pupils to go, and

that it is their responsibility if they are locked out. They protest but are pushed out and the door is locked. Both pupils are in your special group and you can hear their incoherent protests above the noise of the wind and the rain.

Exercise 7: thinking about stress

The purpose of this exercise is to compare perceptions of the sources of stress in your situation and to identify areas producing general problems. There are many ways of doing this. For example, Grunsell (1985) suggests filling in equations of this sort: stress $= x + y - z$. Below are some points which should guide thinking, and they themselves have benefited from anger management techniques described in a recent book (Hughes, 1988). Participants should spend ten minutes considering them alone before dividing into groups of three or four. Group work may need up to thirty minutes before sharing conclusions in plenary session.

1. Exactly describe one cause of stress to you. Briefly but specifically note exactly what happens.
2. Identify any organizational features or other forces that create or maintain the unwanted situation.
3. Write down your goals or ambitions in this situation. Could they be altered, and if so in what way?
4. You should now be able to identify those aspects of the problem directly under your control, and those that are external stressors. Using a popular analogy, you should be able to separate that part of the problem that is an excessive load on the bridge, and that part caused by weakness in the bridge.
5. Be clear about those parts of the problem that are yours and that will form the basis of any self-assertion strategy. List some alternative actions that you could try in your stressful situation. Note the preparation and self-statements you would need. Consider what might happen with each alternative.

In groups compare your problems, share solutions, and try to analyse and suggest remedies for each other. You will certainly find that there are different hierarchies of stressful situations. You may even discover that one person's stressor is regarded favourably or with indifference by others. This illustrates the role of perception in stress. The plenary session may identify school-wide problems which require continued staff co-operation and management.

Exercise 8: confrontation with Malcolm

For this exercise the group should divide into pairs or threes to permit full contributions from all participants. Twenty minutes is usually sufficient time in small groups before sharing ideas in plenary session. The purpose of the exercise is to identify examples of the points discussed above; to identify points at which the teacher could have taken alternative action and in particular any examples of inappropriate action. One way of learning from this case is to begin with one teacher empathizing with Malcolm and another with the teacher. If groups are in threes, the remaining member may try to consider the situation from the viewpoint of a colleague or one of the other pupils.

There cannot, of course, be a model solution to this or any other example: the value lies in practising confrontation management techniques. The paragraphs are numbered to facilitate reference in discussion. The course leader should read the comments on the exercise before the plenary session.

Incident report from a teacher

1. The trouble began when I set them to do the exercise. Malcolm said 'It's boring!' and shut his book with a loud snap. I told him he would have to do the work like everyone else and if he didn't do it now I would see he did it later. His reply to that was a lot of very foul language – he said 'Just try and make me' or some challenge like that.

2. I went straight up to him and opened his book at the page and I tried to make him be sensible – I spoke to him very quietly and reasonably – but he just threw the book down on the floor and rocked back on his chair. I just couldn't let him get away with that. I knew there was no point in ordering him to pick the book up so I did and put it on his desk again.

3. As I attended to another pupil I heard him rip the book in half. I didn't turn round straight away – I was telling some others to get on with their work – they were watching his performance. They were looking to see what was going to happen next. Then I saw the book fly across the room.

4. I explained to him how patient I was being and how I had defended him against other teachers' complaints on more than one occasion. His response was more swearing.

5. I told him not to be silly and went back to my desk but he then took other pupils' work and threw it on the floor. It was just out of control and he was obviously heading for a showdown.

6. I warned him that if he didn't grow up I would bring the deputy

but he just laughed and said 'Go on and fetch her'. Those are not the actual words he used. I ordered him out but he defied me again.

7. The class went very quiet, he was standing up in an aggressive style. I turned to go for the deputy and he then came up behind me and punched me hard in the back. When I came back he was in his place and the deputy took him away. He had calmed down then. It was a good thing the lesson was nearly over as the kids were really high.

Comments on the exercise

Too much should not be read into the actual wording or the form of this report. Although it is based on a real report extra information has been added to give a full enough picture for analysis.

1. Malcolm's action should have caused an alarm bell to ring in the teacher's mind: here is a typical cue to avoid unconsidered responses and get control of self. Here the teacher's positional authority as a teacher is rejected. Note the suggestion that the work must be done at any price, the threat that 'I would see' that it was, and the feeling of being challenged. The teacher is personally involved from the outset. Accepting the comment on boring work may have avoided further activity.

2. A juxtaposition of a challenging response (opening the book) and conciliation (speaking quietly and reasonably). The teacher's personal reasonableness joins the professional authority on the floor. The teacher is driven by imperatives: 'couldn't let him get away with that'. You could let him get away with it and others might accept this exception being made: perhaps a comment like 'Malcolm's not himself today'.

3. Here we see recognition of the role played by the audience. The pupil's further provocation suggests that it is affecting his behaviour too.

4. Personal reasonableness takes another blow. The feeling of hurt expressed here suggests that this pupil is seeking revenge: the teacher is receiving punishment belonging to some other person in some other relationship.

5. Apparent evidence that the pupil is determined to continue irrespective of teacher's response, and the teacher's feeling of inevitability confirms this. Accepting the inevitability of events hastens and does not hinder their progress.

6. In the light of (5) ordering the pupil out seems unwise. It might have been appropriate, even at this late stage, to specify some simple

achievable behaviour and withdraw. 'Grow up' is both imprecise and insulting – although it cannot be denied it is deserved.

7. This conclusion is doubly distressing for the teacher: having been assaulted the teacher brings help to what appears to be a situation of no threat, easily managed. Staff support groups and discussions would be helpful here and will be explained in Chapter 7.

Chapter six

Individuals in context

In this chapter the focus is on the classroom and school contexts in which the pupils' behaviour may be understood and operated upon. First, we will look at the classroom itself and describe a method of analyzing and altering behaviour; second, we will consider the influence of the organization and climate of the school. We are principally concerned here with troublesome pupils and not implying that all pupils, or even a majority, will necessarily be adversely affected by the contexts discussed – nor that all can be influenced by the manipulation of them. Pupils, like any other people, are not infinitely malleable. As Eisner (1985) puts it: 'Children have an enormous capacity to learn how to cope with treatments that they wish to manage for their own purposes.'

The classroom

Schostak (1986) quotes Bain's assertion of a century ago that 'for the single pupil individuality may be studied and appealed to, for the class, individualities are not considered'. Caspari (1976) describes some aspects of behaviour in groups which indicate some of the behavioural features to expect in classrooms that may be missing from individual and small group interaction. These are: that members are more dependent on the leader, who may be used as a target for negative feelings that are felt for others; that to gain attention in groups, forcefulness is necessary; and that it seems to be easier to be destructive than positive. It is this last point that is often made by those advocating one of the more widespread interventions in disorderly classrooms: a programme based on the principles of behaviour modification or behaviour management as it is now more often called (typical texts are Galvin and Singleton, 1984, Cheeseman and Watts, 1985; and Wheldall and Merret, 1984. The strength of this approach lies in its ability to offer practical programmes and solutions: there is something straightforward that can actually be tried. Desired behaviours are rewarded, or positively reinforced, and unwanted behaviours are negatively reinforced and extinguished by having their reinforcers withdrawn.

A pupil who rarely sits at his or her desk would receive smiles, sweets, or other attention when found to be sitting and would be ignored when leaving the desk to pester the teacher for attention. In some cases, approximations to the desired behaviour are rewarded with the long-term intention of shaping the end result by encouraging improvements towards it. A procedure known as task-analysis may be used to determine the sequence of small steps which, when rewarded, will add up to or lead towards the desired behaviour.

Punishment may take the form of withdrawal of reinforcement or removal from an interesting activity. This is called time-out and may involve a few minutes' exile within or outside the classroom. Behavioural programmes may be useful with dull or very young children and significantly, the textbook examples do not usually include pupils over the age of twelve. However, Porter (in Coupe and Porter, 1986: 64) notes that, even for children with severe learning difficulties, the behavioural approach 'should not be viewed as a panacea'. Older or more reflective pupils readily see that they are being manipulated and are able to thwart a simplistic tactic that does not recognize motive and action.

The limitations of behavioural programmes and their distorted view of human action are handicaps that have been recognized, not least by therapists themselves, faced with outcomes that were only partially or temporarily successful. A major drawback is that they take little or no account of the constraints of classroom management. Doyle concludes that the weight of the evidence is against them: '. . . early recommendations for elaborate and complex systems of token economies, systematic contingency management, and ignoring undesirable behaviour while praising desired behaviour were impractical for individual classroom teachers' (Wittrock, 1986: 423). On a related issue, Evertson and Emmer (1982), not that 'instructional approaches (for example, an individual diagnostic-prescriptive method)' that do not take account of the pressures of the classroom setting are not easily or correctly implemented. The claim that it was safer and more objective for teachers to attend only to the behaviour, ignoring other factors and possibilities, is now seen to be over-optimistic. Certainly time can be wasted in futile speculation but to ignore the social context is to limit one's vision. It is similarly limiting to ignore the subjective motives and intentions of the parties: for it is an objective fact that people are subjective. Further doubts are sometimes expressed about the wisdom of using external reinforcement, its effect upon the pupil's intrinsic motivation, and the apparent lack of attention to the nature of the learning that the pupil is being trained to accept. Attending only to what can be observed and measured can result in pupils' intentions and meanings being ignored: but it is often these motives that determine what the behaviour actually is. It is difficult to describe a human action without including or implying a motive or other state of mind. A pupil may swear at a teacher in order to win esteem from a delinquent peer group; another pupil's swearing may spring from frustration, personal failure and the prospect of future unemployment. Without attention to the pupil's meaning, intervention is likely to be ineffective or aggravating. The same difficulties apply to determining what counts as ignoring, or as a reward or punishment. The success of the behavioural approach hangs on an uncertain congruence of view between teachers and pupils in these matters.

These limitations have led to the typical product of behavioural programmes being described as the pupil who '. . . stays glued to his seat and desk all day, continuously looks at his teacher or his text . . . does not talk to or in fact look at other children . . . does not laugh or sing . . . and assuredly passes silently in the halls' (Winnet and Winkler quoted in Hughes, 1988: 20). In reality, however, this parody has proved more an indictment of the intention than the result. Behaviourally orientated authors have expanded their repertoire in order to meet some of these difficulties. Wheldall and Merrett (1984) pay attention to environmental antecedents; Cheeseman and Watts (1985) throw in a list of strategies '. . . tried, tested and approved by teachers . . .' – or tips as they might be called. It still may be, as Docking (1980) suggests, that behavioural methods are appropriate only for novices or the inexpert, and even then so long as control does not become an end in its own right.

Hughes (1988) describes a more radical extension of the behavioural approach into a new specialism, termed cognitive behaviour therapy. This discipline takes account of the active role of human perceptions and the extent to which we act in environments created by ourselves. The cognitive behavioural approach retains the interest of behaviourists in experimental verification of carefully defined programmes but with a new emphasis on interaction between therapist, or teacher, and pupil. More time is spent in showing the pupil what to do, taking turns to practise alongside him or her, and working together co-operatively. The pupil is no longer a passive object of therapy but is fully involved in the aims and direction of the programme and regarded as its legitimate owner. Pupils are encouraged to talk themselves through their problems and practise controlling their impulses and wayward inclinations. Teachers help by giving the pupil encouraging explanations for failure: for example, that it is a temporary setback that does not preclude future success; that it is at least partly a matter of bad luck; and that the pupil has the ability to succeed with a little more persistence and effort. Pupils are invited to consider alternative strategies, and their different consequences, that might be more appropriate in situations where they habitually resort to violence or disruption. If troublesome pupils are to have a fair chance of using the new strategies it is often necessary to involve their classmates. Hughes (1988) warns that other pupils may react on the basis of reputation rather than current efforts and unintentionally thwart troublesome pupils' attempts to improve.

A troublesome pupil's classroom behaviour may be a partial result of his or her experience of trying to establish a role in the group. For example, an insecure or semi-literate pupil may have found other pupils respond to his or her tumbling on to the floor with rewarding smiles and laughter; the teacher may respond by describing the pupil as naughty or as a distraction – labels the pupil may see as a suitable cover for his or her lack of achievement. The pupil, over time, may develop and elaborate an identity as a mischief-maker which may both disguise and excuse an inability to read. There is, in fact, a well-established correlation between inability to read and troublesome behaviour (Laing and Chazan, 1986) although the direction of causality is impossible to identify with certainty. One study does suggest that poor verbal skill at the age of three is associated with difficult behaviour at the age of eight (Stevenson, summarized in Cohen and Cohen, 1987). It is necessary to precisely identify the unwanted behaviour, discover any predisposing conditions and unintended rewards, and devise a strategy for change.

Precise identification

To describe pupils as noisy, cheeky, uncontrollable or hyperactive is insufficiently accurate to focus observation and improvement. A pupil can be noisy in many ways that may be identified with more precision: sings, drums feet, whistles, shouts to pupils or teacher, scrapes chair, drops equipment. Being cheeky can be pulling faces, staring, parodying or repeating the teacher, packing books away before the proper time as well as offering rude comments. A teacher's rules take meaning from particular contexts (Hargreaves *et al.*, 1975) and therefore it is not enough to know, for example, that a pupil 'will not stop talking': this may mean that he or she is cheating, interrupting, being rude, disturbing others, or refusing to work. The physical setting and the expectations associated with it also influence the meaning of behaviour: conversation that is appropriate in CDT may not be so in history. Pupils may regard some areas with awe and fear but see others as 'soft' (Delamont and Galton, 1986). In some specialist rooms, there is more scope to demonstrate the intrinsic worth and practical value of what is being taught (Schostak, 1983): the discipline of the subject can aid the discipline of the group.

Precision is more easily achieved with some behaviours rather than others. It is in principle impossible to know with certainty whether someone is paying attention or not, for example, as we cannot think another person's thoughts. In such cases a rough approximation has to serve and pupils are usually regarded as paying sufficient attention if they are facing the teacher and apparently engaged on the task. It is an unnecessary use of time to go to absurd lengths in precisely describing pupil misbehaviour: an example sometimes quoted is the definition of 'out of seat' as being 'when no part of the seat part of the person is in contact with the seat part of the seat'. It is possible to use elaborate and detailed checklists for recording behaviour and examples may be found in Galvin and Singleton (1984), Coulby and Harper (1985) and Grunsell (1985).

Measuring the extent or frequency

If progress is to be measured then some sort of baseline must be established: we need to know how often a particular unwanted action occurs or what proportion of a typical lesson is spent in unwanted behaviour. If the unwanted behaviour is a discrete action, for example leaving the seat and kicking another pupil, then the number of occurrences can be counted. This can be done over a single lesson, or teachers can collate figures for several lessons. If this shows wide variations in the frequency of the misbehaviour, then this is itself a piece of useful information. Where the behaviour is not measurable in this simple way then the co-operation of a colleague may be necessary. Observations are taken at intervals: every minute or every two minutes the pupil's behaviour is recorded; this produces a measure of the frequency of the unwanted behaviour. Generally speaking misbehaviour measured in these ways turns out to be much less prevalent than expected: it is common to find that a pupil is able to give an impression of perpetual disruption while attending the lesson, or being harmlessly disengaged, for two-thirds of the time. Congruent with this phenomenon is the observation reported in Wragg (1984) that in some classes which are apparently totally out of control, two-thirds of the pupils are in fact on task. This discovery is welcome news to the teacher and helps to get the management programme off to an optimistic start. Some pupils are sometimes able to record their own off-task activity rate and in such cases the additional attention and teacher interaction make the pupil's aims in misbehaving redundant.

Picking a target

There is often a whole range of behaviour exhibited by a problem pupil. It is tempting to begin work on eradicating the most serious, even if it not the most frequent. Unfortunately, the most serious behaviours are often the most difficult to eradicate and the close observation and analysis programme is therefore vulnerable to a speedy and unsuccessful end. It is wiser to focus on any easy target first, particularly if it is a high frequency behaviour: often relatively trivial misbehaviour is a necessary precondition to committing more serious offences. For example, a pupil who hits others and spoils their work is also off-task and out of his or her place. The most profitable procedure therefore is to increase on-task activity and decrease the time the pupil spends out of seat. Choosing to reward an appropriate behaviour that is incompatible with an unwanted alternative has the added advantage of creating a more rewarding environment for a pupil accustomed to ignoring punishments.

Unwanted behaviour may need teacher co-operation for it to occur: pestering for attention is one example. It is usual to advise ignoring such behaviour but this is rarely possible in the classroom or indeed in principle: to deliberately ignore is to attend in a negative way and the pupil usually knows this. A determined pupil may then escalate the attention-seeking until the teacher gives way: all the pupil has learned is to be persistent and the behaviour is therefore made worse not better. An equivalent strategy to ignoring is to attend to the pupil in a detached and distant manner – denying eye contact and moving away whilst speaking, for example. As soon as the pupil is observed on-task, the teacher can give full and rewarding interaction. In extreme circumstances it may be necessary to remove the pupil from the classroom and as far as possible from stimulating and interesting surroundings. Behavioural psychologists term this treatment, time-out. Few schools have an appropriate spare room, or even a walk-in cupboard, that can be made available even for the few minutes that may be necessary. However, many of the features of time-out and ignoring can be produced by the planned and deliberate coolness described above.

Predisposing and confirming circumstances

There are some very simple aspects of classroom environment that influence attentiveness and distraction. Bull and Solity (1987: 137) provide a list of such things as seating, task difficulty, teacher behaviour. Chapter 3 deals with such factors. Curricular variety and relevance at the primary and secondary level have their equivalents in pre-school contexts; and evidence from nurseries can help observation of older age-groups. Smith and Connolly's study of three and four-year-olds (summarized in Cohen and Cohen, 1988: 139) showed that ample play equipment reduced conflict but also reduced sharing activities; reducing the quantity of toys encouraged more conflict but also more sharing, and fewer children were left out of activities. Severe crowding (less that 15 square feet per child) reduced the scope for rough-and-tumble play but increased aggression. This work shows that if provision is always lavish some children will be denied opportunities to learn to share. Interestingly, Laslet (1977) suggested that although maladjusted pupils need exceptionally patient teachers, they should be exposed to less tolerant outsiders too. Research discussed by Laing and Chazan (1986) suggests that a 'tight organizational pattern' which required young children to participate in activities in a pre-arranged rota 'whether they were interested or not' created disruption opportunities for some pupils. Organizational patterns of this sort are an inevitable feature later on.

The close recording and measurement of behaviour may reveal other previously hidden factors. For example, it may be noticed that the pupil under observation is not the only one involved in many of the incidents. Sometimes several pupils co-operate in mischief, perhaps inciting the target pupil to join in. When the teacher notices and corrects them, all but the target pupil fall into line. Hargreaves (1980) describes an example of this. It is therefore important when observing to take the whole context, which includes other pupils, into consideration. Some pupils create trouble only in some subjects, or with some teachers or at certain times of the day. These conditions are not usually easy to remedy but in serious cases a change of timetable or personnel may be considered justifiable. Sometimes, of course, teachers may need the advice in Chapter 3.

It is more common to find misbehaviour being unintentionally rewarded so that, from the pupil's viewpoint, its utility is confirmed. With younger pupils the reward for unwanted behaviour often consists of isolation with a kind and sympathetic teacher – for example, after throwing a spectacular scene. It is not unknown for some senior pupils to behave badly partly because suspension from school gives them freedom and the opportunity to earn money. In other cases appropriate behaviour is insufficiently rewarded, leaving the remnant of good behaviour at the mercy of the more exciting bad. Unrewarding teaching, unimaginative learning methods and scant attention to pupils' productions are ways of weakening the incentive to co-operate.

Charts and records

Younger pupils benefit from having a visual reminder of their improvement target. This should relate the behaviour that is to be increased or decreased to something of interest to the pupil. Figure 6.1 shows examples of charts made by pupils and which had the incidental but important consequence of involving the pupils' peers in their reform. Coulby and Harper (1985) provide some other examples. For teenagers, such methods may be inappropriately juvenile. Some will find recording their classroom activity graphically, perhaps through a simple histogram, an interesting and instructive activity: pupils are often amazed at the amount of time they waste. This activity can be introduced to the whole class as a maths project and those with alarming results encouraged to continue monitoring their own progress.

Many schools use lesson record cards or report sheets for persistently disruptive offenders. These are ineffective with some pupils and are often difficult to fill in honestly and accurately. Typically, a pupil will behave

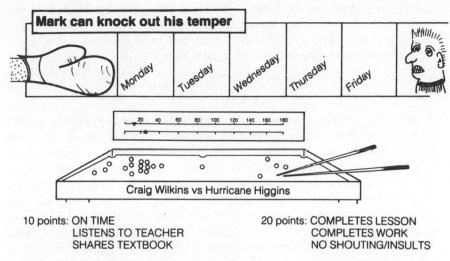

10 points: ON TIME
LISTENS TO TEACHER
SHARES TEXTBOOK

20 points: COMPLETES LESSON
COMPLETES WORK
NO SHOUTING/INSULTS

Higgins scores 10 points every time Craig shouts or swears, leaves seat, distracts others.

Figure 6.1 Examples of record charts

in his or her usually disruptive way until close to the end of the lesson. Some may make no effort to behave but try to persuade a weary teacher to moderate the truth for the promise, likely to be unrealized, of co-operation next time. As the pupil moves through the day, succeeding teachers become reluctant to be the first to record total non-co-operation: some may even suspect that their lesson is at fault and not the pupil.

Figure 6.2 shows an alternative. First, the card is specific, easier to fill in accurately, and a better basis for discussing the required behavioural changes with the pupil. Second, the behaviours required are mostly expressed positively. Third, and most important, it is weighted in the pupil's

On time?
Went to proper place?
Neatly turned out?
Smiled or greeted teacher?
Done homework?
Properly equipped?
Paid reasonable attention?
Did most of work set?
Contributed to lesson?
Helped other pupil?

Helped give things out?
Helped clear away?
Answered question?
Accepted correction?
Finished set work?
Did not shout out?
Stayed to end of lesson?
Any other good point?
50% bonus points?
SCORE out of 20:_____

Figure 6.2 Disruptive pupil's lesson record card

favour since many of the listed behaviours are easily achievable. If the pupil gains nine or more ticks a further two points are automatically earned. As each series of lessons is recorded, perhaps over a few days, the scores provide a clear measure of progress.

Classroom climate

A positive classroom climate where praise is regularly available is recommended. Teachers who measure their own performance usually find that they issue more negative remarks than positive - in a ratio of about two to one. It is not particularly difficult to reverse this ratio and to do so may help to increase the amount of praiseworthy behaviour, thus reducing the amount of space available to the unwanted. The effectiveness of the lavish use of praise is often presented as if it were a modern discovery but it has a longer history. Curtis (1963) quotes Ascham's 16th century text: '. . . there is no such whetstone to sharpen a good wit, and encourage a will to learning, as is praise.' This advice has to be followed with discretion in the case of older pupils. Most primary school pupils are proud to please adults; most secondary school children respond better to praise when it is given privately, and not just because they wish to cultivate a rebellious image: many adults do not know how to accept praise and they find it difficult and embarrassing. Although it sometimes appears that some pupils offer little behaviour worth praising, close observation usually shows this not to be the case. Demanding pupils create this impression because during their periods of orderliness the hard-pressed teacher's attention is being given elsewhere. Observations by supporting colleagues not infrequently find that pupils who are apparently totally uncooperative are in fact behaving themselves for as much as one third of the time. Hard though it may be to accept, these are most important opportunities to influence troublesome pupils. The same principle applies to pupils' work which is often too poor to be genuinely praised. Imaginative teachers can do their best: for example, some misspellings, like 'foggot' (forgot), improve the meaning of the original word. Rather than reacting only to errors and misbehaviour the advice is to 'catch the pupil being good'.

When a disruptive pupil has been settled, or even excluded, another pupil sometimes steps into the role: this alerts us to the social characteristics of the classroom. It can rarely be the case that classrooms can be wholly free of some degree of unwanted behaviour if only because people's differing values produce gradations in the desirability of behaviours. This social phenomenon is described in Durkheim (1893/1933). Understanding and accepting this fact, and appreciating pupils' perspectives, is an essential part of learning to work with other people. In some classrooms there seems to be a need, whose source is difficult to identify, for an array of roles to be occupied (Hanko, 1985). The pupils and their teacher must reconcile their differing images of self, and their intentions, in an environment constrained by expectations and regulations from without. The resulting conflicts, negotiations and compromises constitute commitments to, and are the substance of, the classroom system: put simply, some classes seem to need a dunce, a clown, a scapegoat, a baby, or a tyrant – someone to be excessively smart, or weak or tough (Hanko, 1985). A teaching programme or style that is restricted to telling or to free activity, a work programme that is drearily predictable or giddily indeterminate, and an evaluation scheme that is ambiguous or harsh may themselves make unwanted pupil roles and activities worthwhile. In extreme circumstances some pupils may feel unable to do anything to satisfy the teacher: the only possible way of finding success is to be the best at being the worst. Classroom observation is incomplete without considering these possibilities.

Using support teachers in the classroom is a recent alternative to the removal of pupils to the charge of a separate teacher (Bell and Best, 1986). This tends to avoid the dilution of curricula and expectations, focuses attention on the possible shortcomings of the ordinary classroom, and helps to prevent pupils and teachers becoming stigmatized in a separate room where the testing and assessment of one pupil become a substitute for the reform of curricula for all. Support teaching as a form of co-operative or team teaching requires planning: roles need to be rotated to prevent one teacher becoming the leader and the other feeling de-skilled and unable, for example, to address the class in the absence of the dominant colleague (Denscombe, 1984). There are lessons for all schools in research in playgroups and nurseries reported by Bruner (1980): '. . . teachers in fact develop reputations for the particular services they supply and children come to them for those services . . . the children in a playgroup or nursery school may prevent the teacher from changing her role.' Resource-based learning helps to prevent polarization of teacher roles: the necessary block timetabling distributes discretion and authority to individual teams, enhancing the interest and feeling of significance in the work. The original problems are tackled in their original context; all pupils benefit irrespective of their needs; and a co-operative climate should lead to motivational, intellectual and social gains. For the teachers, such co-operation is both a source of personal support and an opportunity to develop competence in new subjects: a sort of classroom-based, rather than school-based, in-service development and training. The additional noise and movement create problems for teachers although it has been suggested that pupils are less troubled by it. Delamont and Galton (1986) point out that what counts as inappropriate movement is culturally specific, and by implication alterable: Islamic and Jewish pupils, for example, may rock and chant when reading. Denscombe (1985) claims worries about noise derive largely from taking it as evidence of disorder in the traditional closed classrooms into which we cannot see. Quietness in classrooms is 'an impression to be sustained to outsiders who have meagre information on which to assess the extent of control exercised behind closed doors' (Denscombe, 1985: 11).

Individual teachers' expectations of pupils are often said to be a vital aspect of the classroom context (for example DES, 1984) although the research literature is inconclusive. In a review of attempts to induce expectations, laboratory type experiments and naturalistic studies, Rogers (1986) concludes that the evidence for the straightforward effect of expectations is lacking. However, there does seem to be support for the view that those teachers whose expectations are related to social class may influence younger children. It is also likely that artificial attempts to induce expectations may fail, not because teacher expectations are irrelevant, but because experimenters are unable to overcome the expectations and typifications that teachers already have. Hargreaves *et al.* (1975) construct a theory of typing involving the three stages of speculation, elaboration and stabilization. They say that teachers attend principally to appearance, conformity and ability when allocating or withholding the status of normality. Some classroom categories receive considerable acknowledgement in the organizational system and climate of the school and will be discussed in the next section. There seems little doubt that some pupils receive profane labels because of some teachers' preconceptions. Keddie (1971) recorded an example of pupil questions being accepted or rejected on the basis of their ability group.

Consideration of the classroom context, therefore, needs to include teacher attitudes and behaviour as well as those of the pupils. It is a universal phenomenon, and essential to thinking, for human beings to sort, categorize, type, label, and to entertain expectations in relation to these classifications. Division of labour improves intellectual efficiency as any other: the world of experience, past, present and future, is too rich and complex to be apprehended in any other way. Left undisturbed and unchallenged categorizing leads to ossification of routines, expectations and preferences: an autocratic classroom environment is more likely than a co-operative climate to allow one person's errors and prejudices to handicap those less powerful. Expectations and typifications may be self-confirming for pupils already vulnerable through other difficulties in their lives. Each antagonistic episode may be a small thing, local, insignificant, and apparently leaving room for the pupil to improve and pull his or her socks up: each is a stitch in a tapestry depicting the distinctive nature of each pupil. Standing back, in what we imagine to be objective detachment, we view our product as a massive picture, too real, too substantial to be merely something of our own creation. We see the natural abilities associated with that sort of child, the type of behaviour to be expected from that sort of family: and are not our beliefs daily confirmed by the way the pupil reacts to the curriculum offered and the discipline we insist upon? Even we as its creators resist its influence with difficulty – it all hangs together too well. For those ignorant of its construction it represents the true nature of things as they really are.

The school

In one sense pupils attend classrooms not schools. The different and particular features of group life in classrooms, compared with the briefer, shallower and more insubstantial school experiences, create a feeling of insulation between the two for both pupils and teachers. Nevertheless, school climate, culture or organizational arrangements constitute a context within which classrooms and their populations function. In classrooms, the official systems of the school coexist with the unofficial peer-group systems of the pupils (Pollard in Hammersley and Woods, 1984).

For some, the school is necessarily a conservative force, condemned to reproduce cultural and social inequalities, and where the activities of the classroom are ultimately determined by the social relations of production (see Bourdieu's paper in Eggleston, 1974). Soder argues (in Barton and Tomlinson, 1982) for a direct link between the number of unemployed in an economy and the number (ideologically defined) in need of special education: it has been suggested by others that Warnock's apparent raising of the proportion of the population in need of special education was just in time to help blame some of the unemployed as victims of their own incompetence. As Soder says, the links 'can be difficult to find without in-depth analysis'. There is a sense in which troublesome pupils can be regarded surplus to the political economy of the school: they produce nothing and do not consume the goods produced by others, but attractive comparisons are not evidence for correspondence.

Walker in Hammersley (1986) says that descriptions of classroom activities that cannot be related to the social structure and culture of society are conservative. For some, the relationship is seen as so complete that change, viewed as impossible, is not attempted – a conservative result. A school's organizational structure may be perceived as both immediate in its constraints and remote from our influence: it is commonly the case that social structure appears as objective and immutable (Berger and Luckman, 1971); yet social structures persist only with the support (active, passive or unintended) of their constituents. Change is always possible: those persons within a school who wish its organization to be other than it is are that part of the organization that is already changing. To believe that only thought is unconstrained, and that the economic and political system blocks progress, is only partly true – if true at all in respect of life in classrooms. That schools, that is teachers, have some degree of autonomy, is said to be widely accepted even by Marxists (Blackledge and Hunt, 1985: 114).

Structures are created and maintained by the aggregation of multitudinous individual commitments – the perceptions, motives, and objectives of people – and therefore cannot be forever free from change. Knowledge of this fact of social life is the first step in gaining the power to cope with and control one's social environment. Those enthusiastic for change need to remember that changes have costs as well as benefits. For those content with things as they are, the former will hide the latter from view. Writing of the role of a consultant sociologist in a school, Reynolds (in Woods and Pollard, 1987) advises accepting a school's goals, not questioning them on the first encounter. He suggests helping the school to become more effective in its own terms and treating value issues as they arise, later in the consultancy. In practice this may be a difficult act to maintain: giving people the advice they are believed to want, while harbouring fundamental doubts, can drop the consultant into a tangled web of patronizing deception.

A school's organizational ethos, distribution of authority, systems of appraisal, as well as the rewards offered to both pupils and teachers are the subjects of, and influences on, perceptions, decisions and actions – whether to comply, disengage or rebel. Eisner, discussing the contributions of educational radicals such as Holt and Kohl, comments: 'The reward system of the school – the covert, muted one – speaks loudly' (1985: 72). Cusick (1973) suggests that the remoteness of the organizational level of structure itself forces pupils to look to their peers to give meaning and purpose to their lives in school. This will often involve not attending to the work priorities of the teachers. The pupils may see the teachers' agenda as a part of the organizational structure and distribution of power: a feature in which pupils are dominated but otherwise uninvolved makes 'goofing off' a rational strategy (Everhart, 1983). The differentiating and polarizing effects of streaming and banding upon pupils have been documented (Hargreaves, 1967; Lacey, 1970; and Ball, 1981). Bird *et al.* (1981) have pointed out that these structural labels create more problems for pupils than the temporary, and possibly inconsistent, labels used in specific lessons. An attempt to find a statistical relationship between such pupil-processing features was unsuccessful however (Galloway *et al.*, 1985). Allocation to categories (stream/not stream) does not capture the climate in which policies become practice – statistics destroy information.

Teachers too are influenced by selection and appraisal processes of a similar sort, but they are not easily researched. In an authoritarian school, teachers may feel constrained to act so as to please the boss and against their judgement, and like their pupils, they may opt either to comply or rebel (Hanko, 1985). Teachers cannot easily be self-critical, reflective, or sensitive to pupil needs if their performance is measured by a single criterion – exam results or classroom silence for example – and no account is taken of their personal values and aims. Staff can be differentiated and polarized as Hargreaves and others found pupils to be. A critical atmosphere of assessment is not compatible with an honest and critical approach to self, others or situations. Eisner (1982) deplores the ill-effects of the education system's preoccupation with, and valuing of, only the verbal and mathematical. He compares the situation to one where good chess players are unacknowledged because the only game that is played is poker. Becker (1952) wrote: 'All institutions have embedded in them some set of assumptions about the nature of the society and the individuals with whom they deal.' A social structure's available roles have psychological implications, for people are to some extent composed of the roles which they enact (Schostak, 1986). Pupil behaviour can only be completely understood if the school's differentiations and categories are identified, and the related penalties and benefits taken into account. Central to schools' differentiation systems is ability: the criteria used; mode of identification; rewards or stigma attached; and rights to resources of space, time and personnel. How private, personal abilities become public property is an important influence on the attitudes and behaviour of both pupils and teachers.

School organization may influence a wider section of the pupil population than those who are openly troublesome. Tattum (1982) suggests that some disruptive pupils may represent the discontent of a larger but relatively silent group. As Bird *et al.* (1981) put it: 'Most disaffected behaviour could best be understood as an implied, if inarticulate critique of schooling.' Willis (1977) has documented the extreme views of some pupils on the irrelevance of schooling to their lives. It may seem difficult to accept that these pupils speak for those who evidently fear and avoid them. Hargreaves (1967) and Lacey (1970) both found extreme pupils (Drac and Badman respectively) to be disliked and isolated. Nevertheless, it is likely that disruptive pupils express frustrations that are more widespread and possibly in an attenuated form. There is no particular reason why other pupils should thank them for inarticulately expressing fears and uncertainties that are widely shared.

Schostak (1983, 1986) has explored pupil frustrations and seems to propose radical upheaval as a solution. Reynolds (in Gillham, 1981, and a number of other papers) has claimed that a less coercive and more incorporative atmosphere, with low levels of institutional control, is likely to reduce disaffection and disruption. Rutter *et al.* (1979) appeared to find that schools organized and conducted on traditional lines were the more effective: for example, where there was an academic emphasis, a prompt start to lessons, homework set and marked and where heads ran 'a tight ship'. Rutter's book was much criticized though it is worth noting that, compared with many studies, there was considerable work and detailed analysis on which to pounce (see, for example, Acton, 1980; Rutter *et al.*, 1980; and Tizard *et al.*, 1980). A comprehensive collection of papers on these issues is edited by Reynolds (1985). Perhaps one source of the contradictions is in the pupils themselves: they expect the traditional teacher to be in control but respond to being treated with flexibility and respect. Perhaps different pupils are being measured, or similar pupils at different times and in different circumstances. Conflicts among research findings are indices of the complexity of human affairs, in which, to paraphrase Edmund Burke, there is no certain truth and all our knowledge is but a woven web of guesses.

The school features which are associated with co-operative and orderly behaviour have not been identified to the satisfaction of all observers and researchers. Reid, *et al.* (1987) in a comprehensive and detailed review of the school effectiveness literature note that, although it is assumed the ineffective can be distinguished from the effective, there is no consensus on what constitutes an effective school. This does not mean we can ignore the significance of the school in the creation, maintenance and eradication of disruptive behaviour. Trying to understand necessarily requires us to distance ourselves from problems: as was argued in the context of pupil perceptions and motives, this is an important method of coping with problems which are otherwise felt personally: distance, in this sense, lends detachment.

DES in their pamphlet (HMI Report No. 5) *Education Observed* (1987) identify some principles said to maintain high standards of behaviour and discipline. These are explicit and consistently applied policies, a positive climate, good teaching, and quality relationships among pupils, teachers and the wider community. Rewards are said to outnumber sanctions and these latter are applied with flexibility and discrimination. By contrast, policies are said to be firmly and consistently applied. Sound advice – but not easy to see how any school, except perhaps the most appallingly disorganized, could develop action from it. Reid *et al.* (1987) present a similar list which includes effective leadership, happy and efficient staff, a concern for academic standards allied with empathetic pupil care, a curriculum accessible to all pupils and opportunities for all to participate in the running and organization of the school.

These descriptions as well as the generalized school types developed in Chapter 2 do not provide an explicit and unambiguous agenda for school reform: resulting as they mostly do from school level measurements this is not surprising. Even if a list of factors could be agreed upon the magnitude of their effects might be very small: perhaps 6 per cent in Rutter (1979) for example. For present purposes we need know only which factors are possible influences upon pupil behaviour: in looking at each pupil, or group of pupils, it is possible to ask in each case which factors are significant. It is then a question of judgement, or possibly experiment, to discover whether the observations and enquiries are correct or not.

The ways in which school factors enhance or handicap pupil progress and behaviour are often invisible to those who work in them and little clearer to a visitor. It is far from simple to adopt the standpoint of a stranger and not to see what is customarily there to be seen. Even when features contributing to disaffection have been identified, and there is consensus in respect of their influence, it is rarely a simple matter of removal and replacement.

It has been accepted for some time that the sort of streaming systems described by Hargreaves (1967) and Lacey (1970), where similar groups of pupils are together for much of their time in low status classes, necessarily lead to a degree of disengagement, disaffection and perhaps open rebellion. Less rigid groupings, broad bands for example, seem to be less likely to produce polarized attitudes (Ball, 1981). Demands from without the school for standards and qualifications in knowledge of a certain sort (mostly knowledge about things) are best met, in many teachers' experience, by sorting pupils into homogeneous groups.

Delamont and Galton (1986) note that teaching pupils, through the covert curriculum, that they belong to different groups may subvert attempts to get pupils to work in small groups together. They found young secondary pupils feared being put with a member of the other sex: Peter and Gita, sat together, were shamed and did not work. Allied to this may be an emphasis on a single academic criterion for success. The content of assemblies, the pupils praised and indicated as models, the nature of teachers' encouragement in the classroom, and the phrases used on reports all indicate to some pupils that they have failed. Many find that to turn their personal failure outwards, and blame the school for failing them, is a more satisfying way of accommodating their difficulties. In the exchange of punishment which follows, the uncomfortable role of the academic weakling may be swamped by the tough and powerful role of the disruptive hooligan. Paradoxically, the more successfully a school engenders a spirit of academic achievement, the greater will be the sense of betrayal felt by those least successful – confirmed when examination selections are made. The older the pupils, the more the hierarchy of authority, the stratification of knowledge and its separation from their lives becomes apparent, and the greater becomes its influence upon their thinking and action.

These academic responsibilities cannot be abandoned by schools but their influence can be moderated. Schostak (1983) notes that the term, curriculum, derives from curricle, a chariot – a curriculum may be seen as a route chosen in the hope of gaining success. A variety of success criteria and a number of different curricular routes which are valued and defined as successful are ways of engaging a larger proportion of the pupil population in the school's activities.

Lacey (1970) describes two pupils who did not fit with the assumption that middle-class pupils tend to succeed and working-class pupils fail in the grammar school. Priestley was a middle-class drop-out interested in commerce and economics which were two subjects not catered for in the school; Cready was a working-class success, whose fine singing voice had engaged him in the school via its choir. Had the music teacher dissolved the choir and begun an economics class, the school lives of the two boys may have been reversed. Pring (1976) mentions a pupil whose interest in electronics passed unnoticed by the school until it led him, through theft, into court. One essential consideration therefore is to ensure that the school offers a multitude of options in addition to its core curriculum. It is also necessary to give these options a high visible status – ample equipment, good rooms, senior staff – their value must be emphasized in actions.

Most secondary schools offer at least twenty options to years four and five but some make available as many as forty. Some schools make a particular effort to mix abilities and social classes in as many options as possible, thus blurring the distinctions associated with the subjects traditionally taught in homogeneous groups. The effort of producing such an extensive menu results in many teachers devising courses closely related to their own personal interests or expertise. For teachers to engage in activities alongside their pupils, and share real interest and enthusiasm, is one way of showing disaffected pupils that schooling is not artificial and irrelevant. The broader the menu the greater the likelihood of giving and receiving satisfaction. There is a sense in which a disorderly class, or an abusive pupil, is an unrecognized talent, an unrewarded effort, a blocked ambition.

Where setting by ability is not minimized (by resource-based organization of learning for example) it is possible to camouflage the hierarchy to some extent, and for some of the time. Set numbering can be displaced by naming: theoretical maths, applied maths, vocational maths, maths studies, technical maths, craft maths, culinary maths are preferable to maths sets 1 to 7. The content and focus of the different maths groups might also reflect the interests of the pupils and enhance their motivation and achievements. It is important here too that those subject groups vulnerable to being dismissed as unimportant have their value confirmed by their allocation of staff, space and equipment.

From the first days in school children begin to be transformed into types and categories of pupil: in playgroups common categories are 'noisy/quiet ones', 'big/small ones', and of course boys and girls. The categories in public use in the classroom, and supported and confirmed in school-wide practices, are available for pupil identity construction and for some pupils they are a source of conflict, a possible source of disaffection, and a step on the route to disorder. As King (1978) found in infant schools differing expectations are associated with the categories into which pupils are sorted by their teachers: girls can be trusted to hang their coats outside the classroom but boys cannot. Those girls and boys who find their teachers' typifications a poor fit may find themselves labelled 'really peculiar' (Sharp and Green, 1975) and in the embryo stages of a deviant career.

School organization in respect of pastoral care has a direct bearing on relationships between pupils and their tutors. The introduction of pastoral responsibilities into schools was in part a response to the belief that schools were growing in size and organizational complexity, becoming more goal-directed and impersonal. In contrast, many felt the ideal teaching relationship was more personal, concerned with individual needs and interests rather than organizational goals and valuing both education and pupils for their own sakes. For many young people school is their first acquaintance with a social unit larger than their family: relationships are less certain and emotions more thinly spread. Those whose domestic experience has been characterized by misfortune or chaos are in particular need of considerate supervision in school. The establishment of a bureaucracy of pastoral care is not a guarantee of its being practised. Since control of one group by another is a central feature of any administrative structure it is not surprising that pastoral systems become entangled and merged with discipline systems. This can shift their focus away from personal and affective concerns towards the goals of the school's senior managers: the particular problems of troublesome pupils are not inevitably foremost among their concerns.

Many schools arrange for tutors to retain responsibility for their groups as they progress through the year bands. This is intended to assist the development of relationships but in itself is insufficient. Tutoring in some schools is a nominal role with no discretion, responsibility or power attached. Tutors are often among the last to be informed of matters relating to individuals in their group.

Some schools ensure that relationships of trust have an opportunity to develop by devolving powers to tutors. The problems that could arise through weakness or inexperience can be pre-empted by using pairs of tutors with some groups: this reproduces in the pastoral sphere the benefits of support teaching within classrooms. Empathetic relationships develop, and tutors and pupils come to understand one another's perspectives and the constraints under which they operate. This can lead to conflict between teachers. A tutor may be regarded as too sympathetic to a pupil who may have grossly offended a colleague: to attempt to explain or even defend misbehaviour is readily viewed as disloyalty. Staffroom folklore reveres the headteacher who backs his or her staff, right or wrong; some heads present this as wise policy. In time of war it most certainly is. One aim of pastoral care, however, is to maintain the peace.

After some crises it helps to make the peace terms explicit in a formal contract: sometimes these are signed in a solemn session in the headteacher's office. The contract need not represent the school's final aim in respect of any pupil. It may be seen as a first achievable step: a negotiating baseline. An extreme example of a contract that some might view as a defeat for the school is printed below.

> The school agrees: not to demand homework or schoolwork; to allow the pupil to withdraw to the year area if in danger of losing self-control; to allow the pupil to consult and be accompanied by her tutor in any enquiry into any incident or report.

> The pupil agrees: to attend school regularly; to be on time for classes; to remain in the place indicated by the teacher; not to abuse, threaten or assault pupils; not to leave the school grounds at lunchtime.

Few demands were made upon an extremely troubled pupil: the school presented its concessions as the natural right of a person who was emotionally disabled – analogous to those made for pupils with physical disabilities. For the school in question it was a preferable alternative to exclusion and demonstrates what is possible even in extreme situations.

Graham (1988) mentions some American, pupil-led, radical alternatives to pastoral systems such as the appointment of a mediator. A good pastoral system should pre-empt the need for this. The school as a whole enjoys benefits from ensuring that pupils' interests are well represented, and of institutionalizing representation. First, it channels and controls pupil hostility, and with luck diminishes the impulse to violence; second, it wins time and allows all parties the chance to negotiate and compromise; third, it helps to persuade pupils who feel victimized that some adults can be trusted; fourth, it allows the tutor and the pupil to exchange real understanding in situations of crisis, far removed from the abstracted skills and processes of some personal and social education programmes. This is not to say that tutors should adopt the pupil's viewpoint: as with solicitors and their clients, representation does not preclude offering vigorous advice and reprimands. The tendency for some pastoral care lines of communication to become clogged and carriers of only bad news is documented in Spooner (1979), Best et al. (1983), Coulby and Harper (1985) and Galloway (in Reynolds, 1985). This can undermine the purpose of pastoral systems to the extent that they become viewed by pupils as another antagonistic, disciplinary instrument. The lateral distribution of authority and responsibility helps to remove the blockage.

Exercise 9: fixing the coffee machine

The purpose of this exercise is to discover any aspects of your school environment unnecessarily conducive to troublesome behaviour. If any are identified, it does not follow that they ought to be altered: alterations, as well as existing arrangements, have costs and benefits for various pupils which must be taken into account. The exercise should increase understanding of some pupils' situation and therefore help in coping with them. The task is in two parts, the first of which was prompted by the analogy of society as a fruit machine (see Taylor's work, described in Furlong, 1985). The second part of the exercise is the difficult task of trying to look at your school in a detached way, as if a stranger, and through the eyes of a troublesome pupil. The more entertaining first part is to put you in a suitable frame of mind.

Part 1

A school can be thought of as in some respects like a coffee machine. Everyone has an equal opportunity to get a drink out of it, if they bring the correct change with them. Coffee machines do not serve all equally, however. Some do not get what they want and some get nothing – no money or faulty machine. Disappointed customers, or pupils, take one of several attitudes. They may continue to put money in without hope of success (plod through lessons, bored and without commitment). They may give up and refuse to use the machine (truants). They may try to wreck it to stop others using what they see as failing them (disrupters). Some may pretend to use the machine while quietly sipping their own drinks (some say these are mostly girls). Many will say they do not want coffee anyway, for in their neighbourhood everyone drinks tea.

The machine's minders, or teachers, have their own range of responses. Some want to make it more attractive and effective: put plants on it, see it is plugged in on time and not switched off early, assistants in uniform, a drink every time. Some want to get a new machine that dispenses different drinks; others want to keep the present machine for some customers, and add a different one for the tea-drinkers; a few think they should settle for water. A few think we should discard the machine and go back to making our own coffee, at home.

Divide into groups of five or six to explore how far your school fits or does not fit the analogy of a typical (faulty) coffee machine. Spend about fifteen minutes on this part.

Part 2

In the same groups, answer these questions in respect of your school. Group work will take about forty-five minutes before comparing results in plenary session. Although this exercise focuses on the school, it can be adapted to analyse a department, a teaching team, or a teacher and a single class.

1. What categories are used to describe, label, differentiate and allocate pupils? Think about the formal, official, system (for example, Fifth Year, A stream, TVEI band) as well as the informal, unofficial system (for example, the bouncy ones, the just-not-interested, the real troublemakers).
2. Briefly list the benefits, rewards, deprivations and rules, both formal and informal, associated with these categories and statuses (for example, mentions in assembly, free study time, warm part of the school). Do not ignore seeming trivialities. For example, if one class always has the job of chair-stacking after assembly, in what ways is this a benefit and in what ways a deprivation? How do the pupils, stackers and non-stackers, see it?
3. How do pupils learn of their category or interpret the school's arrangements? What things are communicated formally, and what learned informally? Is the message transmitted the same as the one received?
4. Consider how a particular troublesome pupil or class experiences life in your school as you have analysed it under the above three points. Are there any unintentionally pejorative categories or deprivations? Is it possible to have non-evaluative categories at all? Does the communication system need attention? Are any changes needed, and are they feasible? Are those with the power to make changes convinced that changes are needed?

Exercise 10: the case of Carl, aged six

This exercise requires the pre-reading of a case study and is the only detailed case described in this book. As with previous exercises, discussions begin in small groups. The course leader should read the comments on the exercise before chairing the plenary session. This case is assembled from interviews and reports and is presented mainly as it was told by the principal teacher involved.

The case of Carl, aged six

Carl joined his new primary school halfway through the term having moved from another city. First impressions were of a 'grubby, sturdy boy' who had little to say and was quiet for the first few days. The school was open plan and he began to wander, would not be occupied by anything offered him and rapidly became loud and disruptive. From the start his eating habits had attracted attention: rapid, omnivorous and with his fingers. He gathered food from other pupils' plates and from the waste bin – including banana skins. When crossed by pupils or teachers he bit and spat. The bites were severe enough to produce bleeding.

Action 1

The school was accustomed to coping with difficult children and prepared to give Carl a fresh start. During the first week the headteacher from his previous school (more than 200 miles away) telephoned to apologize for the delay in passing on records and to say that the abrupt removal had been due to domestic violence: Carl was ungovernable and had had an NTA to himself. The teachers were not particularly interested in his records however. They decided to ignore as much as possible: the open plan, partly resource-based organization allowed a good deal of movement and noise so Carl's wandering was not particularly disruptive. Fruit, bought with school fund, was used as a reward for co-operation. The tolerance did not include the biting and spitting, where intervention was instant.

Result 1

The fruit reward had a slight effect but was limited to the mornings: by lunchtime it was all used, and after lunch he did not seem so hungry. The spitting continued in two or three tantrums a day during which one or two people would be bitten. One side effect of Carl's fruit eating and spitting was to teach the staff a little chemistry: fruit acid saliva bleaches clothes. He began to strip in assembly and refuse to leave the hall afterwards. In one scene he totally wrecked an area of the school - the equivalent of a classroom – but a teacher succeeded in making him restore it during the lunch break.

Action 2

Carl was referred to the Educational Psychological Service. The visiting psychologist approved the fruit rewards and ignoring regime, suggested using time-out and ensuring that 'cuddles' were not used to reward angry behaviour. He arrived at an opportune moment from the teachers' point of view: Carl was naked outside the staffroom. They listened with interest to discover how a psychologist dressed an unwilling child. Except for repeating 'good boy' as he worked the technique was the familiar one of cajolery, coercion and exasperation.

Result 2

The medical room was used for time-out but had to stop when Carl began kicking the window. As the school was single storey, and every area had an outside door, time-out became locked out: when serious trouble started Carl was put out of the door and all the other teachers locked their doors. Carl never attempted to run away from school. The policy began to produce other problems. His running around the building trying to get back in upset the teachers. Some felt that not only their teacher authority was threatened but also their natural, adult feelings for children. Carl was suspended from school and the statementing process began.

Action 3

An extra NTA was appointed to ensure supervision of Carl at all times. Time-out could now be safely in the medical room. The earlier regime of ignoring and using fruit and cuddle rewards continued. The boy's mother was encouraged to visit school and she happily joined in helping clean cupboards and engaging in similar activities. Whenever Carl came near her, however, she told him to go away – sometimes using obscene language.

Result 3

In the teacher's own words:

> He's calmed down a little – a bad scene once a week now – maybe three days' peace and three days' hell. With consistency we feel we have progressed. He doesn't undress near me because the first time he tried it I helped him off with his clothes. I just laugh or joke or sidestep him. I'm the sort of person who withdraws when I'm cross – maybe that helps. It's such a shame because he's such a lovely boy – bright too we think. There are two others in the family coming up from the nursery and we've heard that one of them is worse.

A day or two in mother's life

The following statement is the mother's account of the events leading up to her child attending hospital with a suspected skull fracture.

> My cheque did not come but I did not go phone as I had been up with Carl and his earache. I left it a day as sometimes it's in the next post but it wasn't. I left Carl in bed and took the two youngest with me to find a phone that was working – they're mostly vandalized round here. When I got through they kept me waiting and passing me from this department to that. I still hadn't got anybody to help when all my 10p coins ran out. So I just went back home trailing the kids, no money and no prospect of any.
>
> Carl was worse so I thought I'll have to get a doctor. The woman next door offered to watch the two youngest while I took Carl down the clinic. I had no money left at all so she had to let me have the bus fare. I managed over the weekend by borrowing and on the Monday I set off down the DHSS with the three kids. I didn't have an appointment of course so we just had to settle down and wait

our turn. By the time I got to the front of the queue I was at my wits'
end with trying to keep the kids down and then I had to go through
all the long list of details relevant to my claim because they didn't
have my card. I didn't know whether to scream or cry.

It was nearly dinner time when I got my money – they even gave
me some heating backdated that they'd refused me before. I thought
it would be nice to give the kids a treat so we went into MacDonalds
even though it's too expensive really. I let them choose something
but Carl wanted a big expensive icecream so I said no. When the
burgers came he wouldn't eat his so I just left it in front of him. He
was still going on about the icecream. Then he just pushed it off the
table on to the floor. I just snapped. I lashed out at him and he fell
over backwards and cracked the back of his head on the floor. I only
went in there because I'd been on at them all day. I wanted to cheer
us all up.

Discussion should cover these points:

1. How, if at all, did your feelings about this case change on reading
   the mother's account? What conclusions do you draw from your
   reactions?
2. Consider the personal skills and moral qualities needed by those
   living in poverty.
3. Reflect on the weaknesses, wastage, and risks to which the poor
   are exposed.
4. Consider the experiences, knowledge, feelings, expectations Carl
   carries into school.
5. What coping strategies are available to him?
6. List the appropriate personal qualities, expectations,
   understandings, perspectives, stategies conducive to success with
   pupils like Carl.
7. Consider aspects of school organization and ethos that would help
   or hinder pupils like Carl.
8. Finally: What has this exercise accomplished? Has it shifted the
   blame for individual venality to society? Has it shown how public
   issues are transformed into private personal troubles? Has it altered
   your perceptions of, attitude to, and capacity to cope with
   'emotional and behavioural problems'?

Comments on the exercise

1. We often say that pupils' behaviour and effort is to be expected
   'when you look at their homes': the implication and shared
   understanding is that chaos at home is confirmation of the futility

of trying to educate or make progress with them. Many people will want to modify their opinion after reading the mother's story.

2. Thrift, effort, determination far beyond the average are required to survive in poverty. Some years ago Matthew Parris MP tried and failed to live for one week on the dole. The prime minister was rumoured to have scorned his attempt and insisted that she could have managed without difficulty. No doubt she could. Anyone can do it for a limited period that has a certain end. The inclination to survive with dignity comes harder when there is no past to reflect on and no future to look forward to. The demands of children are not easy to resist and easily wreck efforts to be thrifty.

3. In these circumstances spending scarce resources on a video and TV seem understandable extravagances. So does leaving the children alone, or with an unvetted babysitter, in order to nip out for a quick drink. Money is similarly wasted on costly, TV-advertised toys, many needing batteries and most quickly broken. Overcrowding and shared beds may make some families vulnerable to unwarranted allegations of abuse: their hostile and unskilled reactions likely to act as confirming evidence from the viewpoint of some professionals.

4. Carl's experience of undependable, unpredictable, irritable adults may lead to caution or distrust of adults in school. He may be aware of material deficits in respect of clothes, toys, trips or accommodation.

5. Children may cope by withdrawing into themselves. Some indulge in wild or bizarre behaviour to distract themselves and others from their difficulties. Some children try both extremes prompting the diagnosis that such grossly unpredictable behaviour must evidence deep neurological defects.

6. The teacher's account gives clues: impassive, reliable, not easily manipulated. She was detached enough to see a funny side of it all (for example, the acid saliva, the reception given the Ed. Psych.). She was able to ignore some of the behaviour and helped to extinguish it (for example, the stripping). In her final statement she shows her affection for the boy and her high expectations of his capability. It is common for teachers reporting cases to training groups to express a liking for troublesome pupils, and as often to seem surprised at this themselves. There is an example in Caspari (1976: 48). Kohl (1970) writes: 'I like defiant, independent and humorous people and my preferences naturally come out in my teaching.' Teachers like this are a considerable asset and are best viewed as the pupil's defence counsel in situations where aggrieved teachers may question a colleague's loyalty. Note also the lack of interest in the boy's records. This attitude, often the despair of

administrators, is common among teachers who wish to make up their own minds before looking at other people's opinions. Novice teachers and students, however, are thirsty for prior information (see Wragg, 1984 and Chapter 2 of Calderhead, 1987).

7. School-wide practices and expectations can create problems for pupils who have no ready access to money nor a stable home life. Imagine the 'tight ship' ethos recommended by Rutter (1979): homework done, PE kit clean and complete. Endless letters asking for cash for cookery and CDT, school trips or treats cause additional worry and aggravation. School refusal, theft and revenge begin to look like rational strategies in these circumstances. Note how the open/resource-based learning environment helped the school cope with Carl.

8. This is not an invitation to radical political action although this case does flesh out the dry bone structure of school and society. The understanding it gives may spark some additional professional commitment to troublesome pupils which is the aim of this book. 'For we struggle not against flesh and blood, but against principalities, against powers, against the rulers of the darkness of this world, against spiritual wickedness in high places' (Ephesians 6:12).

Chapter seven

Putting learning into practice

Serving stone soup

On the fifth morning of the famine the villagers awoke to find a stranger among them. Relief had been promised but this person looked unsuited to the office. Perhaps he too was looking for nourishment? There is no food here, he was quickly told.

'I am here to help you', said the stranger, 'I can show you how to feed yourselves.' He held out three smooth stones. 'With these you can make a soup sufficient to feed everyone here.' Hunger and despair overcame the villagers' disbelief. Someone fetched a huge cauldron. Others filled it with water. A fire was lit beneath it. Then they waited.

The stranger dropped the stones into the simmering water. 'It won't take long now,' he said, sniffing at the steam. 'An onion would improve the flavour.'

'I have an onion,' said one of the villagers. 'You are welcome to it. It's of no use to me on its own.' Others murmured that they too had redundant onions. Soon not one but seven onions were produced and added to the pot.

The stranger continued to stir. 'A pity there isn't a carrot or two,' he said. Several people thought they had a carrot lying somewhere. They were found and added to the broth. The stranger continued to sniff and stir. He thought a potato would give it more body. Potatoes were produced. The villagers began to take the initiative, suggesting and offering various vegetables that remained in their larders, each in itself too small a thing to make a meal.

The stranger decided that the soup was ready and, as he had promised, everyone was able to eat till they were full. The stranger himself joined in their feast and smiled at the praises and thanks lavished upon him by the grateful villagers. When all were fed, the stranger reached into the pot and held up the three stones for the astonished villagers to see.

'I will make you a present of these,' he said. 'If ever you find yourselves in distress again, just do as we have done today.' The delighted villagers congratulated each other on their good fortune. So overcome with happiness were they that they did not see the stranger slip away. As he set off along the road, he stopped and gathered three more stones.

Evaluating short courses

This section and the next discuss some of the issues surrounding the assessment of in-service interventions in schools and may be skipped. Those wishing to prepare their own in-service work on troublesome behaviour should turn to the last section, 'The development of understanding and coping in schools'. Evaluation of one's own work is plainly vulnerable to criticism and error, but so also is any evaluation of anything. Evaluations, by definition, are judgements. To ask for an objective standard to which they can be referred is to ask for the values to be taken out, thus destroying what is distinctive about a judgement. An evaluation that is not infused with values – and therefore the possibility of disagreement – is not an evaluation but must be something else. Stenhouse, in Hamilton *et al.* (1977), claims that objectivity is possible in examining our own ideas and further that the only ideas we can examine objectively are our own. In opposition to this view, Scriven, in the same book, says that 'we would never accept an evaluation by a co-author of his own materials as meeting even the minimal methodological standards for objectivity' (Hamilton *et al.*, 1977: 133). Scriven defends a style of evaluation analogous to a consumer report: courses are evaluated without contact with their authors and oblivious of their objectives: we buy good products not good intentions. Gomm, in Smetherham (1981), lists some of the strategies used to present evaluators' failures as successes of a different sort: the limitation of the brief, the shortage of time and resources and other problems may be listed to pre-empt criticism. Appropriate jargon may transform a bad job into a good one and the final report displays the qualities of the true star of the show – the writer.

It is an error to believe, however, that quantitative evaluative representations are necessarily truer than qualitative: to prefer 'an ounce of data to a pound of insight' (Eisner in Hamilton, 1977: 90). The converse may also be the case. Eisner notes that quantities presuppose qualities and that the less expressive a description is, the truer it is taken to be: 'Yet if there is an absence of emotional or qualitative content, the description risks leaving out more of what is important in the classroom' (1985: 158). He compares preoccupation with quantitative data to ineffective attempts to improve football skills by attending only to the final score (page 179). McIntyre and Macleod however (in Hammersley, 1986) find quantitative statements – 'quite a lot . . . very rare . . . we often heard' – in the work of 'Case Study' researchers. All evaluations necessarily use both qualitative and quantitative data. Attending to this fact helps to prevent errors and omissions even though we may still be doing no more than to add one variety of theoretical findings to another (Atkinson and Delamont in Hammersley, 1986). More than a century ago these same qualitative and quantitative evaluation issues were raised during the operation of Robert Lowe's Revised Code, popularly known as 'payment by results'. In 1863 Matthew Arnold HMI complained of the restricted and rigid examination procedures constraining his work and compared them unfavourably with his former inspections: 'The whole life and power of a class, the fitness of its composition, its handling by the teacher were well tested . . .' (Curtis, 1963: 262).

There can probably never be certainty in any evaluation work that the data are objective and valid. Writing on research into language use in classrooms, Stubbs notes that some researchers believe evidence may be justifiably gathered by selecting 'any feature of language which appears intuitively interesting' (in Adelman, 1981: 116). Glaser and Straus (in Hammersley, 1986: 55) state that researchers 'can easily find examples for dreamed up, speculative or logically deduced theory after the idea has occurred'. In seeking for confirming evidence for theory, rather than looking at data in search of theory, we are less likely to notice contrary examples. It is sometimes suggested that where the evidence is gathered on tapes and films, any sceptic may examine it to test the accuracy of the findings. This is seldom a feasible operation, and the existence of hundreds of hours of tapes and thousands of pages of transcripts may serve only to lend a spurious objectivity and authority to an evaluator's report.

Added to these pitfalls are others of a different sort. The observation by Eisner (1985) is seriously, if unintentionally damaging to any claim that the course affected teachers' practice. Like other teachers, I tend to judge success by 'the extent to which students appear engaged, immersed, caught up, and interested in the activities of the classroom' (Eisner, 1955: 70). Even in the small scale evaluation I have carried out, the quantity of data is too bulky to reasonably expect someone to spend time working through and checking. A colleague examined a random sample of the data and sorted it into categories as a cross-check on my own. The selection was done in a simple and crude way: all the question/comment sheets and the interview reports were put in a pile, a nail was driven through and every sentence, phrase or comment thus pierced was selected for re-examination. Where the data is on paper, this method is a quick and effective way of generating a random sample. Some paragraphs of data give up only one sentence to the selection and this further helps to provoke fresh thought.

This technique drew attention to previously unnoticed items even before the selection was independently examined. When the open-ended comment sheets were treated in this way, six of the sixteen comments nailed did not fit into the categories used to discuss the data in the first draft of this chapter. Two suggested alternative ways of organizing the course and two commented on the teaching method. The other two comments were criticisms, passed over in the first trawl for categories into which to sort the information. One suggested that practical ideas for involving staff in formal discussions of problems was lacking; the other thought the suggested strategies needed uncommon confidence. Random sampling has one other benefit in that all the data so selected can be quickly examined to test the claims made for it.

Theory and practice

Eisner (1985) questions whether education research can inform education practice. He unsuccessfully tried to collect examples from university teachers: most were unable to say how their personal work had been affected by research findings other than to claim it functioned in the background. Woods and Pollard (1987: 11) argue that education research has altered practice and claim that 'It can, in fact, transform one's view of life'. They mention the sensitivity to issues of race, gender and social class as well as streaming, school organization and the eleven-plus. For example, understanding the societal location and widespread prevalence of discipline problems is said to liberate teachers from 'false notions of personal inadequacy and blame': the more common a problem is the less likely is it that 'it is of the teacher's own making'. In Reynolds' own chapter of the book he lists the benefits of consultancy to a case study school as: more positive self-images among the staff; greater group co-operation with ability to share problems and anxieties; greater initiative and 'line leadership' both within the school and in local education politics. Some of these benefits may not have been part of the intervention's explicit programme but one of the hidden consequences of being involved in educational discussion and having one's ideas treated seriously. To paraphrase Dewey, it is a fallacy to believe that teachers learn only one thing at a time. Some of the teachers' comments suggest that they learnt that working with troublesome pupils is as theoretically and intellectually demanding as any other teaching and that it can be fun. These aspects were not part of the original plan but they are undeniably important in lifting morale and generating a determination to persist and succeed. As Eisner (1982) argues, cognition is not restricted to the discursive and mathematical – affect and cognition are inextricable – like all other information, emotions are encountered by minds.

Wilkin (in Woods and Pollard, 1987) notes that changes in practice need not be directly derivable from theory: practice may be affected by theory functioning in the background in an illuminative way. This latter may be one way of escaping the admission that theory and practice do not connect, and this seems to be the construction put upon similar comments received from faculty staff by Eisner (1985). His own impressions of teaching quality in university faculties are that the variance is as wide and the mean no higher in education than in other departments. He observes that those best informed about educational research 'seldom use the fruits of their labours either to make practical decisions or shape intellectual policy in the institutions where they work' (Eisner, 1985: 256). He suggests that research has followed practice (for example in group work, open plan schools, images of children) rather than initiated it. He mocks such commonplace findings as that 'time on task' is associated with gains in test scores. However, Rutter (1979) severely weakened this sort of argument by listing 'obvious' findings that were not in fact among his team's conclusions. A problem is raised by Mac an Ghaill (in Woods and Pollard, 1987) who found some teachers claiming that awareness of the structural constraints upon their classrooms and the education system had confirmed their feeling of powerlessness. However, interviews with the colleagues of these teachers seemed to show that the cognitive and affective components of the attitudes revealed to Mac an Ghaill did not match the behaviour observed by colleagues in school.

Eisner (1985) notes that even where research findings do seem to penetrate teachers' thinking, they do so in a vulgarized form bereft of qualifications, caveats and reservations about experimental design. Misunderstanding can go further still. Sometimes teachers on my course provided information which they believed illustrated a theme of the course but which directly contradicted it. The importance of strict rules on school uniform was offered in support of Reynolds' notion of 'truce'. After discussing the need for staff to co-operate in respecting pupils' dignity, one teacher agreed and spoke approvingly of how his headteacher supported staff in dealing with miscreants: '. . . he really tears them off a strip and sorts them out, strips them down, strips them right down . . .'

American research reviewed by Eisner (1985: 261) showed that most experimental interventions in schools lasted little more than one hour. He comments that one cannot 'become familiar with the richness of classroom life' on such educational 'commando raids'. Changing people's attitudes, however, need not require extended intervention, as is often assumed by those mourning the passing of long, full-time courses for teachers: the trend, says Watson (1988), is 'towards short courses aimed at specific skills training and away from longer courses which allow time for reflection and change'. It is not the length of a course, but the nature of it, that determines whether it will produce change or not. New perspectives are adopted at a moment, and often following the introduction of a single piece of information. The longest of the courses from which this book is derived was nine sessions of two hours. Most of the school-based sessions were only three hours and the minimum input has been only one-and-a-half hours. To these times must be added any sessions held by school staffs after the courses, along the lines suggested, and with handout material for guidance.

Complexity of teaching

Teaching, whether of pupils in schools or teachers on in-service courses, is a highly complex activity. The difficulties encountered in assessing classroom effectiveness are doubled in attempts to assess the power of in-service training to alter classroom practice. Eisner speaks of the kaleidoscopic moments in teaching, the unexpected opportunities for explaining, demonstrating, signifying, and the difficulty of specifying objectives (as opposed to general direction) until after the lesson or programme is completed (in Hamilton, 1977: 88–90). He makes much of the uniqueness of schools and the central importance of nuance to the quality of classroom life: 'the sense of engagement when a class is attentive will always elude the language of propositions . . . yet it is precisely these qualities that the teacher must address' (Eisner, 1985: 256). Hamilton and Parlett describe the complexity and diversity of the learning milieu: a social, psychological, material, cultural, institutional network of interacting variables producing unique patterns of circumstances, customs, opinions and workstyles (Hamilton *et al.*, 1977: 11). As Eisner puts it, in arguing that propositional language is inadequate to the task of educational description and evaluation and defending his notion of connoisseurship: '. . . the simultaneity found in patterns of context is lost in the sequence of propositions' (Eisner 1985: 266).

This cannot permit anything to count as evaluation. Walker (in Smetherham, 1981: 148–51) points to the importance of taking note of personalities and offers a fictional account which he claims allows the signalling of 'ideas, meanings and significances'. This raises as many problems as it tries to solve, not least of which is the quality of the writing as a work of fiction in its own right. Jenkins' account (in Hamilton *et al.*, 1977) of Mr Bondine's lesson is also vulnerable to the charge that it is as partial and incomplete an account of the lesson as any behavioural or propositional description. Yet the Jenkins piece, witty and apparently effortlessly crafted, rings truer than that by Walker. It is not possible to say whether this is because it described reality or not: Jenkins' fictional account of styles of innovator also has the ring of truth (OU course E283). To say that Jenkins is just a better writer is to re-phrase the problem not to solve it. In passing it must be noted that unlike Jenkins, Mr Bondine judged the lesson a success. Partial representation is a problem in all accounts however: statistics, whether simple or sophisticated, can disguise and misrepresent.

I have used this fiction technique in preparing some of the case studies used as exercises in the course. Also, as a method of eliciting information in interviews I prepared a fictional account of participants' opinions of the course, giving the worst possible interpretation of it. This procedure has been used before (Hamilton, 1977). These examples underline the importance of 'methodological self-awareness' and the need, in the 'unravelling and explication of mundane beliefs and actions' to suspend common sense not endorse it (Atkinson and Delamont in Hammersley, 1986). Evaluation in education has more in common with the evaluation of a marriage than the evaluation of a horse-training programme: it benefits from uncommon awareness and sensitivity.

Aims of the course

Presenting repeated versions of the course led to some modification of its aims. I began to see the session on teacher skills as serving to inform teachers of my understanding of, and respect for, the ordinary teaching job: it was a display of credentials that made teachers more receptive to more contentious work later. I began to see the sessions on altering teacher's perceptions of classroom deviance as central to the popularity and effectiveness of the course; and the examples from my own experience of troublesome pupils seemed to have more importance than simply as illustrations of themes. As part of the emphasis on changing teachers' attitudes I paid more attention to lifting morale through stressing the high level of professionalism inherent in teaching troublesome pupils.

I began to refer to theoretical work in more detail: for example, Dreikurs and Reynolds became seminar topics in their own right. The amusing anecdotes which had earlier served to keep tired teachers awake through evening sessions began to function as a 'hidden curriculum' which taught that working with troublesome pupils could be fun. Conveying enthusiasm became more difficult as the same material was faced time after time: it became necessary to change the order of presentation and especially to do fresh reading in search of a new idea or focus for repeated sessions.

To summarize, the focus of the course shifted from changing skills to changing perceptions and attitudes. It was my assumption, and part of the teaching, that in interpersonal relationships a change of attitude is in itself a change of behaviour. That is to say, viewing an aggressive pupil as making an unskilled attempt to find a trustworthy and indestructible adult necessarily altered that pupil's experience of adults: being restrained by an adult who understands your problem is a different experience from being restrained by one who sees you as simply evil. In a chapter of Woods and Pollard (1987: 162), Reynolds sees his role as a school consultant as to change behaviour, from which, through reinforcement, change in attitudes, values and perceptions will follow. There is no necessary reason for this distinction and it is difficult to visualize how this would happen in practice. It is similarly difficult to understand his other suggestion that methods and means can be made more effective without regard to aims and ends. How problems are perceived, and therefore the teacher's experience, is a product of the individual's internal system as well as the qualities of the environment. The qualities of the environment are multiple. Which features are salient, and the meaning attached to them, partly depends upon each particular act of perception. Eisner (1985) refers to the concept of 'anticipatory schemata' developed by Neisser (1976): these schemata influence the form our experience takes. Perception is constructive, an anticipatory cognitive event, an active seeking, not a passive receptive mould (Eisner, 1982: 41, 49). 'What we experience depends in part on what nets we cast' and the nets we cast are the nets we weave.

It follows that what people learn from their experience is in part a function of what they have already learned: how they look at the world influences what they see and the meanings they attribute. Eisner (1982: 37) points out that when we say that some people fail to learn from experience we may be failing to recognize that 'the experience we assume they are having, from which they might learn, they, in fact are missing'. It is also the case that what people may believe experience has taught them, they have in fact taught themselves: travel does not broaden closed minds. It was the aim of the course to get teachers to look for a range of possible significances in their classrooms and to be willing to see some things differently.

Evaluation data

Teachers seemed to look for, and sometimes to find, a number of things in the course: some found new ideas or practical approaches; some found reassurance that their present practice and performance was legitimate; others found that their problems were insignificant in relation to some of the cases introduced on the course; a number had particularly valued the opportunity to share ideas with others without being able, apparently, to specify what they had found worthwhile.

It soon became clear that teachers distinguished learning of explicit rules and procedures from learning in a nebulous, but nevertheless valued way, from experience – in this case vicariously through case studies and examples. This response is an illustration of Smythe's (1987: 3) claim that professional knowledge – derived from cases – cannot always be codified: embedded in practice and inseparable from it, we display skills we cannot adequately describe. Some distinguished between those aspects of the course that had helped them personally and those which they thought useful procedures for beginners. In general there was a tendency to value explicit rules and pieces of advice for use with inexperienced (and inexpert) teachers and to value more diffuse experiential learning for themselves. Some of the value attributed to the section on pupils' motives and strategies appears to have been due, at least in part, to the plenitude of examples used to illustrate the themes. Berliner (1987) emphasizes that experts are distinguishable by their ability to learn by reflection upon experience: the ability to follow rules is insufficient. Clark and Yinger (1987) conclude from their research into teachers' planning that expert teachers solve problems by drawing on a repertoire of practical knowledge that generates exemplars such as case studies or significant examples.

Much of teachers' activity is not appropriately described as problem solving. Bromme (1987) suggests that the analogy with medical diagnosis corresponds to reality only in certain limited circumstances: remedial teaching is one such. Generally, however, teachers' attention is said to be focused on the lesson as a whole – its content, the likely pupil response and the need to maintain 'instructional flow'. There is here a parallel with Jackson (1968): teachers' thinking is in the form of a sandwich with reflection enclosing a thick filling of interactive spontaneity. This phenomenon has been discussed in respect of student teachers by Mardle and Walker (1980b): college-based analyses of pupil problems make no impact on common-sense understandings in the classroom. The authors suggest that teacher training begins in infancy and continues throughout schooling with only a brief and temporary disturbance during formal teacher training. Trainee teachers make use of theory only when it is congruent with existing (that is prior to teacher training) beliefs. However Lacey (1977) noted occasional situational influences upon students' decisions in acknowledging their beliefs: for example, some might argue points to annoy other members of the group. Clearly, the absence of theory from practical activity is a barrier to improving classroom responses. In assessing the worth of in-service work it is necessary to distinguish between perceiving the material as relevant at the time of delivery, and finding it so back in the hurly-burly of the classroom.

In interviews and on comment sheets a large number of remarks, both spoken and written, expressed inexplicit thoughts about the course as a whole: such comments as good, useful, enjoyable or 'Dodgy ground. Depends on relationships too much.' The sessions on pupil motives and strategies were most frequently remarked upon as having been valuable. In the view of one headteacher, this particular topic had made a difference to teachers' staffroom discussion following a half-day session held in his school.

> I have noticed that discussion of pupils has been much more analytical. I'm thinking in particular of what I would call hard members of staff – they've not been so ready to dismiss kids – it's certainly affected their way of thinking and that's very good I think . . . very professional.

Perhaps the hard persona he referred to was a defence against the feeling of being under attack. When the unwanted behaviour is viewed differently, the need for defence disappears. The nature of the cases used to illustrate this particular topic, and the examples given from the literature, had persuaded some that their own problems were minor. A primary school head wrote: 'The wide range of examples helped us to place our own problems into a more sensible perspective.'

The next most frequent comment indicated that the course had been reassuring in some way.

> Ideas I've been developing over fifteen years (about motives) . . . it's a good feeling to know they are correct. It was useful to know that the way I operate with difficult situations is generally accepted as being effective for more extreme cases.

These comments express the feeling that teachers' ways of working, perhaps developed in isolation, are supported by the literature. It may also be that the course's claim that professionalism consisted to some degree in being able to avoid habitual, common-sense punitive responses was a morale booster in a time of morale attack: 1987/8 saw teachers' contracts, the national curriculum 'consultative document', repeated criticism in the press and parliament of the quality of teachers and unfavourable comparisons with a supposedly dynamic and enterprising industrial sector.

Teachers generally felt that the approaches proposed were practical: 'Down to earth – real world'. Remarks about practicality were often accompanied by comments upon cases mentioned. Some commented upon the benefits to be derived by exchanging experiences with others and adding to their own repertoire of experience: 'Helpful to hear the views and difficulties encountered by others – we are not on our own!'

Many teachers found the contrasts between experienced teachers' reactions and those of students enlightening. Students' comments were intro duced to illustrate the range of responses possible and to show course members that much of what they took to be common sense was in fact a type of specialized, professional knowledge. The strategies of the inexperienced startled some of the teachers: reminding them of their own early errors confirmed their present expertise, and further supported their confidence in their professionalism. A boost to morale may help teachers to cope irrespective of the precise advice and information accompanying it. Many thought that establishing school-based study groups was likely to be the most important outcome for them. 'I feel I have got something very positive to offer the school's INSET programme.'

The development of understanding and coping in schools

Knowledge has scant effect upon practice if introduced piecemeal. One enthusiast for change on a school staff is unlikely to be any more effective than inviting an expert to visit, pronounce and depart. A school that wants to reappraise its strategies with disaffected pupils, that wants to gain the capacity to control problems in context must organize. As Dreikurs (1957) says, it is not always possible to consider a child in terms of underlying causes when confronted by difficulties in action in the classroom. The way to learn to see things differently, so that one is no longer confronted by the inexplicable, is through discussion of cases with fellow professionals. The first step is to fix a series of meetings for the express purpose of discussing one or two individual cases. It is best to build these meetings into the school's training timetable and not wait until crises have occurred: the stressful atmosphere following a serious disruptive incident is not the best climate to begin thinking dispassionately about a problem. A time limit of an hour or so concentrates the discussion and encourages members to look for agreement: open-ended meetings may stray into pessimistic generalizations about the modern world: one pupil's case must be discussed in its context and not used as an illustration of 'what things are coming to'. It is sometimes helpful to listen to members draw parallels with their own feelings of anger, attention seeking, or revenge in situations where they are ignored, rejected or demeaned. Probably three meetings covering three pupils make a safe start. The principal headings used in this course provide suitable items for the agenda of such meetings: sometimes information will be available; sometimes the meeting will expose gaps to be filled. A sample agenda is reproduced at the end of this chapter. Thorough exchange of perceptions, opinions and information should lead to an agreed, whole school policy; and it should alter teachers' anticipatory schemata, what they expect, perceive and comprehend in the classroom.

Discussions allow anxiety to be shared, worries faced, strengths and weaknesses acknowledged. The pupil's behaviour is seen in the whole context of his or her personal, domestic and school circumstances and the intractable becomes redefined as vulnerable: understandings, perceptions and expectations alter. We learn to respond professionally and to set aside our 'untutored selves' (Kahn and Wright, quoted in Hanko, 1985). Hanko quotes a teacher who claimed that she had come to like difficult pupils through working in the group. This is reminiscent of Kohl's comments (see the notes to the exercise for Chapter 6). Learning to separate untutored responses from professional responsibilities is to accept that tackling deviant behaviour is as much part of teachers' professional task as it is for police, barristers, priests and parents. It is true that teachers recognize that 'success at their job necessarily involves a capacity to establish and maintain classroom control' (Denscombe, 1985). However, Doyle reports the finding, in respect of problem pupils, that teachers 'did not always see the solving of these problems as part of their duties as classroom teachers' (Wittrock, 1986: 423). Planned sharing through open talk not only removes this misperception but as Dyke (1987) puts it: 'The simple act of "wondering why" creates the space for something new to happen'.

It is not always possible to alter all the circumstances that are thought to be inducing or contributing to a pupil's troublesome behaviour. There may be good reasons for retaining them irrespective of their effect upon an individual pupil. A secondary school cannot drop examinations nor ignore curriculum legislation, but where unmodifiable factors are identified this knowledge becomes part of the understanding. Similarly, a nursery class reading programme cannot be abandoned in the face of parental opposition even if it does frighten one or two pupils into phobia or rage. Focusing on the behavioural problems, as we have in this book, does not mean that the educational functions of school can be discarded: we think of the emotional and intellectual spheres as separate but it is a mistake to regard them, in school life, as separate and competing. Teaching maths and correcting exercise books is a way of demonstrating concern and regard for a pupil; and emotional therapy is an inescapably intellectual enterprise: everything, as it were, goes in through the mind. Identifying disturbing features focuses attention on fundamentals: there is a whole world of difference between being labelled as a child with emotional and behavioural problems who cannot read, and being labelled as a child who cannot read, with behaviour problems in consequence. One will receive potentially helpful attention; the sort of attention given to the other may well make the matter worse.

Those who take the lead in introducing staff-training and discussion programmes need to take care not to slip into the role of outside expert, lecturing teachers on their responsibilities. To be of value, meetings must generate information and leave the teachers in control and committed to tackling the problem (Hanko, 1985: 63) The chair or meeting-convener must encourage open discussion and honesty by his or her own non-judgemental attitude, and by gently preventing others from competitive contributions: the common staffroom claim, 'she's all right for me', must become data for consideration, not implied criticism of colleagues.

Meetings can be convened with hidden agendas. For example, a request for in-service work on the contribution of school ethos to behaviour problems can sometimes be an attempt to compel some staff to obey a contentious, school policy: wheel in the expert and hit the staff with that version of the Rutter report that made the popular papers. Hanko (1985: 140) suggests that 'one accepts the teachers' views of their difficulties as the essential and only possible starting point in a mutual pooling of expertise'. This is essential but far from easy: and sharp clashes of view on both particular and general matters, compounded by differences in status, can make even the most turbulent class seem docile by comparison. One way of keeping the meeting on task is to be open about the disagreements and the feelings engendered by them: to accept them as the reality, without approval or disapproval, inviting members to account for them and share other points of view. It is useful to remember that many of the features of group life in classrooms can appear in problem-focused meetings. A judgemental atmosphere will force teachers defensively into fixed roles: defensive communication does nothing for our problems and creates fresh ones of its own.

With experience, it may be possible to include consideration of teachers' needs: for example, to be recognized as competent and to feel valued. As groups grow in confidence the feelings of teachers can be discussed with less fear of offence being taken. Teachers sometimes communicate more than they realize. For example, a teacher who had made a number of witty interventions during a course chose to introduce a case giving him concern. This case concerned a pupil who was said to seek constant attention – 'the class clown' – and the teacher's response had been such things as making him stand in the corner. The group quickly identified the incorrect strategies and proposed a better approach. When discussion turned to why the teacher was so concerned about such trivial behaviour, some suggested, in the light of his earlier contributions and the manner of his presentation, that perhaps he saw unwanted aspects of himself in this pupil. His instant response was a mocking, cock-a-snook gesture – thus neatly confirming the group's diagnosis. Hanko (1985) gives examples of how, 'with lightness of touch', it is possible to find some of the reasons for being upset by behaviour in ourselves: coming late to complain about the problem of lateness, hyperactively describing a hyperactive pupil, and failing to prepare a case presentation on a pupil who refuses homework.

Another problem which might seem a nice one to have is a too rapid improvement in a pupil's behaviour. Dramatic changes are sometimes claimed. Hanko (1985) mentions teachers who come to meetings, having prepared to open the discussion on a pupil giving trouble, but who say 'Strangely enough, the case I was going to present, he was okay today'. She warns against expecting instant effects to last if the effort that produced them is instantly abandoned. Caspari (1976: 52) notes that it is difficult to pinpoint what is happening in such cases. The effort of understanding alters the perception, and the resulting change in teacher attitude improves the pupil's experience of school life. Where problems seem to vanish abruptly, it may be an instance of W. I. Thomas's rule, which paraphrased is, a threat defined as unreal is unreal in its consequences. Hanko (1985: 53) says it is unclear how far benefits to the child are due to teachers having 'a better understanding of his needs or to the support which they themselves received in relation to their own concern about handling him'.

Our habit of deference to experts sometimes causes us to regard insights as a gift from without, and teachers fall back into the belittling role of receivers of advice from superiors. Sometimes after what seems an ineffectual if explorative meeting, a course leader will be thanked for his or her helpful advice: having given none, this can be startling. The meeting leaders must resist the temptation to take the credit, for assuredly, there will be blame to allocate in due course. Discoveries, insights and solutions, where they occur, are communal productions arising from the strengths of the group: to see them any other way is to return to the arid enterprise of importing dead knowledge from outside. Dead knowledge, as White-head said, does not keep any better than fish.

Conclusion

Let us return to some of the issues we began with. This book has addressed a problem that it has declined to define, and possibly disappointed those who hoped that a definition of good and bad behaviour would clarify issues and suggest a remedy. The government's *Enquiry Into Discipline In Schools* put this as its first question when it began taking evidence in 1988. Sometimes the request seems to be accompanied by the hope that knowing the thing's name will deliver some power over it. It is not possible to produce a definition that is both helpful and satisfies all teachers – leaving aside the agreement of outsiders and parents. Teachers differ in what they find acceptable or serious and in what they feel they can cope with and control. As we have seen, some regard rudeness as part and parcel of everyday life and correct it without allowing it to halt their lessons or unduly upset them; others regard it as the thin end of a wedge and may send a pupil out of the room to a senior teacher. Those who are able patiently and tolerantly to use skill, stealth and what I have termed, disarming strategies, seem to feel more competent and to actually be more successful in winning co-operation in the long run; those who always react confrontationally and coercively are most stressed, more likely to aggravate situations and more likely to be pessimistic about the future. Definitions serve no useful purpose and statistics gathered on the basis of them are unreliable. The more experienced and competent the teacher, the more likely they are to question and challenge attempts to present examples of 'serious incidents'. Confident teachers see hope and possible strategies in any incident described to them: some worried teachers find every sort of behaviour threatening. Behaviour in school is too complex to be bounded by definitions. As in a friendship or marriage, a definition of what is right or good depends on the parties to the definition and its value is limited: when things are going well no-one thinks of it; when a crisis occurs, definitions are not uppermost in people's minds.

Evading the question of definitions evades the question whether disruption is getting worse or not, and the ambiguous results of surveys were discussed in the first chapter. Of the many cases I have discussed, with almost 1,000 teachers over three years, few have been assaults – and often those presented were not regarded as counting as assaults by some of the teachers present. Many teachers feel there is more rudeness and inattention but there seems to be little reliable evidence that circumstances have changed much in the past twenty years or so. There are some teachers less able to cope than others – as there always have been and by definition always will be – but they are neither numerous nor totally beyond help.

To ask for the causes of troublesome behaviour is another deceptively simple question. Disruptive incidents or confrontations arise when certain factors are present on both the pupil's and the teacher's side. Causes may be found in the persons involved, their families and friends, and their classroom and school circumstances. For example, a pupil from a family living on unemployment benefit, who is accustomed to undeserved anger and punishment from unhappy and pessimistic parents, and who is aware of his relatively deprived home life, may withdraw into silence or choose to work out his or her frustration on a teacher by open defiance. The type of lesson and the mood of his or her peers may amplify or mask whichever strategy the pupil adopts. Further, the teacher may understand the pupil's motives and problems and may react in a cool, dispassionate manner, accepting the unwanted behaviour and selecting a more appropriate moment to improve it. Another teacher, ignorant of the pupil's circumstances and unobservant of behavioural clues, might view the unwanted behaviour as a personal insult: an unrewarding exchange, accompanied by attempted coercion, might lead to what will later be described as an assault.

It is my belief that the 'discipline problem' is best understood as a part of the communication, debate and dispute between school and society. Those predisposed to blaming schools and teachers for the imagined or real ills of society, argue illogically from single incidents to 'widespread disorder'. Some teachers, in particular their unions, hope to present their job as more deserving of sympathy and salary by claiming that pupil behaviour is ungovernable. The 'discipline debate' is one aspect of an ideological dispute between those who think teachers are venal and those who think they are undervalued. The discipline issue is similar therefore to the professionalism issue. The word profession has become an ideological tool in a struggle between some teachers and some of their employers. Teachers are sometimes told that they are professionals: therefore they should selflessly serve the community, refrain from challenging policy and abandon the right to strike. On the other hand teachers may assert that they are professional: therefore they should be given autonomy, have their advice followed by ministers, and be highly paid. It has become a futile exercise to try to give a yes/no answer the once popular question – is teaching a profession? Similarly it has become futile to hope for yes/no answers to questions in the discipline debate.

The solution, if there is one, lies elsewhere. I believe that teachers must rebuild confidence and restore personal esteem from within. We need to accept that our responsibilities are much greater than the simple ideal of teaching docile pupils in pleasant surroundings, revered by parents and lavished with resources and emoluments by governments. Problems and privations have always been a part of normal life as they always will be. It needs to be understood that teachers can no more abolish troublesome behaviour than the police can abolish crime or doctors banish illness. We need to learn to cope as best as we can but most of all to learn that the overwhelming majority of teachers already are performing at maximum human efficiency. It may be objected that I seem to be ignoring the specialist agencies expressly established to assist teachers with troublesome pupils and sometimes to relieve them of the burden. Do not other professionals turn to experts when they meet difficulties in their work? Certainly the psychological and social services can be a useful resource but they are not professional experts in the matter of teaching. The study of psychology and two or three years' teaching experience is no substitute for twenty years of reflective practice in the classroom: as we approach the end of the century more than two-thirds of the teaching profession have more than twenty years' experience in their job. The real experts to turn to are our colleagues, even if their expertise consists only in the ability to engage the trust and attention of just one troublesome individual. That is what our job is about and competence in it is no small thing.

In short, teachers need to acquire increased confidence and changed attitudes to difficult behaviour: to see it as tractable, as something to be tackled dispassionately, as part of their job and not just as grit in the machine. The fact that so many experienced and competent teachers single out reassurance as one of the most valuable results of in-service training supports the view that the 'discipline problem' is as much to do with ideology as reality. As for the role of government and other outsiders: anything that lifts the morale and confidence of the profession will reduce the complaints from teachers about unruly behaviour. Perhaps we cannot expect too much in that respect. The responsibility for our professional development must be our own.

Exercise 11: a suggested agenda for a first case meeting

1. Retrieve and identify pupil motives or reasonable strategies.
   Mirrors, parallels, avoid re-enacting.
   Identity display, testing, attention seeking, power/revenge.
   Sources of hostility and avoidance strategies.
2. Classroom and teacher factors.
   Skills, varied teaching and learning styles.
   Unintended discrimination or undervaluing.
   Group roles.
   Behaviour: identify/measure, predisposing/confirming
   circumstances, unintended rewards.

Catch the pupil being good.
Priorities, charts, records.
3. School.
Categories and differentiations.
Pupil experience of rewarding/stigmatizing labels.
Roles/routes/choices available.
Shadow or imagine the pupil's experience.
Contracts.
4. Domestic context.
Family roles, purposes, experiences.
Dependable/reliable adult, hostility.
Avoid reproducing/re-enacting domestic fears in school.
5. Shared understandings.
Re-define the intractable, alter perceptions/attitudes.
Share anxieties, recognize strengths.
Sense of scale, worry in advance.
Professional vs. untutored responses.
Agreed whole school policy.

Further reading

There are several general overviews and introductions. Laslett and Smith (1984) is a brisk, succinct guide which benefits from experience with pupils in schools for the maladjusted. Robertson (1981) is good on classroom skills. The original research on which much classroom management is based is to be found in the mammoth American Education Research Association's publication edited by Wittrock (1986). Wragg (1984) reports British work. Reid *et al.* (1987) is a handy encyclopaedia of research on effective schools. Cheesman and Watts (1985) is a cheerful introduction to the behavioural approach. Readers attracted by the work in Chapter 4 would enjoy Dreikurs (1957), Balson (1982) and Stott (1982). Hanko (1985) is very helpful for those intending to lead discussion groups, as is the *Journal of Educational Therapy* (26, Chesterfield Gardens, London, NW3 7DE). Teachers considering this area for a higher degree will find Furlong (1985) useful.

Bibliography

Acton, T. A. (1980) 'Educational criteria for success: some problems in the work of Rutter, Maughan, Mortimore and Ouston', *Educational Research*, 22: 3.

Adelman, C. (1981) *Uttering, Muttering: Collecting, Using and Reporting Talk for Social and Educational Research*, London: Grant McIntyre.

Atkinson, P. and Delamont, S. (1977) *'Mock-ups and Cock-ups'* in M. Hammersley and P. Woods (1984a).

Ball, S. J. (1981) *Beachside Comprehensive*, Cambridge University Press.

Balson, M. (1982) *Understanding Classroom Behaviour*, A.C.E.R.

Barton, L. and Tomlinson, S. (eds) (1982) *Special Education and Social Interests*, London: Harper and Row.

Barnes D., Britton, J. and Rosen, H. (1969) *Language, the Learner and the School*, Harmondsworth: Penguin.

Bastide, R. (1972) *The Sociology of Mental Disorder*, London: Routledge and Kegan Paul.

Becker, H. S. (1952) 'Social class variations in the teacher-pupil relationship,' in B. R. Cosin, I. R. Dale, G. M. Esland, and D. F. Swift (eds) *School and Society*, London: Open University and Routledge and Kegan Paul.

——(1963) *The Outsiders*, Free Press, New York.

Bell, P. and Best, R. (1986) *Supportive Education*, Oxford: Blackwell.

Berger, P. and Luckman, T. (1971) *The Social Construction of Reality*, Harmondsworth: Penguin.

Berliner, D. C. (1987) 'Ways of thinking about students and classrooms by more and less experienced teachers,' in J. Calderhead, (1987).

Bernstein, B. (1961) 'Social class and linguistic development: a theory of social learning', in A. H. Halsey, *et al., Education, Economy and Society*, London: Collier-Macmillan.

——(1971) 'On the classification and framing of educational knowledge', in MFD. Young (ed.) *Knowledge and Control*, London: Collier-Macmillan.

Best, R., Ribbens, P. M. and Jarvis, C., with Oddy, D. (1983) *Education and Care*, London: Heinemann.

Beynon, J. (1985) *Initial Encounters in the Secondary School*, Lewes: Falmer.

Bird, C., Chessom, R., Furlong, V. J. and Johnson, D. (1981) *Disaffected Pupils*, Middlesex: Brunel University.

Blackledge, D. and Hunt, B. (1985) *Sociological Interpretations of Education*, London: Croom Helm.

Blishen, E. (1980) *A Nest of Teachers*, London/Lewes: Hamish Hamilton.

Booth, T. and Coulby, D. (1987) (eds) *Producing and Reducing Disaffection*, Milton Keynes: Open University Press.

Brennan, W. K. (1979) *The Curriculum for Slow Learners*, Schools Council Working Paper No. 63.

Brice-Heath, S. (1986) 'Questioning at home and at school: a comparative study', in M. Hammersley (ed.) (1986b).

Bromme, R. (1987) 'Teachers' assessments of students' difficulties and progress in understanding the classroom', in J. Calderhead (1987).

Brophy, J. E. and Evertson, C. M. (1976) *Learning from Teaching*, Boston: Allyn and Bacon.

Bruner, J. (1980) *Under Five in Britain*, London: Grant McIntyre.

Bull, S. L. and Solity, J. E. (1987) *Classroom Management: Principles to Practice*, Beckenham: Croom Helm.

Calderhead, J. (1984) *Teachers' Classroom Decision Making*, London: Holt Rinehart and Winston.

Calderhead, J. (1987) (ed.) *Exploring Teachers' Thinking*, London: Cassell.

Caspari, I. (1976) *Troublesome Children in Class*, London: Routledge and Kegan Paul.

Cheesman, P. L. and Watts, P. E. (1985) *Positive Behaviour Management*, London: Croom Helm.

Chessum, R. (1980) 'Teacher ideologies and pupil disruption', in Barton, L. *et. al.*, *Schooling, Ideology and Curriculum*, Lewes: Falmer.

Chisholm, B., Kearney, D., Knight, G., Little, H., Morris, S. and Tweddle, D. (1984) *Preventive Approaches to Disruption*, London: Macmillan.

Cicourel, A. V. (1968) 'Police practices and official records', in R. Turner (ed.) *Ethnomethodology*, Harmondsworth: Penguin.

Clark, C. M. and Yinger, R. J. (1987) 'Teachers' Planning', in J. Calderhead, (1987).

Cohen, L. and Cohen, A. (1987) (eds) *Disruptive Behaviour*, London: Harper and Row.

Corrigan, P. (1979) *Schooling the Smash Street Kids*, London: Macmillan.

Coulby, D. and Harper, T. (1985) *Preventing Classroom Disruption*, London: Croom Helm.

Coupe, J. and Porter, J. (1986) *The Education of Pupils with Severe Learning Difficulties*, London: Croom Helm.

Cronk, K. A. (1987) *Teacher-Pupil Conflict in Secondary Schools*, Lewes: Falmer.

Curtis, S. J. (1963) *History of Education in Great Britain*, Foxton, Cambridge: University Tutorial Press.

Cusick, P. A. (1973) *Inside High Schools: the Students' World*, New York: Holt, Rinehart and Winston.

Cuttance, P. (1985) 'Frameworks for research on the effectiveness of schooling' in D. Reynolds (1985) *Studying School Effectiveness*, Lewes: Falmer.

Davies, B. (1984) 'Friends and fights', in M. Hammersley and P. Woods (1984b).

Davies, J. G. V. and Maliphant, R. (1974) 'Refractory behaviour in school and avoidance learning', *Journal of Child Psychology, Psychiatry*, 15: 23–31.

Davies, L. (1984) *Pupil Power: Deviance and Gender in School*, Lewes: Falmer.

Delamont, S. (1976) *Interaction in the Classroom*, London: Methuen.

Delamont, S. and Galton, M. (1986) *Inside the Secondary Classroom*, London: Routledge and Kegan Paul.

Denscombe, M. (1985) *Classroom Control: a Sociological Perspective*, London: George, Allen and Unwin.

DES (1975) *Survey of Violence, Indiscipline and Vandalism in Schools*, London: HMSO.

——(1978) *Behavioural Units*, London: HMSO.
——(1980) *Truancy and Behaviour Problems in Some Urban Schools*, London.
——(1984) *Education Observed 2*, London: HMSO.
——(1987) *Education Observed 5, Good Behaviour and Discipline in Schools*, London: HMI report.
Dewe, P. J. (1985) 'Coping with work sress: an investigation of teachers' actions', *Research in Education*, No. 33; 27–40.
Docking, J. W. (1980) *Control and Discipline in Schools*, London: Harper and Row.
Doyle, W. and Carter, K. (1986) 'Academic Tasks in Classrooms', in M. Hammersley (1986a).
Dreikurs, R. (1957) *Psychology in the Classroom*, London: Staples Press.
Driver, R. (1983) *The Pupil as Scientist*, Milton Keynes: Open University Press.
Dunkerley, D., and Salaman, G. (1986) 'Organisations and bureaucracy', in M. Haralambos (ed.) (1986) Developments in Sociology, Vol. 2, Ormskirk: Causeway Press
Durkheim, E. (1893/1933) *The Division Of Labour In Society*, London: Free Press.
Dyke, S. (1987) 'Psycho-analytic insight in the classroom: asset or liability?', *Journal of Educational Therapy*, 1, 4: 43–64.
Edwards, D. A. and Furlong, V. J. (1978) *The Language of Teaching*, London: Heinemann.
Eisner, E. (1982) *Cognition and Curriculum*, New York: Longman.
——(1985) *The Art of Educational Evaluation*, Lewes: Falmer.
Eggleston, J. (1974) (ed.) *Contemporary Research in the Sociology of Education*, London: Methuen.
Everhart, R. B. (1983) *Reading, Writing and Resistance*, Boston, Mass.: Routledge and Kegan Paul.
Evertson, C. M. and Emmer, E. T. (1982) 'Effective management at the beginning of the school year in junior high classes', *Educational Psychology*, 74, 4: 485–98.
Finlayson, D. S. and Loughran, J. L. (1975) 'Pupils' perceptions in high and low delinquency schools', *Educational Research*, 18, 2.
Fontana, D. (1985) *Classroom Control*, London: Methuen.
Furlong, V. J. (1985) *The Deviant Pupil*, Milton Keynes: Open University Press.
Galloway, D. (1985) *Schools, Pupils and Special Educational Needs*, Beckenham: Croom Helm.
Galloway, D., Ball, T., Blomfield, D., Seyd, R. (1982) *Schools and Disruptive Pupils*, London: Longman.
Galloway, D., Martin, R. and Wilcow, B. (1985) 'Persistent absence from school and exclusion from school: the predictive power of school and community variables', *British Educational Research Journal*, 11, 1.
Galvin, P. and Singleton, R. (1984) *Behavioural Management*, NFER.
Gannaway, H. (1984) 'Making sense of school', in M. Hammersley and P. Woods (1984b).
Garfinkel, H. (1967) *Studies in Ethnomethodology*, Englewood Cliffs, New Jersey: Prentice Hall.
Gathorne-Hardy, J. (1977) *The Public School Phenomenon*, London: Hodder and Stoughton.
Gillham, B. (ed.) (1981) *Problem Behaviour in the Secondary School: a Systems Approach*, London: Croom Helm.
Goffman, E. (1968) *Asylums*, Harmondsworth: Penguin.

Graham, J. (1988) *Schools, Disruptive Behaviour and Delinquency*, Home Office Research Study No. 96, HMSO.

Gray, H. and Freeman, A. (1988) *Teaching Without Stress*, London: Paul Chapman Publishing.

Gray, J. *et al.* (1983) *Reconstructions of Secondary Education: Theory, Myth and Practice Since the War*, London: Routledge and Kegan Paul.

Grunsell, R. (1985) *Finding Answers to Disruption*, London: SCDC.

Hall, E., Woodhouse, D. A. and Wooster, A. D. (1984) 'An evaluation of in-service courses in human relations', *British Journal of In-Service Education*, 11, 1: 55–60.

Halsey, A. H., Floud, J. and Anderson, C. A. (1961) *Education, Economy and Society*, London: Collier-Macmillan.

Hamilton, D., Jenkins, D., King, C., MacDonald, B. and Parlett, M. (1977) (eds) *Beyond the Numbers Game*, London: Macmillan.

Hammersley, M. (1986a) *Controversies in Classroom Research*, Milton Keynes: Open University Press.

——(1986b) *Case Studies in Classroom Research*, Milton Keynes: Open University Press.

Hammersley, M. and Woods, P. (1984a) *Classrooms and Staffrooms*, Milton Keynes: Open University Press.

——(1984b) *Life in School*, Milton Keynes: Open University Press.

Hanko, G. (1985) *Special Needs in Ordinary Classrooms*, Oxford: Basil Blackwell.

Hargreaves, A. (1978) 'The significance of classroom coping strategies', in M. Hammersley and P. Woods (1984a).

Hargreaves, D. H. (1967) *Social Relationships in a Secondary School*, London: Routledge and Kegan Paul.

——(1980) 'Teachers' knowledge of behaviour problems', in G. Upton and A. Gobell (eds) *Behaviour Problems in the Comprehensive School*, Cardiff University College.

——(1982) *The Challenge for the Comprehensive School*, London: Routledge and Kegan Paul.

Hargreaves, D. H., Hestor, K. H. and Mellor, J. M. (1975) *Deviance in Classrooms*, London: Routledge and Kegan Paul.

Her Majesty's Stationery Office (1977) *The Pack Report*, London: HMSO.

Hewett, F. M. and Blake, P. R. (1973) 'Teaching the emotionally disturbed', in R. M. W. Travers (ed.) (1973).

Hoghughi, M. (1978) *Troubled and Troublesome*, Burnett Books.

Holman, P. G. and Coghill, N. F. (1987) *Disruptive Behaviour in School*, Bromley: Chartwell-Bratt.

Hughes, J. N. (1988) *Cognitive Behaviour Therapy*, Oxford: Pergamon.

Jackson, P. (1968) *Life in Classrooms*, New York: Holt, Rinehart and Winston.

Johnstone, M. and Munn, P. (1987) *Discipline in Schools: a Review of the Literature*, Edinburgh: Scottish Council for Research in Education, Edinburgh.

Jones-Davies, C. and Cave, R. V. (1976) *The Disruptive Pupil in the Secondary School*, London: Ward Lock.

ILEA Research and Statistics Group (1986) *The Junior School Project*, London: ILEA.

Keddie, N. (1971) 'Classroom knowledge', in M. F. D. Young, *Knowledge and Control*, London: Collier-Macmilan.

King, R. (1978) *All Things Bright and Beautiful?*, London: Wiley.

Kohl, H. (1970) *The Open Classroom*, London: Methuen.
——(1986) *On Becoming a Teacher*, London: Methuen.
Kounin, J. (1970) *Discipline and Group Management in Classrooms*, New York: Holt, Rinehart and Winston.
Kyriacou, C. and Sutcliffe, J. (1977) 'Teacher stress: a review', *Educational Review*, 29, 4: 299–306.
——(1978) 'A model of teacher stress', *Educational Studies*, 4, 1: 1–6.
——(1979) 'Teacher stress and satisfaction', *Educational Research*, 21, 2; 89–96.
Lacey, C. (1970) *Hightown Grammar*, Manchester University Press.
——(1977) *The Socialisation of Teachers*, London: Methuen.
Laing, A. F. and Chazan, M. (1986) 'The management of aggressive behaviour in young children', in D. P. Tatum, *Management of Disruptive Pupil Behaviour in Schools*, Chichester: Wiley.
Laslett, R. (1977) *Educating Maladjusted Children*, London: Staples Press.
——(1982) *Maladjusted Children in the Ordinary School*, Stratford: National Council for Special Education.
Laslett, R. and Smith, C. (1984) *Effective Classroom Management*, London: Croom Helm.
Lawrence, J., Steed, D. and Young, P. (1977) *Disruptive Behaviour in a Secondary School*, University of London.
——(1984) 'European voices on disruptive behaviour in schools: definitions, concern, and types of behaviour', *British Journal of Educational Studies*, 32, 1.
Lloyd-Smith, M. (1984) (ed.) *Disruptive Schooling*, London: John Murray.
Longworth Dames, S. M. (1977) 'The relationship of personality and behaviour to school exclusion', *Educational Review*, 29: 163–77.
Mardle, G. and Walker, M. (1980) 'Strategy and structure: a critique of teacher socialisation', in P. Woods (1980b).
Marland, M. (1975) *The Craft of the Classroom*, London: Heinemann.
Marsh, P. *et al.* (1978) *The Rules of Disorder*, London: Routledge and Kegan Paul.
Marshall, S. (1963) *An Experiment in Education*, Cambridge University Press.
Martin, N. C. (1976) *Writing and Learning Across the Curiculum*, London: Ward Lock.
MacLure, M. and French, P. (1980) 'Routes to right answers: pupils' strategies for answering teachers' questions', in P. Woods (ed.) (1980a).
Marsh, P., Rosser, E., and Harre, R. (1978) *The Rules of Disorder*, London: Routledge and Kegan Paul.
McManus, M. (1987) 'Suspension and exclusion from High Schools: the association with catchment and school variables', in *School Organization*, 7, 3.
Mead, G. H. (1934) *Mind, Self and Society*, Chicago: Free Press.
Mehan, H. (1979) *Learning Lessons: Social Organisation in Classrooms*, Cambridge, Massachusetts: Harvard University Press.
Mercer, N. and Edwards, D. (1981) 'Ground rules for understanding', in N. Mercer (ed.) (1981) *Language in School and Community*, London: Edward Arnold.
Meyenn, R. J. (1980) 'School girls' peer groups', in P. Woods (1980a).
Mortimore, P., Davies, J., Varlaam, A., West, A., Devine, P., and Mazza, J. (1983) *Behaviour Problems in Schools*, London: Croom Helm.
Musgrove, F. (1979) *School and the Social Order*, Chichester: Wiley.
Nash, R. (1973) *Classrooms Observed*, London: Routledge and Kegan Paul.

Pack, D. C. (1977) *Truancy and Indiscipline in Schools*, Edinburgh: Scottish Education Department.

Partington, J. A. and Hinchliffe, G. (1979) 'Some aspects of classroom management', *British Journal of Teacher Education*, 5, 3: 231–41.

Phillipson, M. (1976) *Sociological Aspects of Crime and Delinquency*, London: Routledge and Kegan Paul.

Pik, R. (1987) 'Confrontation situations and teacher support systems', in L. Cohen, and A. Cohen (eds) (1987).

Pollard, A. 'Goodies, jokers and gangs', in M. Hammersley and P. Woods (1984b).

Posner, G. J. (1980) 'Promising developments in curriculum knowledge', paper presented to American Education Research Association, quoted in Y. C. Sheeran (1988) 'A sociocultural approach to children's writing', M. Phil. Thesis, University of Leeds.

Pring, R. (1976) *Knowledge and Schooling*, London: Open Books.

Reid, I. (1986) *The Sociology of School and Education*, London: Fontana.

Reid, K. (1986) *Disaffection from School*, London: Methuen.

Reid, K., Hopkins, D. and Holly, P. (1987) *Towards the Effective School*, Oxford: Blackwell.

Reynolds, D. (1985) (ed.) *Studying School Effectiveness*, Lewes: Falmer.

Reynolds, D. and Sullivan, M. (1981) 'The effects of school: a radical faith restated', in B. Gillham, *Problem Behaviour in the Secondary School*, London: Croom Helm.

——(1979) 'Bringing Schools Back In', in L. Barton and R. Meighan, *Schools, Pupils and Deviance*, London: Nafferton.

Robertson, J. (1981) *Effective Classroom Control*, Oxford: Blackwell.

Rogers, C. (1969) *Freedom to Learn*, Columbus, Ohio: Merrill.

——(1986) 'Teachers' expectation and effects', in M. Hammersley (ed.) (1986b).

Rutter, M., Maughan, B., Mortimore, P., Ouston, J., and Smith, A. (1979) *Fifteen Thousand Hours*, London: Open Books.

——(1980) 'A response to the discussion papers', in B. Tizard, *et al.* (1980).

Schostak, J. F. (1983) *Maladjusted Schooling*, Lewes: Falmer.

——(1986) *Schooling the Violent Imagination*, Lewes: Falmer.

Shostak, J. F. and Logan, T. (1984) *Pupil Experience*, London: Croom Helm.

Schutz, A. (1972) *The Phenomenology of the Social World*, London: Heineman.

Sharp, H. and Green, A. (1975) *Education and Social Control*, London: Routledge and Kegan Paul.

Smetherham, D. (1981) *Practising Evaluation*, Driffield: Studies in Education Limited.

Smythe, J. (1987) (ed.) *Educating Teachers: Changing the Nature of Pedagogical Knowledge*, Lewes: Falmer.

Sockett, H. (1983) 'Towards a professional code in teaching', in P. Gordon (ed.) *Is Teaching a Profession?*, Bedford Way Paper 15, University of London.

Spooner, R. T. (1979) 'Pastoral care and the myth of never ending toil', *Education*, 2.2.1979: 251–2.

Stenhouse, L. (1975) *An Introduction to Curriculum Research and Development*, London: Heinemann.

Storr, A. (1968) *Human Aggression*, Harmondsworth: Penguin Books.

Stott, D. H. (1978) *Helping Children with Learning Difficulties*, London: Ward Lock.

Stott, D. H. (1982) *Helping the Maladjusted Child*, Milton Keynes: Open University Press.

Stubbs, M. and Delamont, S. (eds) (1976) *Explorations in Classroom Observation*, London: Wiley.

Tattum, D. P. (1982) *Disruptive Pupils in Schools and Units*, Chichester: Wiley.

——(1986) (ed.) *Management of Disruptive Behaviour in Schools*, Chichester: Wiley.

Tickle, L. (1984) 'One spell of ten or five spells of two', in M. Hammersley and P. Woods (1984a).

Tizard, B., Burgess, T., Francis, H., Goldstein, H., Young, M., Hewison, J., and Plewis, I. (1980) *Fifteen Thousand Hours, A Discussion*, University of London.

Topping, K. J. (1983) *Education Systems for Disruptive Adolescents*, London: Croom Helm.

Travers, R. M. W. (1973) (ed.) *Second Handbook of Research on Teaching*, Chicago: Rand McNally.

Wagner, A. C. (1987) 'Knots in Teachers' Thinking', in J. Calderhead (1987).

Watson, J. (1988) 'One-year courses: the teachers' views', *British Journal of Special Education*, 15, 2.

Welton, J. (1982) *Meeting Special Needs*, Bedford Way Paper 12, University of London.

Werthman, C. (1963) 'Delinquents in schools', in B. R. Cosin (ed.) *School and Society*, Milton Keynes: Open University Press.

Wheldall, K. and Merrett, F. (1984) *Positive Teaching: The Behavioural Approach* London: George, Allen and Unwin.

Wideen, M. F. and Andrews, I. (1987) (eds) *Staff Development for School Improvement*, Lewes: Falmer.

Willis, P. (1977) *Learning to Labour*, Farnborough: Saxon House.

Wills, D. (1945) *The Barns Experiment*, London: Allen and Unwin.

Wills, D. (1967) *The Hawkspur Experiment*, Harmondsworth: Penguin. (First published 1941.)

Wittrock, M. C. (1986) (ed.) *Third Handbook of Research on Teaching*, New York: American Education Research Association, Macmillan.

Woods, P. (1980a) (ed.) *Pupil Strategies*, London: Croom Helm.

——(1980b) (ed.) *Teacher Strategies*, London: Croom Helm.

——(1983) *Sociology and the School*, London: Routledge & Kegan Paul.

——(1984) 'Teaching for Survival', in M. Hammersley and P. Woods (1984a).

Woods, P. and Pollard, A. (1987) (eds) *Sociology and Teaching*, London: Croom Helm.

Woodhouse, D. A., Hall, E., and Wooster, D. A. (1985) 'Taking control of stress in teaching', *British Journal of Educational Psychology*, 55: 119–123.

Wragg, E. C. (1984) *Classroom Teaching Skills*, London: Croom Helm.

——(1987) *Teacher Appraisal: A Practical Guide*, London: Macmillan.

York, R., Heron, J. M. and Wolff, S. (1972) 'Exclusion from school', *Journal of Child Psychology and Psychiatry*, 13: 259–66.

Index

Acton, T. A. 128
Adelman, C. 142
Andrews, I. 61
Atkinson, P. 56
attention seeking by pupils 84–5

Ball, S. J. 51, 52, 126, 129
Balson, M. 10, 15, 27, 53; pupils'
    motives 71, 79, 84, 85, 86, 92, 94
Barnes, D. 18, 47, 55, 74
Barton, L. 25, 37, 125
Bastide, R. 8, 9, 39, 41, 83, 98
Becker, H. S. 3, 37, 127
behaviour: attention-seeking 84–6;
    and grouping of pupils 129; power-
    seeking 86; of pre-school children
    87–8; and revenge 85–6; teachers
    56; see also troublesome behaviour
Bell, P. 123
Berger, P. 108, 125
Berliner, D. C. 148
Bernstein, B. 18, 26, 27
Best, R. 123, 132
Beynon, J. 9, 52, 75
Bird, C. 97, 126, 127
Blackledge, D. 126
Blake, P. R. 3
Blishen, E. 3
Brennan, W. K. 44
Brice-Heath, S. 18
Bromme, R. 148
Brophy, J. E. 56
Bruner, J. 35, 123
Bull, S. L. 50, 53, 119

Calderhead, J. 50, 65–6, 105, 139
Carter, K. 54
Caspari, I. 114, 138, 152; teachers'

skills 55, 58, 98, 107; pupils' identity
    76, 82, 88, 89
causes, common sense of troublesome
    behaviour 6–11
Cave, R. V. 5
changing perceptions of classroom
    deviance, teachers 146
Chazan, M. 117, 119
Cheeseman, P. L. 9, 114, 116
Chessum, R. 18
Chisholm, P. 9, 44
Cicourel, A. V. 36
Clark, C. M. 148
class preference by teachers 55–6
classroom: climate 122–5; and
    individual 114–25; and schools
    125–6
classroom management skills 44–69;
    basic 45; clearing up and exit 60–2,
    64; desk work activity 52; early
    encounters 49–52, 62; main part of
    lesson 53–7, 62–3; research on 61–2;
    response to trouble 57–60, 63–4;
    start of school year 51–2; and
    teacher qualities 44–69; traditional
    lessons 47–9
Coghill, N. F. 6, 7
Cohen, A. and L. 88, 105, 117, 119
confrontation: and attack 107; and co-
    operation 108–9; manipulation of
    104–5; and procrastination 107–8;
    and pupils 106; 'ratchet' statements
    and 106–7; repairing relationships
    108; and stress 96–113
Corrigan, P. 76
Coulby, D. 118, 120, 132
Coupe, J. 115
Cronk, K. A. 10, 13, 71, 76, 86, 88–9